I0148848

Luck on the Wing

GEN. WILLIAM MITCHELL, COMMANDER-IN-CHIEF
OF THE AMERICAN AIR FORCES AT THE FRONT.

Luck on the Wing

Recollections of an American Aerial Observer
During the First World War

Elmer Haslett

LEONAUR

Luck on the Wing
Recollections of an American Aerial Observer During the First World War
by Elmer Haslett

First published under the title
Luck on the Wing

Leonaur is an imprint of Oakpast Ltd

Copyright in this form © 2013 Oakpast Ltd

ISBN: 978-1-78282-130-4 (hardcover)
ISBN: 978-1-78282-131-1 (softcover)

http://www.leonaur.com

Publisher's Notes

The views expressed in this book are not necessarily
those of the publisher.

Contents

Some Words in Explanation 9

Introduction 17

Beginner's Luck 21

Hardboiled 34

My First Scrap 52

Brereton's Famous Flight 66

Troubles on the Ground 85

The Wild Ride of a Greenhorn 98

Eileen's Inspiration 110

Down and Out and In 126

The Court of Inquiry 143

Becoming Kultured 160

Escaped Almost 172

The Privileges of Prisoners 181

"Coming Out" 195

To
My
Mother

Some Words in Explanation

If anyone should be interested enough to inquire as to the reason for my becoming a sky spy, an aerial observer, a deuce, or whatever one chooses to call it, I should certainly speak the truth and affirm that it was not the result of calm, cool and deliberate thought. I have always had a holy horror of airplanes and to this day I cannot say that I exactly enjoy riding in them. My sole reason for flying now is that I am still in the Air Service and there is not an excuse in the world for a young man being an air officer if he does not spend a part of his time in that element. Every boy in his own heart wants to be a soldier whether his mother raises him that way or not: as a boy and as a man I wanted to be an infantryman.

Upon being commissioned in Infantry following the First Officers' Training Camp, I was about to have a lifetime's ambition gratified by being placed in charge of a company at Camp Lewis, Washington, when along with two hundred other new officers I was ordered to Fort Sill, Oklahoma, for assignment with the Missouri and Kansas troops. I had been enthusiastic over the infantry, I liked it fine, and most of all I wanted to train my company and lead them into action. Arriving at Fort Sill, we found that the troops had not arrived and would not come for at least a month. Meanwhile we stagnated and lost our pep. The papers were full of the pressing need of help at the battle front and still all around I could see nothing but destructive delay. It was the old call of the individual—for though my heart was set upon the ideal of training my own men for the supreme test yet I could not stand the delay. I was determined to get to the front and with that as my paramount ideally I would take the first opportunity that would lead to its realisation.

The chance came one morning early in September, 1917, when one of my friends, Lieut. Armin Herold, caught me going out of the mess hall late (as usual) for breakfast and excitedly told me that the division adjutant had just tacked a little notice on the door at Headquarters, in response to an urgent request from General Pershing, that ten officers who ranked as First or Second Lieutenants would be detailed at once for training as airplane observers, and would be sent to France immediately upon completion of their training. Volunteers were requested. That part about "training as airplane observers" was Greek to me—I did not know that such things existed—but at the word "France" I pricked up my ears like a fire horse at the sound of a bell. My decision was formed then and there. I was going to be an aerial observer, whatever that was, and nothing was going to keep me from taking that chance, my first opportunity, to go to France.

I almost lost my breakfast at the thought of having to ride in an airplane, but that promise to send me to France at once was an anaesthetic to my better judgment, and I right away made my first flight, *au pied*, covering that ten acres of ploughed ground over to the Division Headquarters in ten flat. I rushed in and made application.

The divisional signal officer was a major who felt that aerial observation was an extremely technical branch. He did not know a terrible lot about it, and told me that he had placed the bulletin on the board only a few minutes before and was surprised that I had responded so quickly. He asked me a lot of trick questions as to my technical training, and now, since I have made a fair record as an aerial observer, I don't mind making the confession that I, along with other conspirators desiring early action, made several "for the period of the emergency" statements. The major wanted to know if I knew anything about civil engineering. I told him I did, but, as a matter of fact, I hardly knew the difference between a compass and a level. He asked me if I got sick in an airplane. I flinched a little, but told him "No," the presumption of innocence being in my favour.

He then asked me if I had ever ridden in one. I laughed so heartily at this joke that he was convinced that I had. The truth of the matter was that previous to that time if anyone had ever got me in an airplane they would certainly have had to hog-tie me and drag me to the ordeal. He then wanted to know what experience I had with mechanical engines. I told him that my was quite varied and that I considered myself an expert on mechanical engines, having had a course in mechanical engineering. This was all true, yet I do not, to this day, know the principles surrounding the operations of an engine, and if anything ever should go wrong, the motor would rust from age before I could fix it.

My application was hasty and unpremeditated and I did not actually realise what I had done until I got outside—then, just as after the unpremeditated murder, the murderer will turn from the body and cry, "What have I done?"—so I turned from that house with exactly the same thought, and as I walked back to my barracks I kept repeating to myself, "What have I done!" "What have I done!" The big question then was to find out the nature of the new job for which I had volunteered. The first question I asked of the two hundred officers when I returned to the barracks was: "What is an airplane observer?" No one present could enlighten me.

I had volunteered for so many things in this man's army which had never panned out either for me or for anyone else, that I was naturally apprehensive as to the result Having in mind such dire consequences should the thing turn out, and yet hopeful of a more pleasant outcome, I alternately anticipated and naturally brooded a great deal over the thing.

The next morning I learned that the telegram had actually been sent to the War Department at Washington and that my name had been first on the list. The package of fate was not only sealed, but clearly addressed, and I was the consignee.

In a remarkably short time the orders came from Washington and ten of us were loaded in a Government truck and transported to Post Field. Of those ten lieutenants it is interesting to note that seven got to the front, and from those seven one can pick five of America's greatest sky spies. Every one of the seven was decorated or promoted in the field. They were Captain Len Hammond, of San Francisco; Captain Phil Henderson, of Chehallis, Oregon; Captain Steve Barrows, of Berkeley, California; Captain How Douglas, of Covina, California; First Lieut. Armin Herold of Redlands, California, and First Lieutenant "Red" Gunderson, of Spokane, Washington. These were the first officers detailed in the United States to "Aerial Observation."

The Observation School at Fort Sill was just being started and was yet unorganized, so after a very extensive course covering four weeks of about one hour a day, in which we learned practically nothing of real help, we were ordered to France for duty.

After an unusually short stay in the S.O.S., or Zone of the Rear, we got to the Zone of Advance at a place named Amanty, where we were stationed at an observer's school, and, after a very incomplete course there, we were distributed among French squadrons operating over the front, in order that we might get some actual experience, since the Americans had no squadrons yet ready for the front.

But a word as to the reason for this book. Here is how it happened. We were at this school at Amanty, hoping each day for orders to move us on up to the real front. It was in February, 1918, and one day, by a great streak of good fortune, Major Schwab, the school adjutant, picked on me as I was passing the headquarters. "Hey, what's your name!" he said, to which I replied, with a "wish-to-make-good" salute.

"Here!" he continue, in a most matter-of-fact way, "you are excused from classes this morning. Take the commanding officer's car, go down to Gondrecourt, and pick up three Y.M.C.A. girls who are going to give an entertainment out here this afternoon. Report them to me."

This was an unexpected pleasure, so, with all pomp and dignity, I seated myself in the rear of a huge Cadillac, with "Official" painted all over the sides of it. It was my first ride in the select government transportation—I had previously drawn trucks. Then we whisked along the ten miles to Gondrecourt. The surprise was a happy one, because the three girls were peaches, and, an aviator being a scarce article in those days (and I wore my leather coat to let them know that I was one), I was received most cordially.

We had just started back to the camp, and I was Hero Number One of Heroes All, when they all harped as of one accord, demanding if I would not take them up in an airplane. This is a feminine plea which never seems to become old, because every girl you see nowadays still asks the same question. But I maintained silence on the subject of taking them up. So, they talked about aces, seemingly positive that I was one of those things—what a wonderful flyer I must be—and a lot of other bunk, until I began to feel exalted as if I were of the royalty, for it seemed that I was being worshipped.

I interrupted their wild rambling to ask if they objected to my smoking. Of course, being a hero aviator, there was no chance for objection. So, as I unbuttoned my leather coat, threw back the left lapel, and pulled out a stogie from my pocket, the eyes of one cute little frizzle-haired girl fell upon my aviation insignia, which, of course, consisted of only one wing. Wild eyed and with marked disdain, she exclaimed sneeringly to the others, "Oh, he's only an observer! A half aviator!"

Actually I had not claimed otherwise, but, as long as I live, I shall never forget the sting of those words, and especially the biting insinuation on the word "only." To their minds I was a branded hypocrite. Talk about the poor man standing before the criminal judge and being sentenced to the impossible "99 years" in the penitentiary; well, take it from me, this was worse, for my foolish pride had been embellished to an acute cockishness by this preliminary adoration, but my soaring little airplane of selfish egoism took a decided nose-dive—it smashed my whole day's happiness.

The other girls, and in fact this little frizzle-topped girl, too, realised immediately the impropriety of the remark, and tried in the most sincere way to temper the sting and alleviate my apparent embarrassment. The only hollow remark I could offer, in my futile attempt at indifferent repartee, was to the effect that pilots would be aces always, and observers, being the lowest card of the deck, must be deuces. They laughed—I don't know why—perhaps to jolly me along. I intended to say something else, but they took advantage of the necessity of my taking a breath—by laughing—so I dropped the "deuce" gag, but, as the conversation went on, the more chagrined I became.

When we finally got to camp, I turned over the precious cargo to the camp adjutant, and then struck out for a long hike by my lonesome to walk it off.

But, like an "ignorant idealist," heeding the call of the fair sex, I went to the entertainment that afternoon, and, as I left the hut with several other observers, we met the entertainers who were now walking along in company with the commanding officer. Of course, we all saluted, the commanding officer sloppily returned it, and the party passed on. Then this same little frizzle-top, red-headed girl, as if by afterthought, recognised me, turned around, and begrudgingly nodded as if meeting a disgraced member of the family. She disdainfully called the attention of the commanding officer and the other girls to my humble presence by saying, "He is the observer that came out with us in the car—you know the 'deuce,'" and, I might add, she laughed lightly and shrugged her shoulders. I'll tell the world it hurt my pride, and I was off with all of womankind for the time being. I had laboured under the impression that an observer was some big gun in aviation. Believe me, she took it out of me.

In fact, these two incidents with this young lady revealed to me for the first time the real insignificance of my position as an aerial observer. A thousand times afterwards, when I still wore an observer's insignia, people would look at it and, for some psychological reason or other, they always seemed to say either by sound or facial expression, "only an observer." Even today, (1920), as throughout the war, the same haunting epithet follows the observer. In fact, in the American Expeditionary Force, we had an unofficial rating of military personnel which classified the various grades as follows: general officers, field officers, captains, lieutenants, pilots, sergeants, corporals, privates, cadets, German prisoners and last aerial observers. And no matter which way one considered it, the aerial observer was the lowest form of human existence. For a long time he was not even eligible for promotion or command. Indeed, in the game of war, he was the deuce— the lowest card of the deck—and the first to be discarded.

So far as official recognition is concerned the observer is gradually coming into his own. After comparing the fatalities in the various branches of aviation, it is agreed as one of the lessons of the war that the observer has had a hard deal as have also observation pilots and bombardment pilots. In recognition of this principle, the Director of Air Service in a letter of January 5th, 1920, in declining to sanction the word "ace," wrote as follows:

> The United States Air Service does not use the title 'Ace' in referring to those who are credited officially with five or more victories over enemy aircraft. It is not the policy of the Air Service to glorify one particular branch of aeronautics, aviation or aero-station at the expense of another. . . . The work of observation and bombardment is considered equally as hazardous as that of pursuit, but due to the fact that the observation and bombardment pilots are not called upon merely to destroy enemy aircraft, it should not be allowed to aid in establishing a popular comparison of results merely by relatives victories.

I notice that the director, in spite of the nice things he said about the observation and bombardment branches of the service, has expressly referred to "pilots," which of course makes me peevish. But so it is. The director undoubtedly intended to include observers; indeed, the observer is the man who does the shooting from observation and bombardment planes—but it is the same old story—the observer is so insignificant that he was just naturally overlooked. Indeed, an observer is only a *quasi*-aviator, as a friend with a legal mind once said—and after he used that word "only," I hated him. And in public appreciation, they consider the observer as the deuce—the card without value— with no definite status, just an inexplicable freak habitating around aviation. The common acceptation of an aerial observer is a mild, passive, sort of a guy, who wears nose glasses, is mathematically inclined, and who, in battle, is privileged to run from the enemy, being, as it were, tamed and "too proud to fight."

Thus, to present to the public a more consistent version of the real life of the observer at the front in his various roles, and hoping in a way to dispel this very unfortunate public misunderstanding, this book of my own modest experiences as an observer is presented for consideration under the title *Luck on the Wing*.

Elmer Haslett,
Major, Air Service
United States Army

Washington, February, 1920.

Introduction

Major Elmer Haslett has made a valuable addition to the literature of the world's war in writing the volume to which these lines must serve as introduction.

Luck on the Wing has two distinct sources of value: first it presents a dear, graphic picture of the life led by our fighting airmen during the three great actions in which American soldiers played so important a part—Château-Thierry, St. Mihiel, and the Argonne—and best of all the picture is a truthful one: and, second, it, all the more forcibly because often quite unconsciously, 'brings out clearly the lack of understanding of the functions of Air Service, a lack which in the final analysis was responsible for the greater part of whatever of dissatisfaction and disappointment with this branch of the Military Service there existed in the American Expeditionary Forces in France.

Since the armistice there have been published a great number of books on the war, the majority of which have been the work of actual participants—of officers and enlisted men. But so far as the Air Service of the United States is concerned Major Haslett has, in my opinion, in the relation in simple narrative form of some of the adventures he himself met with overseas provided not only the most interesting story but one of the very few which the future historian will find of considerable value when he sets himself to the task of compiling Air Service History.

Luck on the Wing is the story of an American observer. The claims to fame of the fighting pilot were early recognized in the world war. The Ace soon became a public favourite. The war correspondents were quick indeed to realise the news potentialities inherent to the "Knight of the Air" and their dispatches made the world familiar with his extraordinary and ordinary adventures. The peoples of the world followed with the zest that the American baseball fanatic follows the baseball victories, the scores of the world's great Aces. But to the observer fame came in rather homeopathic doses, if it came at all. And most observers are willing to take oath it came not at all.

That there were exceptions to this rule, that the very important work of the observer was not entirely lacking of official and public recognition, is a source of personal gratification to me because as commander of the American Air Forces at the front I personally knew and fully appreciated the great value of the work done by this class of Air Service officers. Major Haslett is deservedly one of the exceptions. The variety of his war service qualifies him better perhaps than any other American Air Service Observer to write of Air Observation: the efficiency of his work is attested sufficiently by the fact that he was rapidly promoted from lieutenant to captain and from captain to major. His personal daring and courage, and the extent of both, need no testimony and indeed could have none more eloquent than the citations he received and the decorations awarded him.

To say that this officer or that officer was the "greatest" fighting pilot or the "greatest" observer in the American Air Service overseas would, assuming that it were possible, and many hold that it is impossible, assuredly be improper; but of Major Haslett it may be said with entire propriety that the value of his services was certainly not exceeded by the services rendered by any other observation officer in the American Air Service. And it must always in after life be a source of great pride and satisfaction to this officer to know that he successfully executed every mission upon which he was sent up to the day that he was shot down far behind the enemy lines in the Argonne after an unequal but protracted combat with superior enemy forces.

Few men even in the Air Service had so many and so astounding adventures as befell the author of *Luck on the Wing*, and of these, fewer still lived to tell the story. In simple but vivid language Major Haslett tells in this book of many of his astonishing experiences. Life at the front with him was just one adventure after another—from his first trip over the lines when he sat in the observer's seat in a French plane perfectly at ease and in blissful ignorance of a French battery's desperate efforts to signal him that there was a squadron of seven German Fokkers over him. Through this first adventure his amazing luck carried him safe (or was it a Divine Providence moving as ever inscrutably?).

And this same amazing luck carried him safely through an even more remarkable adventure. While under heavy ground fire on an artillery mission he was thrown out of his "ship" but caught the muzzle of his machine gun as he went over, and in some way managed to pull himself back into the airplane—and then completed his mission. But on September 30, 1918, even Major Haslett's luck deserted him and he was shot down and captured. The rest of the war he spent mainly in unsuccessful efforts to escape from German prisons.

Luck on the Wing tells of these adventures—and others.

It is appropriate in concluding this brief introduction to tell of some of the work of Major Haslett overseas which he himself cannot well mention. Much of this officer's service at the front was spent as operations officer. As such his duties did not require him to execute missions over the lines himself. Major Haslett insisted always on doing not only the full share of such perilous work as would fall to an officer not in an executive position, but more. His argument to his commanding officer was that only by experience over the lines could an operations officer thoroughly master his work—a theory that he went far toward proving.

Whenever ultra-dangerous work presented itself this officer was quick to volunteer. Major Haslett was more than an observer, he was a student of air operations. He was among the first of the American officers to prove that low flying over German trenches was not only possible but was a method of effective attack for airplanes. At the time that he was shot down he was engaged in working out the problems of adjustment of artillery fire on moving targets by airplanes—a question of prime importance in war-fare of movement.

This officer during the course of his service at the front not only contributed exceptionally distinguished personal services over the lines and as an operations officer but he also contributed ideas and suggestions of considerable value in the development of Air tactics and Air strategy, and as I have mentioned before he had the proud record of successfully executing every mission which he undertook during his entire service at the front with the single exception of the mission he was on when he was shot down by superior enemy forces.

With entire frankness Major Haslett has told the story of how he succeeded in getting an assignment as an observer and in later getting duty with Colonel Brereton's squadron at the front. And by his own account he has shown with equal frankness that he had no hesitation in overcoming obstacles to this accomplishment by any means that came to hand. Perhaps some of the fastidious may find something to criticize in this. But Major Haslett's all-impelling motive was to serve his country by meeting his country's enemies on the battlefield. And it was this same all-impelling motive which gave inspiration to the personnel of the American Air Service, which brought to the Air Service proud achievement and dauntless courage in action. Service against the enemy is a good soldier's ambition. This motive carried Major Haslett to the very front rank of all American observers, and gave him the adventure of which he tells in *Luck on the Wing*.

William Mitchell,

Brigadier-General United States Army.

Washington,

Feb. 24, 1920.

Chapter 1

Beginner's Luck

We had been up with the French Squadron for about three weeks and it had rained every day or something else had happened to prevent flying. We had a wonderful social time, but our flying had been so postponed that I actually began to think that the French did not want us to fly, probably lacking confidence in our ability, so, one day I walked up to the captain and by means of his imperfect English and my perfectly inelegant French we managed to perfect some close, cordial and personal liaison. I told him that we appreciated the long, drawn-out dinners and the very excellent quality and quantity of the red wine and the white wine, but that actually we came up to take our first trips over the line and learn a little about observation. He shrugged his shoulders and said that he felt quite sure that we would be there for three or four months and that there was absolutely no hurry.

I told him he did not know the American Army, for while I would admit that we had not shown much speed up to the present time in getting squadrons on the fronts or in the manufacture of our ten thousand airplanes a month, or our five thousand Liberty Motors, at the same time, somewhere, someplace, somehow, someday, we were going to make a start and that I was quite positive that we were not going to have any observers unless the French got busy and trained some for us, and that in my mind we would be leaving mighty soon and it might look sort of suspicious on paper if we had been with the squadron a month and had never taken a trip over the lines.

This sort of impressed the captain and dear, old fellow that he was, he immediately ordered "Mon Lieutenant Dillard," who was his operations officer, to arrange for me to accompany the next mission over the lines, as a protection. This was scheduled for the next day. A French lieutenant by the name of Jones was to do an adjustment of a battery of 155's, and I was to accompany him in another plane to protect him from any attack by German airplanes.

That night we played bridge until midnight, whereupon we all shook hands, as is the French custom, and departed for our various billets. My bridge had been rotten—my mind was on a different kind of bridge: How was I to bridge that next day—What did it hold? The night was chilly as the devil and as I picked my way in the darkness I could hear very plainly the rumble of guns and could see the artillery flashes very clearly, although the front was twenty kilometres away. I began to think about my first trip over the lines that was soon to come. I was mentally lower than a snake. I hadn't prayed for some time and I was just wondering whether or not I would pray that night. My solemn idea of prayer was that it was an emergency measure. I was always reverently thankful to the Maker for His blessings, but He knew that for He must have known my mind.

I believed that God helped him who helped himself, but when the question was too big for man to control, then it was the time to invoke the help of the Supreme Being. I was inclined to think this case was only a duty of war in which man should help himself. So, I had decided that I would go ahead and handle it as a man to man proposition, reserving invocation for a more serious situation, but as I was getting pretty close to my billet I heard a sudden noise that gave me a real thrill—a big cat jumped out of a box and ran directly in front of me. It was too dark, of course, to tell the colour of that cat, but the condition of my mind convinced me that it could be no other colour than black and that it was an omen that bad luck was sure to come my way. When that cat ran in front of me my "Man" theory was gone, absolutely; I knew quite well that I was going to pray.

I lay abed for fully three hours, going over in detail every piece of the machine gun, what I was to do in case of a jam of the machine gun, and what I was to do in case of stoppage of the gun. I was trying to picture in my mind silhouettes of the different German airplanes that had been on the wall at school, and which I, to my regret, had not studied. Then I remembered reading stories of how poor boys were shot down, and most of them on their first flight, and I thought of airplane accidents and I thought of my girl. In fact, I had such a variety of thoughts that when I finally dozed off, that *quasi* sleep was a nightmare, and when from nervous and physical exhaustion about three-thirty o'clock in the morning I reached the point where I was really sleeping, I was suddenly shaken, and, of course, I jumped as if branded by a hot poker.

It was my French orderly telling me it was time to get up to make my flight. I first realised the truth of that little saying, "There is always somebody taking the joy out of life." He was crying, "*Mon lieutenant! Mon lieutenant! Il est temps de se lever*," which is French for "It is time to get up." I had a notion to direct him to present my compliments to the captain and to tell him that I was indisposed that morning but I couldn't speak French well enough to express myself, so, there was only one thing to do and that was to make a stab at it. I dressed and took my nice, new flying clothes which I received at Paris, and hobbled the kilometre and a half out to the field. The crews were already there and also the other flying personnel. Of course, I put on a sickly smile as if to help things along, but honestly there wasn't much warmth in my handshake.

The Frenchmen were all excited, standing around a telephone in the hangar and I found out from one of them who spoke English, that they were trying to get the balloon to find out about the visibility. This pleased me for my feet were already chilling and I was as strong as horseradish for each moment's delay. In a few moments the lieutenant put the receiver on the telephone and with some sort of an ejaculation I saw the face of Lieutenant Jones, who was to do the adjustment, assume a very dejected attitude, for while these Frenchmen are the strongest people in the world for lying abed in the morning, yet they certainly hate to have their trouble in rising come to naught by reason of impossibility to perform the mission assigned and in this case I found that the visibility was "*mauvais*," or "no good." So, we just hung around.

In a few moments one of the enlisted men came up to me and saluted me smartly, and mumbled a lot of stuff about "*voulez vous*" something, "*voulez vous*" being all I could understand, so I beckoned one of the Lieutenants who spoke a little English and he asked me if I wanted a "*Raelt Saeul*" or "ordinary open sight." I had never had a course in aerial gunnery and I did not know the difference; in fact, my experience in machine guns consisted of two lectures by a guy who didn't know much about it, at Fort Sill, the dismantling of one gun and about an hour and six minutes in an open firing butt at Amanty, France. I was afraid "*Raelt Saeul*" would be something technical, in which case I would certainly demonstrate my ignorance, and to my dazed mind "open sight" certainly sounded frank and on-the-square, so, of course, I just shrugged my shoulders and pointed as if I were perfectly familiar with both but under the circumstances I would take the "open sight."

They were both quite surprised and tried to open the discussion upon the relative merits of each, but I passed this up and made it emphatic that "open sight" it would be. I found afterwards that the "*Raelt Saeul*" was a great deal more accurate. So, they put the machine guns on the plane with "open sight." I wanted in the worst way to get around and monkey with those machine guns, but I knew if I did I would certainly shoot someone up or kill myself, so I laid off. It was a terrible predicament; I knew I had no business going up and my conscience began to hurt me for the sake of the Frenchmen I was supposed to be protecting. Incidentally I must admit, in capital letters, that I had my own personal safely somewhat in mind. But it was too late—I had to go through with it. It was the proposition now of luck, and lots of it. We kept on with preparations; it was still foggy.

At nine o'clock we went in an automobile and got our breakfast, which for the Frenchmen always consisted of hot chocolate and a piece of bread, but for me it usually consisted of ham and eggs, and potatoes, and jelly, and bread, and butter and coffee, and as it usually consisted of that—as this was probably my last breakfast it certainly would not consist of less this time. So, I hied me forth after having my "chocolate" with the Frenchmen, and gave my landlady her usual two *francs*, in return for which I had the repast above accurately described.

We went back to the flying field and waited until about eleven o'clock. I had made up my mind that I was going through with it and the nervousness was beginning to wear off. About noon it got real cloudy and at twelve twenty-six and a half the first drop of rain fell. Believe me, the exhaust action of my Agfa of relief was not unlike one of these carnival, rubber balloons when it is dropped in hot water. They, of course, called it a day, came in and had "*dejeuner*" and gathered around the bridge tables, while Dillard played some very classical airs upon the automatic piano which this squadron carried with it.

In the middle of the afternoon the shower completely ceased, while Sol came out in all his magnificent glory; magnificent I say, to the farmer who wants to till the soil, to the sweethearts who want to go on a picnic, and to the washerwoman who wants to dry her clothes, but for me, it was just like an April shower on a new silk hat—I lost all my gloss—for in a few moments "*mon capitaine*" came in and announced that he felt we could get the planes off the ground. We called up the battery and they were ready so we climbed into the automobile and went out to the field again. The mechanics rolled those two dilapidated Sopwith planes out of the hangars and gave those rotary engines a turn and they began to burr. That whirr and burr felt to me just like the whirr and burr of the dentist's burr that gets in the middle of a wisdom tooth and hits the nerve.

The other two American student observers were out on the field. Phil Henderson, who always was the head of his class and very mechanical by nature, gave me a few added remarks about some technical points of the machine gun, how to do in case of a jam, etc., while Hopkins, the other American, jollied me along. It was the first time I had ever had a ride in a Sopwith. I do not know whether it was from the fact that I was not used to climbing into the Sopwith or that I did not know what I was doing, but anyhow I stepped on that one particular part of the fuselage which is supposed to withstand only wind pressure and as a consequence my one hundred and eighty-two pounds made a nice hole in the canvas.

Of course the Frenchmen had complex fits but the pilot merely shrugged his shoulders as if to say that it wouldn't impair the flying qualities of the boat. I honestly felt that the tearing of the canvas was an omen that I ought not to go. But already the other plane was taxiing out to take off, and it was like a drowning man grasping for the last straw. They came up to see if I was fixed all right. I was fixed, and in more ways than one. I was holding on to the fuselage for all I was worth. Fortunately they noticed that I was not strapped in and so they proceeded to strap me.

They said something about the "*mitrailleuse*" but the "*mitrailleuse*" did not worry me—I said it was all right. I did not know what they were talking about, although I afterwards learned that they meant machine guns, but what they wanted me to do was to shoot a couple of bursts into the ground to see if the guns were working. I tried to twist the tourelle (the revolving base upon which the machine gun turns) around to shoot in the proper direction, but it would not budge. The corporal came around and pressed a little lever which released the mechanism and, of course, the tourelle turned just as easy as a roulette wheel. Then they told me by means of sign language to point it at the ground and pull the trigger. I did, but I almost broke the forefingers of both hands trying to pull the trigger.

The pilot was getting nervous; I think he clearly saw that I was

25

probably like the American airplanes that they had heard and read so much about—I was not coming across. The corporal came around to determine the trouble. I shrugged my shoulders, French fashion, as if to say "*ça ne marche pas*," that is, "it doesn't work," but lovely as that gun lad was he did not give away my ignorance but simply said "*Vous avez oublié*"—"you have forgotten something," and he proceeded to pull down the little latch on both guns which unlocks the entire mechanism. Then he stepped out of my way and I pointed the guns. Having, as I said before, almost broken both my forefingers trying to pull the trigger, I pulled in the same manner, force and fashion, and before I could get my fingers off of the triggers I had almost shot both of the magazines full.

I thought those guns never were going to stop firing. The Frenchmen surely oil their guns and have a similar high strong technique in pulling the trigger that our high-grade artists on the piano have with staccato notes. I could see by the expression on the faces around me that they were indeed surprised at American methods but anyway the guns worked, so I said "tres bien" and my pilot taxied the plane out, gave it the gun, and took off.

This plane did not have telephones; if it did they would have been useless, because I did not speak French understandably, and the pilot did not know a word of English, and we had not agreed upon any signs.

The other plane had gained considerable altitude and after about fifteen minutes I was able to orient myself by means of my map and to know that the aerodrome was directly beneath me. We had gotten about three hundred meters above and two hundred meters behind the first plane. In a few moments the first plane headed due north and we followed. Over to my right I saw very plainly Souilly, which was later destined to play such an important part in the history of the American Army, being the headquarters of our First Army in the Argonne drive. In a few moments more I saw below me the shell-torn country and the two peaks known as "Hill 304" and "Dead Man Hill"—to the French they are known as "*Trois Cent Quatre*" and "*Mort Homme*"—which were so prominent in the fighting around Verdun.

Only a few days before I had visited these same places on the ground and I had seen the myriads of human bones in that mighty cemetery which, though originally properly interred, were being continually brought to the surface by the constant and incessant artillery fire. I thought at the time how terrible it must be to live day and night in the trenches of that graveyard, knowing not but that in the next instant you, yourself, might be the one destined to replace the remains which, from four years of exposure, were crumbling into the dust. On that visit the thing that impressed me was the minuteness of the individual, for both German and French, though the deadliest of enemies in life, found a common resting place, side by side, in the same yard of earth for which they had given their lives to gain.

While on the ground I had seen an airplane high in the heavens and I thought how much more wonderful it was to fight in that broad, open expanse of atmosphere where the extent of one's endeavour is not limited by a section of a trench, but only by the blue heaven, the reliability of the motor and the accuracy of the machine gun. It is strange how one's outlook can change. Man is the slave of temperament and romantic dissatisfaction. Excite him and he pleads for quiet, give him solitude and it becomes unbearably monotonous. I was enwrapped by environment. When in the trenches of that bleached bone-yard the monotony and horror were agony to me—so many bones and those huge trench rats—I wanted in the worst way to get out of those trenches and back to the airdrome, to take my chances mid those silver-winged birds that floated so gracefully above.

But, when I actually got over this same graveyard at six thousand feet altitude that same picture again entered my mind. I knew I would soon be crossing the lines. I began to think of the terrible fall of six thousand feet before hitting that cemetery, and then I thought what I would look like after I did hit. In fact, cold shudders crept through me like a continued electric shock. For once I was downright scared and if I could have changed places with the stalwart guardians of those trenches in the rat-ridden graveyard beneath I would have run for the opportunity. I would, at least, have something solid to stand upon.

We were going straight toward the lines and directly in front of Hill 304 and "*Mort Homme.*" They stood out extremely clear and plain. The perpetual shell fire had left its mark for while the surrounding country was green with vegetation, yet these two hills bulged forth, bald and barren. Hill 304, or "*Trois cent quatre*" was the worse. It had nothing growing on it at all. In fact, it was so bad that one of the polite, French jokes on a bald-headed man was to call him "*Trois cent quatre.*" After flying parallel to the line for a few minutes we turned back toward our own lines. I determined that the French observer had found his target and would soon be calling his battery.

This trip was a complete surprise because I understood from my meagre instructions that even when crossing the line the enemy anti-aircraft artillery, commonly called "the archies," would certainly open fire, but everything was calm and peaceful—except my mind. I looked at my map to find where the panels were displayed. Panels are large, horizontal strips of cloth which are placed on the ground in various symbols near the battery and are used as a means of communication between the battery and the airplane. The airplane communicates with the battery largely by means of the radio telegraphy, but as it was not practicable to receive the radio signals in the plane from the ground, we used these panels.

Among the signals formed by these white panels, which are quite clearly discernible from the air, are those meaning that the "Battery is ready to fire," "Battery has fired," "Fire by Salvo," "Change target," and many, many others including the signal "There is an Enemy Plane near you," which is the most dreaded panel that can be displayed. I might incidentally mention that there is another panel which means "There is no further need of you; you can go home." Now this may not have a great deal of significance to the average layman, but I'll say that when the sky spy has been tossed about for a couple of hours on the archie billows he joins the union which says that "go home, you're fired" is the greatest little panel of the whole panel alphabet. So, in a few minutes I picked up the location of the panels and I had a little chart on my map board showing the meaning of these many panels. I had had some instructions upon them while at Observation School, but I had depended on crossing the bridge only upon arrival thereat, so I did not pay a great deal of attention to them. The descriptive chart on my map board interpreted the panels in French so I was not sure that the chart would do me any good after all for my knowledge of technical or any other kind of French was less than meagre.

I saw the panel "Battery is ready," and then the plane headed toward the lines and in a moment the panel changed to "Battery has fired," so I looked over in Hunland but I could not find where the shells had hit. In my mind they were hitting everywhere so how could I pick out the particular ones that Jones was directing. In a moment I again saw "Battery is ready,"' and again I looked directly toward the supposed target. Suddenly I saw four shells strike real close by and my vigilance was rewarded for I was to witness an actual adjustment of artillery fire against a real enemy. Then I took a genuine interest in the adjustment and paid very close attention to every detail. In fact, I was so attentive that I was oblivious to the fact that my mission was to protect the leading plane.

Delving into this new game I indulged in certain psychological conclusions which took my mind off of the thing that had been troubling me; namely, the unpeaceful condition of my mind. This was most interesting. They had fired about six or seven salvos and were coming very near to the target, which was a cross-road. I thought it must be a wonderful observer to guide the battery with such unfailing accuracy and I looked forward to the time when I too might be a genuine sky spy and with American batteries seek out the enemy and destroy him, for after all was not the position of the aerial observer one of the most dangerous of the army, the spy—for his greatest mission was to find out the intentions of the enemy and if he succeeded in bringing back the information without being seen all would be well, and if he was seen it meant he had to fight for his life. Like the spy he, too, lived within the lines of the enemy.

This was the gist of my thoughts when I suddenly looked down at the panels and saw a huge "Y" displayed. I did not pay much attention to the "Y" but I saw Jones' plane taking a steep spiral toward the earth. I did not call the attention of my pilot to it because I thought "Y" was something usual, meaning, perhaps, that the signals were not understood so Jones was going down low to get closer to the battery in order that his wireless could be heard, but Jones kept going right on down near the battery and finally kept circling around close by at about three hundred feet altitude. I looked around and did not pay any great heed; I thought Jones would soon climb up again. In a few moments I saw the battery take in their "Y" and put it out again; take it in and put it out, as if to attract my attention.

Then I saw them running back and forth with individual panels in different directions, which had a sort of cinema effect. Then they brought out double panels and made a great, huge "Y." Then I thought "Y" must mean something if they were making all that fuss about it, so I thought "Y"—"Y"—"Y"—"Y." It was a memory test for me. I felt I should remember some of those panels and here was the chance to think clear and quick. I went through the various fake memory courses I had taken and tried in every way to determine the meaning of "Y," so after trying to figure it out by the law of association, the law of likeness of sound, the law of impress and five other such hopeless laws I began to regret that I had paid so much for that memory course. Then I casually took out my map chart to find out what "Y" meant.

As I ran slowly down the list of signals I came to "Y" and looking across it I saw "*Attention! Ennemi avion pres de vous*," which in English means "Look out! Enemy plane close to you." I thought I did not know French but I certainly acquired it with the speed of lightning. I dropped my map board like a shot, jumped up in my cockpit, grabbed my machine guns, released the tourelle, and whether I knew anything about that tourelle or not, it followed me as I spun around three times in a complete circle of three hundred and sixty degrees with the speed of a ballet dancer—I was bent on getting anything near me. I stopped—looked frantically at the pilot, expecting to find him dead. He had turned around to find out what the rumpus was about. I did nothing but to give him a sickly smile for I had nothing else to give. They had a signal commonly used among observers to describe a cross with the forefinger and point when the observer saw a German plane, but this was among the thousand things I had not learned about aerial observation. So, he went on, straight flying, just aimlessly drifting on.

I gradually calmed myself and looked into the sky above me and I saw seven airplanes which were hidden from the view of the pilot on account of the position of the wing above him. I was quite sure from the lectures I had had in America from instructors who had never been at the front, that one could easily distinguish an enemy airplane by the huge black cross that is painted all over it, and so I skimmed my eyes over them trying to discern the cross. I could not, and yet the airplanes stayed about six hundred meters above me and kept on circling around. I decided that I was being duped and that there was some under my tail, so I hung my anatomy over the fuselage and after a hasty examination I was convinced that the only airplanes in that sky, except our own, were the seven above me, and Jones, who was down by the battery still circling around.

I looked down at the panels and they were still frantically waving that "Y" and peering at the planes above me I saw that they were still circling around. I did not know what to do. In fact, I did not do anything for fully thirty seconds, except to watch those planes, but they did not make any sudden manoeuvres or show any inclination to attack. I looked down again and they were still putting out that big "Y" and my pilot was just floating along as if nothing had ever happened; in fact he had never seen the panels and was not paying any attention, having undoubtedly an abundance of confidence in the ability of the American observer, and as I could not disappoint him in his splendid judgment as to my ability I just used my perfectly splendid logic and decided that if they were German planes they certainly would have attacked me before this time, and since they had not attacked, they could be no other than French; and the solution was that the battery had probably received notice from the squadron commander that there was a green observer up and so they were undoubtedly flashing this "Y" trying to play a joke on me, believing that I would run home, and thinking, perhaps, that I had not seen Jones go down in his rapid spiral.

So, I decided to show them that they could not fox me and I just stayed up there, floating around. After I had stayed up there for about fifteen minutes Jones pulled out for home, and when I saw him shoot off in that direction I decided that perhaps the signal had been changed and "Y" meant that "there is no further need for you," and that they were just trying to attract my attention so that we would start home. I decided I would not show any more ignorance than I had and would say nothing of the incident. So we went home and I felt pretty good that I was in sight of the airdrome again and still alive and that nothing unusual had happened after all. Jones got there about five minutes ahead of me.

Meanwhile the battery had called up the squadron and told them that the observer in that second plane was either the bravest man they had ever seen or the biggest idiot, that he had stayed up there daring seven Germans to attack him single handed, while they had toiled feverishly for fifteen minutes with "Y's" and double "Y's" trying to give him warning and that his utter disregard of their signals had so unnerved the crew that fifty *per cent*, would be sick for a week. So, of course, the entire flying personnel, including adjutants, sergeants, corporals, lieutenants and aspirants (cadets) were there, as well as the *capitaine*, to meet and greet us. Jones, of course, had gotten out and also told them about our narrow escape from the seven Huns and you can imagine the excitement and ejaculating of a bunch of Frenchmen when anything so preposterous as this should happen, especially with a new American who as yet was untried in valour on the battlefields of France.

They were thoroughly convinced that I was an unusually hard-boiled soldier and that I had just dared the Germans to come down, and knew all the time that they were Germans and that I was really seeking a fight with the seven. Imagine the reception—they all ran up to the plane, double time, including the rather heavy captain, waving their hands and shouting, but their remarks were so jumbled that I could not grasp the entire meaning. They all came up and shook my hand and patted me on the back and said *"Bravo!" "Tres Fort!"* and *"Vive l'Americain!"* and a lot of other stuff. I was not much excited about it because I thought perhaps that was customary as it was my first trip.

Then, just as suddenly as if they were waiting to hear a pin drop, everything became quiet, and they demanded my story. Strangely enough I was perfectly convinced that we had done nothing wrong, so I asked one of the lieutenants who spoke a little English to tell me what it was all about. He threw his head back in great surprise and demanded in low tones, "Did you not see those seven planes above you?"

I quietly answered, "Certainly, I saw those seven planes," for I did.

Then he continued in the same low voice, "And did you not see the battery putting out the 'Y' with the panels?"

I said, "Certainly!"

Everybody and everything was as quiet as death, and then the light began to come to me just as the sun's rays so suddenly and rapidly dispel a fog, and I knew exactly what the next question was going to be. He said, "Those were German planes, didn't you know it?"

At those words I almost faded away but this was the real time for a little "emergency" drama, so I assumed the role of a modern Daniel emerging from the den and shrugging my shoulders with a very much emphasized forward motion of the chest, I bellowed, "Sure, I knew they were Germans all the time. I didn't run (emphasizing "I") because I wanted to say I had shot down some Boche on my first trip over the lines."

Their fond expectations of the bravery of the Americans and incidentally my prowess were met. They were proud of their new ally. Then came many cries of *"Bravo! Bravo!"* and indiscreet whispers of *"Croix de Guerre,"* and we all went home, with the American Sky Spy about the most popular fellow he has ever been.

That night we had a real banquet at which I bought the champagne and the red wine. While we were celebrating I was going over the whole matter and long before I went home that night I realised that it was more than luck and a "handful of Marines" that had saved me from those seven Huns. It was manifest destiny, for I found that the reason those German planes did not attack when they had me cold was that one of the aerial tactics in vogue at that time, was to send one plane low as I was, with a strong pursuit patrol high in the clouds above so that when the enemy attacked the lower plane the pursuit planes high above could dive on the enemy, thus having the great advantages of position, speed and surprise. The seven Huns thought I was a dupe—I was, but not the kind they thought. Mine was a case of ultra-distilled beginner's luck.

CHAPTER 2

Hardboiled

Every soldier from the general to a private sooner or later gets his reputation. It comes through observation of a man's action and attitude by his fellow soldiers. Those who early in the game get a favourable reputation are indeed fortunate while those who get in bad, so to speak, are generally strictly out of luck for reputations are like postage stamps—when once stuck on they are hard to take off.

There was one reputation which many sought but which represented to me exactly what a real man's nature ought not contain—this was the common prefix to one's name of "hardboiled." The accepted meaning of this word varied with localities, but I did not like it even in its most liberal and favourable interpretation.

In every locality except the front, the common acceptance of the term "hardboiled" indicated one who in any position of authority was a pinheaded, tyrannical crab, who was so engrossed in himself and his big stick position that he was entirely oblivious to the feelings and rights of those he commanded. In other words, one who neither sought counsel nor permitted argument. At the front, however, common usage had changed the meaning of this famous term. There it ordinarily referred to the soldier who had the maximum quantity of bravery and the minimum amount of common sense and who purposely flirted with death for the fun of it and who valued life somewhere between eight cents and two bits, war tax not included.

I paraphrase Mr. Shakespeare in that some people are naturally hardboiled, others acquire it and still others have it thrust upon them. I must add another class which has grown quite common since the war is over; that is, assumed hardboiledness, and it is ordinarily recognised in the blowing of one's own horn lest it be not blown for true enough the genuine hardboiled soldier in the fighting interpretation of that word, is strictly a man of action and not words.

It is, of course, safe now for the parlour sofa soldier to explain to his audience just how much help the rest of the army gave him in winning the war. I sometimes pull this gag myself when there is a good chance to get away with it. For those who, during the war, were in the rear waiting for the chance to get to the front it was also healthy to emphatically emphasize just what wonders they would accomplish when fortune favoured them by sending them to the lines. There it was entirely a matter of environment for there was no likelihood of those perfectly harmless bluffs being called since there was no possible opportunity at hand to demonstrate the modest announcements of their prowess.

But take it from me as the greatest lesson I learned, it is the most ill-advised speech possible when one arrives at the front and begins to scatter broadcast promiscuous remarks either about one's own particular courage or anyone else's lack of it, for, believe me, you will no more than get the words into sound than they will be called and called strong. At the front they have the peculiar faculty of making immediately available full opportunity for demonstrating daring, bravery, or any other manly virtue that the newcomer claims as a part of his makeup.

The now famous 12th Aero Squadron formed, with the 1st Aero Squadron, the first American Observation Group at the front. It was located near a little village called Ourches, about fifteen kilometres north-west of Toul. Upon completion of my training with the French, during which time I had just the one trip over the lines, I was assigned to the 12th Aero Squadron. My time over the lines amounted to only fifty-five minutes. The only thing I knew about sky-spying was what I had read in my books and what I had picked up in our embryonic course of instruction at the schools. Just as soon as I had gotten to the squadron I began to hear wild rumours of how the commanding officer was going to send back to the rear all those observers who did not have sufficient experience over the lines and that he expected them all to have had, at least, ten trips over the lines.

I immediately realised that I had no chance whatsoever with that standard, so my only hope was that the commanding officer would be a nice man and that I could talk him into making an exception in my ease. I found out that the squadron was commanded by a young Regular Army officer by the name of Major Lewis Hyde Brereton. No one I could ask seemed to know a lot about him, for the squadron was just being organized and would not operate over the front lines for a couple of days, at least. So I had no dope on the manner of man I was to approach and who fortune had destined should become the leading and controlling influence of my life at the front.

Captain "Deacon" Saunders, who has since been killed, had been one of my instructors at school and he had been designated by Brereton as chief observer. "Deac" was a wonder. It was his duty to round up the wild observers and present them to the commanding officer, who cross-questioned them as to their experience and the like. So, "Deac" grabbed me eventually during the morning of the second day and took me over to meet His Royal Majesty, the commanding officer of an actual American Squadron at the front. He was quartered in a wooden hut commonly known as an "Adrian Barrack."

Saunders gave a sharp military knock of three raps and I, of course, expected to hear a nice, soft, cultured voice say, "Won't you come in?" What I heard, however, was considerably different. "Who in the hell's there?" The voice was sharp and impatient, and it suddenly made me feel "*less than the dust beneath thy chariot wheel.*"

Captain Saunders spoke up, "Sir, I have a new observer reporting and would like to present him to you."

"What's his name?" gruffed the irate voice.

"Lieutenant Haslett, Sir," replied Captain Saunders.

"Who in the devil asked for him?" came from the inside.

"Sir," said my godfather, "he was included in the list sent down by Headquarters."

"Well! Is he there now?" said the power within.

"Yes, sir, right with me now," was the reply, and I began to pull down my blouse and otherwise mill around in preparation for my entrance, for this last question was encouraging.

"Well," came the growl, after a discomforting hesitation, "I don't want to see him. I'm writing a letter to my wife and I can't be bothered."

I felt about as welcome as a skunk in a public park. In all my military experience I cannot re-member anything that really hurt me so much. I wanted like a starving man wants food, to be a plain buck private in the Infantry, for this was the most inconsiderate sort of a bruise; it hurt me more, of course, because I was an officer and was wearing my pride on my coat sleeve. The only thing that bolstered me up was the fact that I had finally gotten to the American front and I was willing to sacrifice practically anything to stay there, but I certainly realised that the man who put the "boiled" in "hardboiled" was no other than Major Lewis H. Brereton.

At noon I saw Brereton for the first time. Someone was kind enough to point him out to me, and I remember thinking at the time, "How can a pleasant-faced youngster like that be so hardboiled?"

That afternoon, around three o'clock, "Deac" Saunders said we would again attempt to get an audience, and just as he introduced me, for some reason, Saunders was called away, and I had no friend to sponsor my cause before a hard judge. Brereton had just finished his after-dinner nap and was in the act of dressing in flying clothes to take a little flight around the field, so being in a hurry, he began throwing out snappy questions at me, as if trying to establish a record in getting rid of me. He lost no time in continuing his dressing, and did not even ask me to sit down or to allow me to relax from my painfully rigid position of Attention. What's your name?" he commanded. Lieutenant Haslett, Sir."

"I've got eyes," he snapped. "I can see your rank all right. How does it happen you are Infantry?"

"I volunteered, Sir, for Aviation and was detailed."

"Volunteered or was ordered to volunteer?" he queried. This hurt for it had been strongly rumoured that in the selection of aerial observers, many line commanders had gotten rid of their undesirables by sending them to aviation—as observers.

"Volunteered, Sir!" I replied, bluffed and bewildered.

His attitude showed plainly that I did not strike him at all well. I was still standing at attention, when he sharply commanded "Sit down!" Believe me, I did.

"How many hours over the lines?" he fired next.

Hours! That word removed the floodgate and the last ounce of my composure ebbed away. My time over the lines was measured in minutes and here was a man talking in terms of hours, already. This was the one thing I must avoid, so I sought to evade the question.

"I have had eight hours in the air, Sir." But I did not lay any stress on "in the air."

"I don't care how many hours you've had in the air. I asked you how many hours you have had over the lines. That's what counts with me," he said emphatically.

There was no escape. If I lied he could look up the record, so, I decided to tell the truth from necessity for this was not the place or time for "period of the emergency" statements.

"Fifty-five minutes. Sir," I confessed.

"I thought so," and he nodded his head in proud self-approval just as does the cross-examining prosecutor when he finally forces an admission from the man at bay. "How many adjustments over the lines?"

"None, Sir."

"None!" he said with a noticeable inflection. "How many in the air at school?"

"None, Sir," I said meekly enough.

"None" he exclaimed emphatically. "How many on paper?"

"One, Sir," I said, hesitatingly, for my energy was getting low.

"Well," he snapped, as if glad to dispose of me on my own lack of merit. "You don't know a damn thing about observation. How in the hell did you get to the front, anyway? I might use you as a mess officer, but if you ever intend to fly over the front you've got to go back and learn something about your job. This is a service squadron, operating over the front. Whoever ordered you to Toul intended to send you to Tours, so I'll call up and get orders for you to go back to the rear."

Tours, by the way, was the great aviation primary school of the American Forces—while Toul in those early days signified the front.

My pride fell like a demonstration of Newton's law of gravity. This hardboiled man could not be approached by man or beast; and it seemed the only thing I could do was to say "Yes, sir" and beat it I had visions of returning to the rear for further instruction, yet here I was at the front—I had finally realised my ambition and yet was on the verge of having it strangled by this man's inconsideration. I could not endure the thought—my attitude changed in a moment—I determined to assume hardboiledness, for after I had gotten that close to the front I certainly was not going back without putting up some sort of a fight. Besides. I had a few days before written my folks and my friends that I was actually at the front, and what kind of a legitimate reason could I give in my next letter when I would have to tell them I was no longer at the front. The only legitimate excuse a soldier has for leaving the front after being fortunate enough to get there, is an incapacitating wound, and while Brereton had dealt me several wounds which were sure enough incapacitating, yet they were not the kind that would put pretty little gold wound stripes on my arm. Sure enough—I was down and about to take the count.

There is always a way to get out of the most entangling net. Sometimes it narrows down to only one way and if the captive fails to choose that one particular hazard out of a thousand plausible ones, he is out of luck. So it was, there was only one way to extricate myself from the web that Brereton had spun so quickly around my whole ambition. Very, very fortunately I had picked the winner. It was a long chance, but I was Houdini this time. This hardboiled monster had to be met with his own style. So, with an assumed role of the hardboiled, man-eating cannibal, I right away cut out that "sir" stuff, took out my pipe and calmly started to fill it with "Bull Durham" tobacco, which was the only brand our little canteen had in stock, and we were really mighty happy to get even that.

Brereton plainly saw that my temper had gotten out of bounds and that I was preparing to come back at his apparently final decision either with tears or blasphemy or both. But just as the matador seeks to infuriate the bull by waving a red flag before slaughtering him, so Brereton seeing me about to fill my pipe with this well-advertised and justly celebrated brand of tobacco, ventured forth.

"Lieutenant," he said, clearing his throat by way of emphasis, "I take it that you are about to use some Bull."

He said this quite seriously, without even a follow-up laugh to dull the cutting bluntness of it. It apparently was his day, for like the infuriated bull, I was seeing red already. I made the final run to gore him or be stabbed myself by his waiting poniard of arrogance.

"You can call it Bull, if you like," I fairly cried, "but, pardon my frankness, the fact that you classify what I have to say even before you have heard it shows your premature judgment, just as you prematurely judged my ability or lack of ability as an observer before even giving me an opportunity to demonstrate it. Of course, I don't know whether you have ever been over the lines or not, but if you have, you will concur with me that the greatest thing an observer needs is 'guts.' I don't say I'm a world's beater in experience, but one thing I have and which can be demonstrated nowhere else but over the lines," and here I threw out my chest, "and that is 'guts' or politely 'intestines.' Now, if that asset means anything to you, you will give me a chance to stay with the 12th. All I want is an opportunity to render good service, and to show the stuff I am made of. Now if you don't want to give me a chance I can do nothing further except to tell you that I will get the chance elsewhere and that I know more about observation than most of your observers ever will know."

Major Brereton was dumbfounded. When he recovered he gave a real, ringing, golden, genuine laugh, came across and said, "Damn it all, my boy, maybe you're right I haven't been over the lines myself yet."

I knew quite well he hadn't. If it had been otherwise I would have mended my speech considerably.

"But, old man," he said, "I was only thinking for your own good. Hell, if you want to be a damn fool and go on over the lines, knowing as little as you do, it's not my worry. Go ahead!"

I thanked him and told him that I had to start some time and I would be all ready to go over at my first opportunity.

Fully decided to make myself at home I went out to the hangars and to my surprise, I saw the same kind of old airplanes we had used in the observation school in France. They were an obsolete type of French service plane, known as "A.B.-'s"—*Avion Renault*—which in English meant "Renault Air-plane." The accepted meaning to the Americans, however, was "Antique Rattletrap." The only good feature about the A.B. was the dependable motor, but they were very slow and did not fly well. They might in those days pass for a second class training plane, but to have them on the line, functioning as service planes, was a great surprise to me. The life of the airman depends very largely on the bus he drives. We all wanted Spads, Salmsons or Breguets, and, of course, any prospect of an American plane in those days was a myth, so there was noticeably keen disappointment when we found that we must fly over the front in those old, discarded and obsolete A.B.'s. However, they were all we had and so far as I was concerned, I knew that my stay in the squadron was largely by sufferance and I could not afford to kick lest I be also kicked out, so I immediately decided to think a lot, but say nothing.

Those first few missions over the lines were tame enough. Happily enough I got in as substitute on the first mission of the squadron over the lines. The only diversion was the anti-aircraft artillery fire, or the "archies," and there was nothing tame about that. However, there was more activity in sight for in a few days Brereton announced that he wanted his squadron to be a specialized one and that he desired the names of a few observers who would volunteer to specialize in "Infantry contact patrol." "Infantry contact patrol" to my mind meant nothing, so from force of habit I volunteered. The only other observers who volunteered were Lieutenant Emerson, a fine, young fellow who was killed a couple of days later, and Captain "Deacon" Saunders, our chief observer.

Though I was not previously known in the squadron I somehow became prominent right off, and with it went the title of "Hardboiled."

So, when several of my newly formed acquaintances solemnly asked me how long I expected to live doing "Infantry Contact Patrols," I hied me forth to the operations room and asked the chief observer what it was all about. I was handed a pamphlet written by Colonel William Mitchell, who was Chief of Air Service at the front It started out with these words, "Infantry Liaison, or Infantry Contact Patrol is the most hazardous, but most important of all missions." My eyes began to bat like a heavyweight's before he falls for the count, and as I read on I came rapidly to the conclusion that the volunteer system was absolutely all wrong and the next time any of these nice, uncertain jobs were offered I'd take my place in the draft.

I found that Infantry Contact Patrol indicated the airplane that gains contact with the infantry in battle, which is done by flying extremely low over the troops, finding the advanced lines, transmitting signals, calling for reinforcements, ammunition or the like, attacking machine guns or anything else which is holding up the advance of the infantry; further, that the great drawback to this kind of work is that the infantry airplane is constantly under fire from enemy machine guns and enemy pursuit planes, which, of course, concentrate to hinder this all important work. I decided that with my huge body in a slow A.B. plane my life on this work would be measured in minutes. It was a real scare.

There was no backing down since I had already volunteered, so I began to study the bulletins, with the greatest care. No attacks, however, took place in this quiet sector so I hit upon the brilliant idea of trying out this new work in practice on the Germans, then I would be properly experienced should there ever actually be an attack. The trenches in the Toul Sector were well marked, especially around Layeyville and Richecourt. So I studied those trenches from maps, photographs and from the air, until I knew them perfectly.

One evening I had as my pilot, Lieutenant Jack Kennedy, who was one of our flight commanders, and who was in for anything new and exciting, so, we fixed it up that we would try out a practice infantry contact on the Germans. When we finished our usual evening reconnaissance of the sector, we played around looking for a good situation that might be assumed. When we got just above Richecourt, which was the beginning of the German lines, I discerned quite clearly, about ten, big, fat Heinies slowly wobbling down a communication trench. It apparently was a relief going into place. The trench was unusually long and was not intersected by any other trenches for some length.

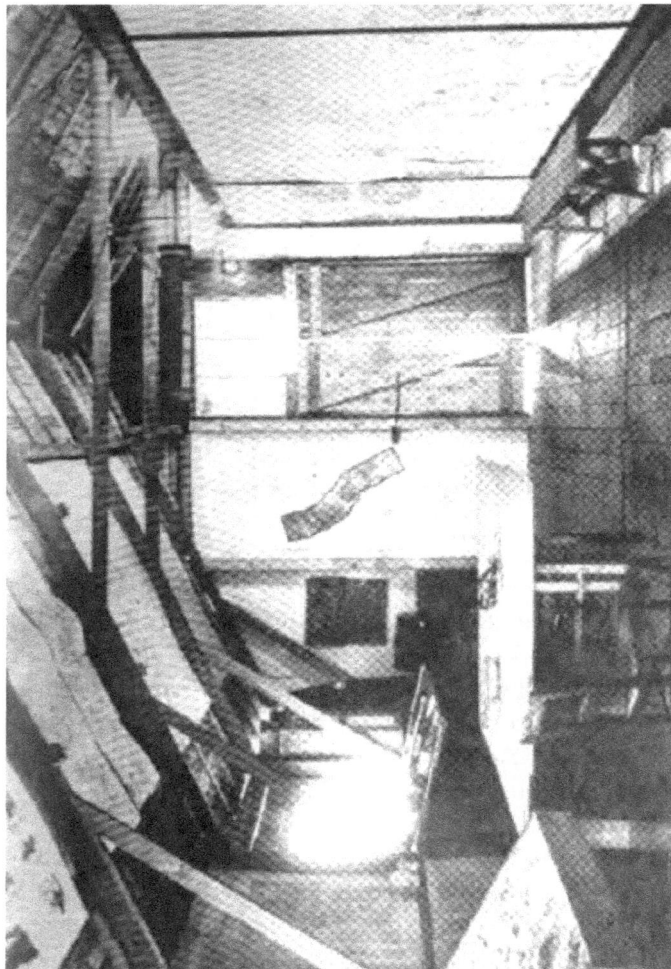

An Operation Room of an American Squadron at the Front, showing battle maps, war plans and photographs

"Those Germans are bringing up ammunition reinforcements for the battle," I assumed. "They must be stopped!" The ammunition was soup.

I called Kennedy, pointed them out to him, and told him my assumption. Without waiting for a signal, he dived like the winged messenger of fate. Kennedy had been trained with the English Pursuit Pilots and he was handling that big, slow, lumbering A.R. like a little fighting scout. We came out of that dive with a quivering groan, and Kennedy, at about one hundred meters altitude, began to circle over that communicating trench, waiting for me to halt the procession. He was too fast for me, but when I finally got my heart gauged down a bit, and my Adam's apple released from its strangle hold on my windpipe, I began to make my final estimate of the situation. The Heinies had stopped and were eyeing us like country boys at their first circus. It was easy. All I had to do was to pull the triggers, for my guns were directly on them and the enemy reinforcements would never reach its intended destination. They could not scatter—they were rats in my trap.

Then an intensely human appeal struck me—poor, belated, unfortunate Heinies—they were not my personal enemies, and if I pulled the triggers it would be little short of murder. To balance this was another series of thought—they were enemies of my country—of the United States—and, if I allowed them to live, would probably kill many of our own brave doughboys; perhaps they belonged to machine gun squads; perhaps it was they who had killed my pals, Angel and Emerson, a few days before. Such were my thoughts when suddenly. *Spiff! Spang!* and two bullets went between me and the gasoline lanky tearing a hole in the top plate. *Spiff!!!* Another went through the fuselage, smashing into bits, my hard-rubber wireless reel. It was no time to indulge in psychological deductions—I realised that I was being fired at from the ground, and like my lumbering old A.B., I was about to pass from obsolescence to obsolete.

The application of proper psychology indicated that since I was being fired at, the war between the United States and Germany had not ended and below me was the enemy. I was conscious of something within calling me to "Do my duty!" I did. The bullets began to sing at the rate of six hundred per minute, and my tracer bullets did not betray me. They were finding their mark. Measured by the standard that an Ace is one who gets five or more Boche, I became an Ace in a day—and also the first American Ace. However, strangely enough, when my friends today ask me, "How many Boche did you get?" I can truthfully say, "Between seventy-five and a hundred," but when they say, "How many Boche planes did you shoot down?" I have to renege for I am not an Ace.

I was quite certain that my assumed reputation of "hardboiled" would be justified by this day's performance. The mechanics took a just pride in the holes in our plane and patched them over, as was the custom, with miniature Iron Crosses, showing the date of the puncture. The next morning I noticed myself being pointed out by several officers of the squadron and this gave me the rather satisfactory feeling commonly described by the English as "cocky."

Brereton had nothing whatever to say about the mission but Captain "Deac" Saunders said "Bully," and called me "Hardboiled," but my reputation lasted only two days, four hours and twenty minutes, for the group commander threw ice-cold water over everything by saying that he considered it very poor work, that it had no military value and that it only encouraged reprisals on the part of the Hun who would soon do the same thing. So, I was temporarily classed as bone-headed, and a "dud" and was in dutch all round. There was one little spark of encouragement in a remark that Brereton made, which got to me through the medium of a friend, and it took away the sting of the group commander's criticism, for to me the only boss I had was Brereton, and what he said was law.

The adverse remarks of the group commander hurt at the time, I admit, but when Brereton said he did not exactly agree with him that the mission had no military value, and also several months later, when this type of mission had so developed that we had special squadrons in the Saint Mihiel and Argonne offensives that did nothing but this particular type of work, I was happy indeed. Later, all types of planes were ordered to fire at troops on the ground when their assigned missions were completed, and the opportunity presented itself.

Shortly after this mission, Henderson, who was the operations officer under Captain Saunders, the chief observer, left for the aerial gunnery school in the south of France, with three other observers, to take a month's course in firing and then return to the front. This left the much coveted position of operations officer open and, of course, everyone was wondering to whom it would fall. It was the biggest job in the squadron next to the commanding officer and the chief observer, and since the operations officer dealt directly with the observers I was mighty anxious to find out who my new boss would be, so that I could make it a point to get along with him.

That night Saunders came around and called me out of a little game we were having—I thought perhaps I was scheduled to go on a special mission of some kind, but there was a surprise, undreamed of, awaiting me.

"Haslett," he said, "Henderson is going to Caseaux tomorrow and I have recommended you to Brereton for appointment as operations officer. He kicks like the devil that you haven't had much experience, but he likes that mission you got away with and thinks you are 'hard-boiled,' so he may come across. He is going to decide before breakfast tomorrow."

I could not believe what he had said and humbly asked him to repeat it all over from the beginning. I slept very little that night, for to me this was the biggest thing in the world, it would clearly indicate that I had made good and that my stay at the front was assured.

The announcement on the bulletin board the next morning was signed by Charley Wade, the best squadron adjutant I have ever seen, and stated that I had been detailed as acting operations officer. I was the happiest lad in the world. I don't believe any success I can ever achieve will make me as happy as I was when I read that order. The first thing I did was to consult Brereton and Saunders as to how they wanted it operated. Brereton gave me no dope whatever, except "to run it as I darn pleased and if it did not please him he would soon get someone who would."

Thus I started. As new pilots reported I always took them over the lines for the initial trip. Saunders asked me to do this for he felt that I was either absolutely worthless or extraordinarily good. If I was worthless there would be no loss if the green pilot killed me, and if on my part, I succeeded in getting the pilot back safe, it would be wonderful training for the pilot. Some logic, I reasoned—thus my job of official breaker-in of new pilots. I say "breaker" for a new pilot coming to the front must be broken in just the same as a horse has to be broken for riding or driving. It is equally true in both cases that the first ride is the worst.

We had one boy who had been with us since the formation of the squadron, but who had been sick and was unable to fly. His name was Phil Schnurr, a young lieutenant from Detroit, Michigan. Phil did not get his first trip over the front until sometime around the first of June. Of course, I was the goat and took him across. It was not new for me as he was about the sixth I had broken in.

I emphasised to him that in my experience over the lines among other things I had found that the best way to get away from the "archies" was to dive when they got near you for the reason that it was much easier for the "archies" to correct deflection than it was for them to correct range. Whatever that means, it's all right. Phil knew.

I decided that we would call on a battery and adjust the artillery on an enemy battery in a woods close by, which was causing our troops considerable trouble, so I explained to Phil just what we would do, going largely into detail

The plane was a little shaky even at the take off, and I decided right away that Phil was not quite in the class with Rickenbacker, but I attributed the cause to his natural nervousness, which would soon wear off. After calling our battery by wireless for several minutes they finally put out their panels and we immediately went over to look for the hostile battery that had been reported the same day. I found it and we just started to cross the lines to go back into France when Fritz played one of his favourite tricks. The Germans allow the observation plane to cross the line and come in for not more than three or four kilometres, then when you turn to come out, having followed you all the time with their range finders, they suddenly open up with all their anti-aircraft artillery and generally catch you in their bracket at the first salvo. You are bracketed when they have fired the first shots—one above, one below and one on each side of you.

It is not a pleasant position in which to be caught. But they did more than that to us—they not only bracketed us, but one shot got us right under the tail and when Phil heard that burst, known commonly as "Aviator's Lullaby," which is the most rasping and exasperating noise it is possible to imagine, he remembered my admonition to dive if they got close, so just as the tail went up from the force of the concussion of the shell directly below us, Phil pushed forward for all he was worth on the control stick. The sudden jarring of the plane from the explosion and the more abrupt dive, released the throttle, throwing the motor into full speed. And with one mighty jerk like the sudden release of a taut rubber band, all three forces working in the same direction, and aided by the flyer's greatest enemy, Newton's law of gravity, that A.B. omnibus started straight down in one terrible dive.

Poor old Phil was thrown completely out of the pilot's seat and was only saved from going headlong into the open air by his head striking the upper wing of the plane, which knocked him back into the seat, dazed and practically unconscious. The "hard-boiled" observer in the back seat did not have a belt, for my famous A.B. plane was not equipped with them. I went completely out of the cockpit and in that brief second I had one of the rarest thoughts I have ever had—I was sure I was going to be killed and I regretted that it was in such a manner, for it was, indeed, unfortunate that I should be killed in an airplane accident when I might have died fighting in combat—there, at least, I would have had an equal chance with the enemy.

As I shot out of that cockpit with the speed that a bullet leaves the barrel of a gun, my foot caught on the wire directly underneath the rim of the cockpit. With superhuman effort doubled by the intuitive hope of self-preservation, I grabbed the top gun which in those days was mounted on the top of the upper plane. Backward I fell. For a moment I was completely free of the airplane, in midair; as I fell my chin hit the outward pointing muzzle of the machine gun; I threw my arms forward and closed them in the grip of death. I had caught the barrels of my machine guns and the next thing I was conscious of was that I was hanging over the side of the fuselage, below the airplane, but clinging on to those machine guns for dear life. The old admonition "to stand by the guns, boys" was tame compared to me. My watchword was "hang on to the guns, boy."

The plane had fallen about one thousand feet and was still going, but stunned as he was, Phil was doing his best to level her off. I was sure if he ever did level her off the strain would be so great that it would fold or strip the wings. I cannot account for the strength that came to me, but I do know that if I ever should get into a good fight, I only hope I may again be that superman, with the agility of the ape riding the flying horse at the three-ringed circus.

I scrambled up on those machine guns, grabbed the rim of the cockpit and the brace of the tourrelle and climbed in. My ears were splitting; I was certain that the top of my head had been shot away, for there was nothing there but a stinging, painful numbness. My heart was beating at the rate of nine hundred and ninety-nine round trips per second. I felt that my whole body was being flayed by sharp, burning, steel lashes. Then I suddenly grew as cold as ice and passed out. It was almost a literal case of a man being scared to death. When I saw the light again I was limp in the bottom of the fuselage. My first sensation was that we had crashed and I was alive in the wreckage, but the drone of the motor brought me to the realisation that we were still flying.

Evidently Phil had gotten control again, so I pulled myself up to my seat in the cockpit and got my bearings—we were headed toward home. Poor Phil had his eyes set straight ahead. At his right he had a mirror which reflected the movements of the observer, thus obviating the necessity of continually turning around. When Phil saw my reflection in that mirror, however, he whirled around at top speed to verify it. His countenance changed from being horrified to complete surprise and then to genuine delight. He had evidently looked around immediately upon gaining control, and not seeing me, had realised that I had been thrown from the plane. He was going back to the airdrome to tell the horrible tale.

I could read the look in his eyes and I do not know what in the world possessed me to do it, but I gave a huge, roaring laugh that would have made the jovial laugh of the old southern mammy sound meagre in comparison. Phil did not laugh, he only gave a sickly, sympathetic smile. The boy was thoroughly convinced that I had suddenly become insane—he had justification for his conviction for there was nothing in the world at which I could find a reason for laughing at that time— either in law, fiction, fact, heaven or earth.

I was still sort of dazed, but we were fast approaching our airdrome. The thing that preyed on my mind was that we had started out to do an aerial adjustment and had not finished it. What would Brereton say—and I was now operations officer—what would the battery say? Could I ever get the results from observers when I did not bring home the bacon myself. There was only one thing to do—the adjustment started must be finished. I shook the plane and spoke to Phil through the old rubber tubes we had in those days. I told him what had happened, but that I was all right now. Then he told me what happened to him.

"How's your head feeling now, Phil?" I asked.

"It's cracked open," he answered.

"Can you go ahead and finish this adjustment!" I demanded.

"Yes, I can," he said, "but I'm not going to, I'm sick."

"So am I, but you know that's no excuse at all. Let's try it," I ventured.

He said nothing but turned his plane toward Germany and we were again speeding toward the lines.

The battery must have realised what had happened or almost happened, so when I began to wireless to them the location of the target, they were sportsmen just like all the rest of that 26th Division and they immediately put out the panel meaning "There is no further need of you, you can go home."

This was commendable on their part and it sorely tempted me to take them up, but I quite well knew there was no excuse to make for going home now since we had both decided to finish it, so I immediately called back and asked "Is battery ready?" They, of course, put out the signal that it was. So I gave them the coordinates of the target and we started to work. We were both extremely nervous and weak and the anti-aircraft kept firing with unceasing violence. We stayed in the air for exactly an hour and fifty-five minutes and fired a total of fourteen salvos. But luck was the reward of our perseverance. On the fourteenth salvo we struck the huge ammunition dump next to the enemy battery and I have never in my experience seen such a huge and magnificent explosion. Our plane, five thousand feet above the explosion, even quivered at the concussion. We, of course, announced to the battery that they had hit the target and then started for home. The last wireless was unnecessary, however, for they had seen the explosion. It was visible for several miles around.

We were so confused and nervous that we fiddled around another half hour before we could find our airdrome. We finally landed and poor old Schnurr was a nervous wreck. Pride forbids me from accurately describing myself.

Schnurr confessed to me later that he barely knew how to fly, having had only a few hours in a plane, but that he was so anxious to get to the front that he managed to slip by the "Powers that be" and finally got there. He begged me not to tell it for fear he would be sent back to the rear. Phil was an example of the high-spirited boys who first led the way for America's aerial fleets. These high-hearted men were America's first and greatest contribution.

However, for Schnurr's own good I decided that he should have more training. I got Brereton off on the side and whispered some things in his ear. He was furious at the fact that a pilot had been slipped over on him who did not know everything about flying, and said that he would send Schnurr to the rear right away, but when I finished whispering these things in his ear he changed his mind, for I repeated to Brereton that in my opinion the greatest thing an aviator can have is nerve, or to again use the army term, immodest as it is, "Guts;" ability is only secondary. Then I told him how Schnurr had gone on and finished the work and had blown up the ammunition.

Brereton agreed to keep Schnurr, and we gave him several hours solo flying under the instruction of more experienced pilots before again permitting him to go over the lines.

What happened to Schnurr? Well, he turned out to be, in my estimation, undoubtedly, the best observation pilot on the entire front, and he went through the hard fighting at Château Thierry, Saint Mihiel and the Argonne, and although he had some of the hardest and most discouraging missions ever given to a pilot, he was one man who could always be counted upon to deliver the goods if it was humanly possible. In fact, he became known as "Old Reliable," for he never failed.

On the matter of promotions and decorations Phil Schnurr had the worst deal that was ever handed to anyone. He started as a Second Lieutenant and ended that. He was never decorated although recommended to my knowledge, at least eight times. Something always went wrong. Where several proposals would go in, Schnurr's would never go through. If anyone in the American Army in this War should have his chest covered with medals and crosses from the Congressional Medal of Honour on down—it is Phil Schnurr.

From this mission, which is small compared to some of Phil's later accomplishments, we were both cited by General Edwards, commanding the 26th Division, as follows:

Headquarters 26th Division
American Expeditionary Force
France, September 17, 1918.
General Orders

No. 78
Extract

******

4. By his accurate registration of Battery F, 101st Field Artillery, on June 10, 1918, First Lieut. Elmer R. Haslett, 12th Aero Squadron, caused the destruction of a large quantity of enemy ammunition, his plane being pierced several times during this dangerous work. The Division Commander takes great pleasure in acknowledging the valuable aid of this officer and congratulates him on his skill and daring.

******

C. R. Edwards,
Major General, Commanding.

After this mission Brereton, himself, classified both Schnurr and me as "sufficiently hardboiled." The boys took up the refrain and thus, after assuming the attitude necessary, I finally acquired the title and had the emoluments and incidental responsibility thrust upon me.

CHAPTER 3

My First Scrap

The early days in the Toul Sector are remembered by the aviators in the observation end of the game as quiet ones. All the time I was there with the Americans I had never even seen a Boche plane. I understand they were around all right, but all of our young pursuit pilots of the 94th and 95th Squadrons were so determined, individually, to become the first American Ace that they scoured the sky from daylight to dusk, and to such a degree of success that the Boche thought it rather risky to even leave their own airdrome.

About the middle of June the Rainbow Division was down in the Bacarrat-Lunéville Sector and having been there some time without aviation, it was decreed that the 12th Aero Squadron, which had done most remarkable work in the Toul Sector, should proceed at once to a little place called Flin, near Bacarrat, to work with the 42nd Division—the Rainbow—in order that they might have more experience in aerial cooperation.

We still had our famous old A.B. training busses, although we had been again promised everything from Spads to Salmsons. So, with our eighteen pilots and eighteen observers and our eighteen A.R. busses we started for our new station, which was about one hundred and fifty kilometres distant.

We were supposed to begin work on the following day, just as in actual battle, for we were simulating a real, active battle move. Our trucks left in the afternoon about three o'clock and without mishap, should have arrived there about midnight. The planes were to wait until the next morning and fly down. The truck train got there all right, and got busy fixing up quarters and getting ready for immediate operations. We expected to see our famous eighteen planes arrive in a well organized, close formation at about eleven o'clock that morning, but at eleven they did not arrive and we heard nothing from them until about three o'clock, when one of our young pilots came from somewhere out of the sky and landed. We asked about the other seventeen, to which question he showed the greatest surprise, and explained that he had been detained by motor trouble and had been unable to get off with the main formation which had taken off four or five hours before him. Immediately "Dame Rumour" stepped forth, and the absence of the other planes was attributed to everything from being lost in Germany to being shot down by a German plane.

While we were discussing the matter someone noticed two planes very high in the air. We thought, of course, that they were our planes and were probably lost. Ideas were rampant as to how we were going to signal them to get them down, when suddenly we heard the *splutter-splut-splut*, intermittently, of machine guns way up in the sky. This was new to me. We thought, of course, that someone was merely trying out his guns. These ideas were soon dispelled for following this short, intermittent sound we heard one, steady, singing stream of sound—then we knew that an air fight was on. We did not have time to realise exactly what was happening for the steady stream of fire suddenly ceased and we saw one of the planes falling, out of control. It was swaying back and forth like a falling leaf, and filling the air with a miserable *swish-swish* sound. The horrible speed of the fall caused both wings to collapse and fold, and the compact mass soon came diving toward earth like a huge torpedo. It crashed with a terrible thud on the very edge of our own field. When the awful horror of the moment passed, we all started to run to see the Boche that had been shot down.

We dragged two crushed and lifeless bodies from the debris and in contrite and humble reverence to our hostile brothers of the air we removed our caps, while the surgeon began to take off their flying garments in order to find their names. It is hard to imagine the ghastly horror of the shock we received, when, upon unfastening the collar of the outergarment the green uniform of the German aviator was not revealed, but instead the Royal Seal of the Crown of England. Two brave, British lads had made the Supreme Sacrifice. It is a memory that will never be obliterated from my mind, and I can well remember how the sentiment of the crowd changed like a burning slap, from icy but human feeling to one of fiery hatred and cold-blooded revenge. High in the sky above the victor was winging his way back to the land of the Hun.

Young Davidson was the only pilot we had there and we had only one A.R. on the field. It was the one in which Davy had just landed. We knew it would be foolhardy to send that Antique Rattletrap up against that Hun, but every man in the squadron from the chief mechanic to the major's orderly and the second cook wanted to go with Davy to avenge our British brothers. Davy and his observer, however, took off but only got several hundred feet when the motor stopped. We had no more gasoline, but the Hun was already too far toward home and our A.R. could never have climbed the altitude at which the Boche was flying, so we were obliged to give it up. There was no loss of morale, however. Matters were too serious to even think of that. The thing that was worrying us was what had happened to our other seventeen planes. Had they all met the fate of the British Tommies? Had they too been caught unawares, for a lot of them had flown with mechanics at the observers' guns. They had undoubtedly lost their formation and in straggling about it was quite easy to suppose that they, too, had become an easy prey for the "Hun in the Sun." Believe me, we worried.

Not very long afterwards a French soldier came along and handed us some messages which had been received at the French telegraph exchange in a nearby village. They were all from our aviators and the wires indicated that they were scattered all over that country from Nancy to Chaumont, and from Colombey-les-Belles to Lunéville. The whole bunch had gotten lost and in trying to pick their separate ways they had certainly made a mess of it. I expected to hear of some landing at Paris or Bordeaux, but while they did not do that, after we finally plotted their various locations on our map, take it from me, it was a study in polka-dots. One by one they drifted in and outside of one valuable plane that had to be salvaged, in a couple of days we were able to work.

Brereton did not arrive with the squadron. He had been ordered to General Headquarters for a conference of some importance, which occasioned him some delay. The morning he arrived, however, he brought Henderson, Herold and Hopkins along. They had been detached from us at Toul in order to take a Gunnery Course at Caseaux, in the south of France.

Henderson again took over his duties as operations officer. Brereton called me in his office and told me a big secret. He stated that there were big things ahead—that we were going to Château Thierry quite soon—that he would be chief of the Air Service for the First Corps and that I would be made a captain and the operations officer for the corps. He asked me how many times I had been over the lines in the last month to which I answered that it was about thirty times. He said that was too much and that I needed a rest. He then told me I should not fly any more for a couple of weeks, so, I took him at his word and settled down for a rest, meanwhile forming plans for my new job. I strutted around the squadron and gave as my reasons for retiring, that it was for my nerves and the doctor had so ordered. The boys all fell for this line and they were very thoughtful of me and asked me many times each day as to the condition of my nerves.

In a few days, the 42nd Division was ordered out of the line in order to prepare themselves for the, affair which we afterwards learned was Château Thierry, and the 77th, which was the first National Army unit to go in the trenches, was ordered in the line. Their Artillery was not yet ready for work, so, some of the 42nd Artillery stayed over to support them. The first morning after the 77th took its place in the trenches the Germans pulled off a raid, the result of which put about six hundred of the 77th in the hospital from gas and wounds.

When the raid came off, the first reports we got were from the French at daybreak. They said that the Boche had attacked along the entire divisional front from Domévre to Badonvillers, and that we should send out a plane at once and find the line in order that the General might know where to send reinforcements. It was Lieut. Hopkins' turn on alert duty, so, he took off right after daylight in the execution of his first mission over the lines. Hopkins had lots of courage—he was a brave fellow—he got tangled up with the "archies" and a huge piece of shell tore away a part of his knee, but he stayed right up there trying to execute his mission until he realised he was losing consciousness from loss of blood. I knew nothing about the attack and was still in bed when they dragged old Hoppy in.

This looked like exciting business for us so when they dragged Hoppy in, I got up and began to pay attention. Meanwhile they had got the next man on the "H" list—Lieutenant Armin F. Herold— whom I knew quite well and he had already been sent out to get the line. I helped lift Hopkins into the ambulance to be taken to the hospital and then went over to get my breakfast. I was about half finished when someone rushed in and said that Herold was also coming in. Of course, we hurried out just as the plane taxied up to the hangar. The mechanics lifted Herold out of the plane with his right leg shattered at the ankle by machine gun bullets fired from the ground. He, of course, had been unable to get the line of our troops, but gamely stated he had gone the limit to find our troops having flown most of the time at about two hundred meters.

I saw Brereton looking around for a new crew to send out. I knew my name began with "H," but I knew also that I had been put on the resting list, and furthermore was sick, according to the doctor, so my mind was perfectly at ease. There were others in our squadron whose names began with "H"—among them, Henderson, Harwood and Hinds, and we were not restricted to "H's." But Major Brereton was known to do funny things. I was starting into the mess shack to finish my breakfast when I heard that familiar voice and its equally familiar inflection demand with a tone of final decision, "Where's Haslett?" I had a creepy feeling run all over my ribs for I knew it was an off-day. Brereton came into the mess hall after me. I certainly had not gone out to seek him.

Then he showed the first and only sign of weakness I ever knew him to display—"Haslett," he said, "do you want to go and finish this mission?" Always before he would have said "Haslett, go and do this mission." I neither answered "Yes" or "No" for I could not honestly answer "Yes" and I dared not answer "No." I simply started to get my flying clothes. Johnny Miller, who had been the pilot for Hopkins on the first attempt, and who afterwards was killed at Château Thierry, begged Brereton to be permitted to finish the job. Brereton agreed.

We got into an A.B. plane and I fairly filled the cockpit with signal rockets for the Infantry. I was determined that there should be no reason for the Infantry claiming that they did not see any rockets. Johnny gave her the gun, but as we left the ground the engine failed. We got the plane back to earth without a crash, although we were quite near to one, and that was a premonition for me. I had always figured that if anything mechanical failed, it was certainly a sign that I had no business in the air that day. When that engine failed I told myself "Goodbye." I felt my time had come.

We jumped out and got into another plane which was the one they had brought Herold back in. The cockpit was spattered from one end to the other with blood, but we did not have much choice in planes, so, we had to take what would run. The sight of that blood and honest-to-goodness, downright fear caused me to grow momentarily weak. I wanted to get out, take the count, and worse. As we were getting ready to take off one of my very dearest, old friends ran out to the plane, all excited, as if the spirit had suddenly moved him.

It was Captain "Pop" Hinds, who was killed later that same day, in an airplane accident. "Haslett, God bless you, old boy," he said, fairly weeping—"something tells me this is an off-day, and that you're not going to come back. You've taken too many chances already. I don't want you to go, old man."

Believe me, that took all the pep I ever had out of me. I leaned over the side of the fuselage and patting him on the back said, "Pop, don't let it worry you. I'm the luckiest guy in the world—they can't get me." And in my soul I thought, "Well, those are my last words—they're not half bad at that. How will they look on my tombstone?"

So, I gave Johnny the high sign and we took off. I could see Johnny was nervous because in taking off, the wing almost scraped the ground. Herold had told me where he thought he had seen a panel displayed by the infantry, so I first looked that place over and then we flew along the front at exactly five hundred meters above where the line was supposed to be. I began shooting off my fire rocket signals to the Infantry in order to get them to put out their white panels from which I could mark their location on my map, but regardless of the many rockets I fired they did not put out a single panel. We went down to four hundred meters, flew along the line for fully twenty-five minutes and fired rockets, rockets, rockets. Still there was no sign of a panel on the ground.

Down to three hundred we went—no panels yet. I felt like going home because I thought three hundred meters was plenty low enough, especially on an off-day, but there was only one thing to do—that line had to be located somehow, so, we went on down to one hundred. No wonder they got Herold, the machine gun fire was something terrible. I had already fired my last rocket and was never so disgusted in my life for there was no response. Finally with the naked eye we located our troops at less than one hundred meters. I hastily plotted their position. If ever a man feels he needs a friend it is when he is going through that awful machine gun fire at two hundred feet and trying to be composed enough to accurately mark on his map the location of things he is seeing on the ground. We developed some very fine observers like Wright, Baucom, Bradford, Powell and Fleeson, who got to be wonders at this work, which is, after all, the greatest work of aviation.

We had been up for about two hours, so, when we landed the whole bunch came rushing out to meet us, including Brereton. It was the only time I ever saw him run. I showed him the line and told him how we got it—the holes in the plane from machine gun bullets convinced him of the truth. I told him I would hazard my little reputation that the dough-boys did not have any panels to put out, for if they had displayed them I would certainly have seen them.

He was genuinely peeved and after telephoning the location of the line to appease the growing anxiety of the French, we got into Brereton's car to go to Divisional Headquarters to find out what was the matter with the infantry.

We arrived at Bacarrat, went to the Division Headquarters, and the signal officer, in reply to our inquiry, told us quite unconcernedly, that the division had panels all right, but this had been their first occasion to use them and they had not been issued for the dough-boys would get them soiled, or might use them for handkerchiefs or the like. Brereton, of course, was in a rage and we demanded to see the commanding general of infantry. On duty at the Infantry Post of Command was a lieutenant colonel in the National Army, who had probably held some big job in civilian life, but who was certainly not born a soldier. He said that the general had been awake all night and had just gotten to sleep after the morning raid and so he did not care to awaken him under any circumstances.

Brereton began to cuss in great style and said he'd be blamed if he'd send his aviators out any more to be killed unless he got some cooperation from the infantry and it was a terrible note when the chief of a service could not see the general when an all-important matter was pending and that if this brigade wanted the Air Service to work with them they had better show some willingness to help. He then demanded that the panels be issued at once. The lieutenant colonel began to show a little concern, and although he was looking right straight at our wings, he asked, "Are you aviators!"

Brereton said, "Yes, of course. What did you think we were?" The old boy then showed some speed; he got hold of the telephone and after saying "Sir" many times in order to appease the wrath of the general who had been so rudely awakened and so as not to increase his disfavour, proceeded to tell him that the Airplane major was here, and wanted to talk to him. Brereton was forced to laugh at this new title and for some time afterwards we all called him the "Airplane Major." The general of course realised the gravity of the situation and was also mighty peeved about the failure to provide the troops with panels. The mission ended with the agreement that the panels would be issued immediately and the general expressed his sincere regret at the loss of our aviators, and, I believe, became converted to the fact that the Air Service was also a factor to be considered in winning a war.

On our way back to the airdrome we stopped at Artillery Headquarters and they wanted us to go up that afternoon and do an artillery adjustment, as a couple of batteries were sorely in need of more accurate regulation in view of further raids by the Germans. When the artillery colonel asked who would do the work Brereton looked at me and I looked at Brereton, and I knew it was settled. "Why, Lieutenant Haslett here has been worked pretty hard and I wanted him to rest up, but I guess he can do this one and then take a rest."

The artillery colonel was surprised, but I was more surprised at what he said—"So you are Haslett! Well, well, I'm glad to know you. Colonel Sherburne of the 26th Division Artillery told one of our majors about a big mission you pulled off for him in the Toul Sector. We sure will be glad to have you work with us." This was the first recognition of this kind that I had ever gotten and coming from Sherburne it was like a million dollars to me, for he was one of the greatest men with whom I had ever worked. Of course, after that compliment I was delighted and I certainly would not have let anyone else do the adjustment at all. I felt like a hero with three wings. I was determined to do the best adjustment I had ever done in my life.

When we got to Bacarrat on the way to the airdrome, an orderly handed Brereton a message which dampened my spirit and determination completely. It read that Captain Hinds—Pop Hinds—the old man who that morning had told me about his premonition that it was an off-day and that I ought not go for I would not come back—was himself killed while taking off from the airdrome, his plane having gone into a tailspin. His observer, another "H"— Henderson, the operations officer, was seriously injured. This news hurt me more than any I had ever received. Pop was about forty-six years old and had gone into the flying game simply from the desire to help along American Aviation, having had some little amateur training before the war.

We had tried our best to get him back from the front because we realised that the old fellow didn't have much of a show against the Hun and under actual fighting conditions, but Pop would not go back. He was always the first to volunteer for any mission. A braver man I have never seen. He was a real daddy to us all and his great human understanding and sympathy caused us to pay him a marked deference and respect. He often won a lot of money from the officers playing poker, but in his characteristic unselfishness, he spent it all for candy, cigars, cigarettes and tobacco for the enlisted men and mechanics. He was their idol and there was little, if anything, that they would not do for him.

Henderson was one of my best friends and happily though he was not killed, it had a peculiar significance to me that one hundred per cent of the day's casualties were "H's." It looked like an off-day for the "H's" without a doubt. There were only three of us left—one was the ordnance officer, Hall by name, who was not a flyer; Harwood, who was busy as could be on some assignments; and myself.

The only "H" left was to do an artillery adjustment that afternoon. I thought it might be a good idea to put off that adjustment until the next day, but I could not get up the courage to tell Brereton my honest convictions.

When we got to the airdrome everyone was feeling mighty low, because these were our first casualties, outside of the loss of Angel and Emerson in the Toul Sector. The bunch all felt that though the sun was still shining and it was a good day for flying that there were better days ahead. Even the squadron surgeon sent out the recommendation that the flying be suspended for the day. I felt quite relieved for I could not conceive of any one going against the recommendation of the *"Medico."* But this did not appeal to Brereton. In his characteristic manner he loudly and emphatically announced that he was not going to let a little thing like that stop the War; if a squadron went to the front they must expect some casualties and that flying would go right on. I did not eat any dinner; I did not care for it; for, as usual, I did not agree with Brereton. I honestly felt that flying ought to be suspended in deference to old "Pop" Hinds if for no other reason at all.

I really dreaded that flight and even the praise of that artillery colonel meant nothing in my life. No one came out to see us off. It was the wrong atmosphere. There was gloom in the sky, gloom on the ground, and gloom within our own beings. In fact, the whole world looked like a dark cloud. The ordinarily jovial mechanics were all acting like a bunch of pall bearers.

Brereton gave me a pilot by the name of West, which to my mind seemed particularly pertinent for I sure felt as though I were going in that direction.

For protection they sent a plane piloted by Schnurr with whom I had previously had a narrow escape and as his observer they sent Thompson against whom I had no complaint at all, for Thompson on his first flight over the lines with the French, shot down an enemy plane. His presence, of course, was no meagre consolation, for while I did not want any drawing cards along, I felt that if the Germans were going to attack it would be a good thing to have someone along who could do the fighting, because my experience in actual fighting up to this time put me in about the same class that the St. Louis Nationals generally have in the Baseball Club standing. I was at the bottom of the list. In fact, Thompson was the only one in the squadron who had so far had a fight and that was while he was with the French.

When we got over our battery I began to call them on the radio and they put out their panels. We picked out the target which we had agreed upon and sent the signal to fire. I had promised to adjust two batteries. The plan was to finish the adjustment of the first battery and then begin the second. So, after an hour and a half I completed the first adjustment after about fifteen salvos, which, I admit, was rather rotten work, then I started on the second.

The name of my second target was "*Travail Blanc*" which consisted of a section of the trench which was especially heavily fortified with machine guns, having a sweep on our lines in the ravine beneath. I had just given them their first signal to fire, and of course, these batteries not having had a great deal of experience in adjusting artillery fire by airplane, were very, very slow in firing. Ordinarily the observer can time the firing, as a prompt battery fires immediately upon getting the signal from the airplane, and the observer can see the burst almost immediately thereafter. It is extremely important to get the first salvo bursts, for from this the observer knows approximately where to look for the next. So, having pressed the key, I was oblivious to all else in the world except the area immediately surrounding Travail Blanc.

I must have eyed it for fully thirty seconds, which is an unusually long time to watch one particular spot on the earth, for with the speed of a modern German airplane against my antique A.B., in thirty seconds the Hun could get in a very advantageous place from out of a cloud or the sun. I was still straining my eyes on *Travail Blanc* when I heard the *rat-a-tat-tat* of something. It was the first time I had heard machine guns firing in the air while in the air myself, so I felt that we had probably lost altitude and that they were firing at us from the ground. I knew that I could not remedy the situation now, so I again turned my eyes toward *Travail Blanc*, when I saw the four bursts of the salvo strike about two hundred yards from the target. I had just started to reach for my key to send the correction to the battery when again I heard the long, continuous *rat-a-tat-tat* of a machine gun getting louder and louder. I leaned over the fuselage to take a look at the ground beneath me. I thought we should be high enough so that they could not possibly be firing at me and I could not figure what it was.

I wondered where Schnurr and Thompson, my protectors, were, so I began to scan the air directly above me. As I threw my head backwards a streak of fire crossed my face barely missing me. I realised that "White Work" (*Travail Blanc*) was all wrong; my immediate target was "Dirty Work," for instead of seeing my protecting plane above me there was bearing down upon us, with a speed that was indescribable, and spitting a thousand balls of deadly fire at me every minute, a German Albatros Scout Fighter, and directly behind it were two others of the same type. The Hun was already not over a hundred feet from me and was coming on every iota of a second with the speed of lightning and with a deadly accuracy of fire that seemed to preclude any defence. I had been caught napping and it was now only a question of which one of the thousands of bullets that were flashing all around me that would get me first. He was so close that had it been necessary for me to move my machine gun one particle of an inch he would have finished with me before I could have fired a single shot.

The Hun very well knew that he had caught me unawares and that I could not possibly do anything to defend myself. Like a flash my finger flew to the trigger of my machine gun, which was resting in its ordinary position on the tourrelle. I did not move it an inch for fortune had pointed it directly in line with the oncoming German. Already the bullets began' singing from my gun and by the grace of good fortune they were going directly into him. On he came and it seemed that a collision was unavoidable, then with the speed of lightning he dived under me. West saw this dive and sharply banked the plane to keep me in a firing position and as the Boche began to zoom to a position under my tail I again let him have it. I was surprised at the apparent accuracy of my guns. The Hun made a loop and dived toward home.

I knew he was disabled and could not come back. There were still two other enemy planes coming on, but strange things happen in the air, for the other two did not fire a single shot, but turned and flew toward a light fringe of clouds high above us. I have never, however, been able to account for their failure to attack simultaneously with the attack of the first. For once I was close enough to a Hun to see not only the Iron Maltese Cross but also the fatal cross that stared me squarely in the face. It is not a pleasant feeling. The first plane got to

Germany all right, but I am quite sure he was forced to land before he reached his airdrome.

I have a hunch, too, that he took his machine guns out on a cement sidewalk and broke them to pieces, for if ever an aviator had the death grip on his adversary they all had it on me. In a moment I saw Schnurr and Thompson, who were flying quite low. It seems that they were attacked first, which accounts for the first gun shots I heard, and the Hun, having gotten on their tail first, they were forced to dive. In a few minutes the two Huns in the cloud were joined by a third, but fortunately the sun was on our side, so the only thing to do was to watch that cloud. Regardless of these Huns, Schnurr and Thompson began climbing and soon reached their position directly behind us.

I wanted to go home in the worst way but the first law we had learned was that the presence of enemy planes is no excuse in observation for failure to perform the mission assigned. For once in my career I had completely lost my courage and pointed toward home. The starch had been taken out of me completely and it was quite immaterial to me what any one wanted to think about our quitting. I felt that enough was enough and I had more than enough. As we passed over our battery, however, my mind turned to that new Division which had just come in that morning and who were doing their first service in the lines; in fact, it was the first time one of our National Army divisions had been placed in the line. They had been gassed on their first day. What would they think?

This thought of what those lads in the trenches, who, of course, had seen the entire fight, would say when they saw an American aviator quit, changed my whole attitude and, to be frank, saved me from becoming a downright coward. I knew that nothing helped the morale of the doughboys more than to see American nerve displayed in the air and, on the other hand, nothing pulled them down more than to see the lack of it. So, I shook the plane and motioned West to turn around. I threw my switch in, clutched the key and with an unsteady hand proceeded to send the correction of the first salvo which I had seen, but which I almost had not lived to report.

I afterwards learned that the boys at the radio receiving set at the artillery checked each other up on the receipt of this message, so dubious were they that it had been sent from our plane. In a few minutes the battery put out the signal "Received and battery is ready." I then told West to fly in the direction of the line and the three Huns, although I knew quite well if we flew that way we were going to be attacked, but it would be a sportier combat, at least, for I had been caught asleep for the first and only time. I gave the wireless signal to the battery to fire, but I confess I was not looking at the "White Work" target, I was keeping an eye on the three Boche in the sky, looking for more dirty work. The Huns made no sign whatever to attack—they simply kept circling above us in that slender line of clouds.

This was the worst adjustment I have ever been guilty of performing. I simply could not watch the target. We went ahead for an hour and fifteen minutes and during that time we fired a total of seventeen salvos, of which I saw but seven, for my mind was not on the work—I was busy with the cloud. At the end of the seventeen salvos, the Huns came out of the sky and started in our direction, then playfully changed their course and flew back into Hunland. I watched them until they were completely out of sight for I knew they would have to go home some time. Actually I was never so relieved in my life, not for the reason that we were safe from further interruption, but from the fact that we had buffaloed them and were the winners of the day's combat against great odds.

But I was certain that it was only a question of time before they would have to leave that cloud for a *chasse* (pursuit) plane does not carry the same large amount of gasoline as an observation plane, and cannot stay in the air as long in a single flight. I was delighted and beaming all over, and especially happy to think, or rather imagine, what was taking place in the trenches below us—those hardboiled doughboys were, perhaps, congratulating themselves that they too were Americans.

Our gas was running extremely low and it was getting late in the evening, but with two additional salvos, when my mind was free from "enemy planes," we succeeded in putting the battery directly on the target. We then signalled for destruction fire and signalled we were going home. Right above the airdrome the motor stopped and we had to glide in. We had used our last drop of gasoline.

As the airdrome was only twelve kilometres from the line everyone had seen the fight and had seen us stick it out. It was really a joyous time and we all got a real welcome. Even Brereton came across. It was the first and only time in my life I ever heard him compliment anyone or anything. What he praised, however, was not "us" but the plane, in that the Antique Rattletrap was not such a bad old bus after all.

Then everyone got around the plane to count the holes made by the enemy airplane. I did not wait to see how it came out for I wanted to get to my bunk and collect myself. I was told later, however, that twenty-one holes were counted—then the mechanics got tired and quit.

CHAPTER 4

Brereton's Famous Flight

The one characteristic above all others that made Major Lewis Hyde Brereton respected by both those under him, and his superiors, was the fact that he flew over the lines continuously and he never assigned, anyone to a mission that he would not do himself. All the boys were acquainted with his record for he not only fought in the air, but also on the ground. He kept his remarkable hold on men for they knew he was a fighter from the word "Go." His whole career had been marked by a series of brilliant ideas which were so radical and revolutionary that they always took him into a fight before obtaining their adoption.

For instance, he came to France with a large number of other officers—about two hundred in all—who accompanied Brigadier General Foulois, the latter having come over to take command of the Air Service of the American Expeditionary Force. The majority of the officers in the party were Brereton 's superiors, and it seemed that he was going to be swallowed up with many others in the service of supply, or in those days, what was called line of communications, which was in the rear, for out of that large number it seemed that but few were destined to reach the front. Brereton immediately asked for the command of a squadron at the front. The authorities, of course, laughed at him and politely informed him that the Americans only had one squadron at the front and it had gone forward only a few days ago and that all the other squadrons in France had competent officers assigned to them; besides, the other squadrons could not go to the front for a long, long time on account of not having the proper planes and equipment, the production scheme in America having fallen down.

This did not sound encouraging to Brereton so he arranged to have himself assigned to a tour of inspection at Amanty, near Gondrecourt, which was the place designated for our future observation squadrons to assemble before going to the front. When he got there he found that it was true that only one squadron had, as yet, gone to the front, but that there were three other squadrons then at Amanty—the 12th, 88th and 91st waiting for service airplanes before moving up for action. All these squadrons had old training planes, the A.R.'s—Avion Renaults,

The squadrons were to leave in the order of the 88th first, then the 91st and then the 12th, according to the rank of the Commanding Officers of each. Major Harry Brown was then in command of the 12th Squadron and Brereton found by accident, that Brown was extremely anxious to get into the bombardment end of the game and was more or less dissatisfied that the 12th was to be made an Observation Squadron. Brereton found that an assignment to bombardment would more than please Brown so he wasted no time on further inspection. He had happened onto his great opportunity, and he departed immediately for Colombey-les-Belles, which was the Headquarters of the Air Service, Zone of Advance.

Arriving at Headquarters, he presented Major Brown's request to be transferred to Clermont-Ferrand to take a course in Bombardment in order that he might command our first Bombardment Squadron. This visit resulted in two orders being issued—the first relieved Major Harry Brown from the 12th and ordered him to Clermont, and the other designated as Commanding Officer of the 12th Aero Squadron, an officer previously unheard of in aviation at the front—Lewis Hyde Brereton.

Brereton asked permission to take his squadron to the front immediately, whereupon they thought him insane. It was pointed out to him that on account of not having service planes the squadron could not possibly get to the front before six weeks. Brereton went into one of his famous "pouts," in which he puckers up his face like a baby about to cry, and said that we would never have an Air Service on the front if they were going to be that particular. His idea was to take what we had and use it. He argued that since the squadron was going to work over a quiet sector they could operate just as well with training planes as with service planes, providing they had machine guns.

Fortunately, he had hit upon the psychological argument for at that time everyone in America was demanding the reason why we did not have squadrons at the front. There was a terrible mess going on

The village of Vaux on the day preceding the Battle of Vaux

about the Liberty motor and the other airplane scandals, so those in power agreed that it would help conditions materially to be able to say that we had squadrons at the front, rather than one squadron, so after considerable argument Brereton was authorized to take his squadron to the front at once with such equipment as they had.

So, the 88th and 91st were left at Amanty and the new comer arrived with orders in his hand to move the squadron forward for action.

Thus when it came time to pick a leader for offensive operations, General Mitchell knew what he was about when he selected Brereton for the Château-Thierry affair. He wanted a fighter and he got a fighter, for with his characteristic foresight Brereton prepared for any eventuality. He quite well knew that something would likely happen any day and he did not intend to let the observation end fall down if it was humanly possible to prevent it. His job was to accomplish the impossible; our "quiet sector" units must be prepared for a great and long offensive, and they must be gotten ready quick.

Brereton selected Lieutenant Ben Harwood as his liaison officer, Lieutenant Mathis as his information officer and put me in charge of the operations, so, we were gone from morning until late at night, travelling between the squadrons, corps headquarters and the various divisional headquarters, getting proper cooperation worked up and, in fact, getting some semblance of organization. The covetous eye of the Hun already looked on Paris. It was only a question of days until the German hand would be extended to grasp what the eye had seen.

The Huns held complete supremacy of the air. They dominated in the ratio of five to one and flew about in droves of fifteen and twenty. Where a fight on a mission had previously been the rare exception to our flyers it was now the common rule. We were very short of pursuit planes. Our Pursuit Squadrons—four in number—were trying to take care of not only our own Corps area, but also other areas held by the French and which adjoined us. As a result, very little direction protection was furnished to the Observation planes. So, the boys knew pretty well when they went out for a mission that it meant a scrap.

There was only one time at Château-Thierry when the Boche did not have the complete supremacy of the air. This was on July first at the Battle of Vaux, at which place Johnny Miller and I did the preliminary adjustment and Brereton and I did the artillery control for the Americans during the battle. We had every American pursuit and observation plane we could get off of the ground. There were not less than ninety-six planes in that formation— their mission being to protect the infantry plane and to protect Brereton and me, who were doing the artillery work. There was such a swarm of planes above us that we practically never looked into the sky, but kept our attention entirely on the work' before us. This was my idea of real protection. It was the nearest we ever came to our big threat to literally blacken the skies by droves of American airplanes.

However, none of these were American airplanes, although the aviators were Americans. This was the first time in the war that the doughboy was brought to realise that there were really other American aviators than those famous ground flyers who took off and landed so often at the famous Hotel Crillion Bar Airdrome in Paris and who were so accurately described by Irvin Cobb.

The Vaux affair seemed to me just like the practice control of artillery fire that I once did on the blackboard in school exercises. It was really one of the easiest jobs I ever did and for which I probably received more credit. The previous day I had passed over the town and was happy for the poor peasants that it had been spared, for even though in the hands of the enemy it was practically intact. Now it was a shell-torn blot of destroyed homes, made more desolate by the scattered bodies of the German dead—and I had been one of the guiding masters of its ruin.

From the first of July to the fifteenth we were continuously engaged in making the best possible preparations for what we knew must come. On the morning of the fifteenth it came. It came from Château-Thierry along to Rheims. The first day we did not worry a great deal for we confidently felt that the Germans would never be able to cross the Marne as all the bridges had been blown up, but on the morning of the sixteenth day things were mighty blue. An American pursuit plane immediately after daylight, reported that the Germans had constructed pontoon bridges in different places and were already sweeping across the Marne.

This flight by a pursuit plane and the resulting information was, I think, unquestionably one of the greatest flights of the entire war. I did not learn until several days later who the aviator really was. No one seemed to know, nor could we find any record on the regular reports. The French Army commander told me the source from which he had gotten this timely information as to the presence of the pontoons. It seems that General William Mitchell, who commanded all American Aviation at the front, had been at the French Army Headquarters dur-

THE VILLAGE OF VAUX DURING THE BATTLE OF VAUX, JULY 1, 1918.

ing the night of the fifteenth, getting the reports from the front and making his aerial dispositions accordingly.

An hour before daybreak on the morning of the sixteenth he left the French Headquarters and without telling anyone his intended movements he drove his high-powered automobile, with all haste, to the American Pursuit Airdrome about fifty kilometres away. Climbing into a single place Spad, the general hastily drew out a pocket notebook and scribbled a few words to his chief of staff, and handed this note to his mechanic. Then the general headed his plane into the wind and with whirring motor sailed off into the sombre darkness. At the first glimpse of dawn he was over Fere-en-Tardenois, fifteen miles within the German lines. He saw the glare of the village, but the usual whiteness of the roads was not there—they were of a greenish hue, like the morning mist surrounding them.

It was hard to comprehend the magnitude of this view. Heading south for five miles, the roads presented the same aspect. From fifteen thousand feet the general swept down to three thousand. Here he could realise the awful fact of what was taking place below him—the whitened roads were green with the thousands of German troops driving on toward the Marne with the steadiness and determination of a huge caterpillar. On south he flew—the Germans were everywhere—infesting the whole salient like a plague of locusts. Beaching the Marne, it was certain the inevitable had happened—one, two, three, four, five—five pontoon bridges already across and the onrushing Huns were marching across in terrible precision.

It was singularly fortunate that the man who undertook this hazardous mission was a rare tactician and strategist. He realised the awful truth where the ordinary airman would not have conceived the possibilities of such a situation. The general knew that the biggest German Army ever concentrated was on the move in a final effort to intimidate and conquer the world.

He made a landing in a small wheat field at the French Army Headquarters. It would have been folly to go on to the American Airdrome for if ever seconds were golden this was the time. He told the supreme commander the extent of his observation and how far back the Germans were concentrated. It was realised that it would be absolutely inconceivable to attempt to hold back this advance by a frontal attack. There was only one thing to do—we must flank the German Army and force them to withdraw or be annihilated. This must be done within three days or the Germans would break the line of our armies and march unmolested to Paris, coming up and flanking our own Northern forces.

Going to his own headquarters, the general was handed the note he had written to his distinguished chief of operations, Captain Phil Roosevelt. It simply stated that if he did not return by eight o'clock that morning to notify Brereton to take command of the American Aviation at the front. The distinguished Roosevelt had also been out doing some rough riding so the note had never reached his hands.

This flight of General Mitchell's needs no comment—it was no less than wonderful, and when the flyers finally heard who had made it, our morale was strengthened one hundred *per cent*. We felt we had a fighting general sure enough.

The Germans continued their crossing on the sixteenth, sweeping on down toward Epernay on the seventeenth and on the night of the seventeenth it rained. It rained all night; and all night long, passing our headquarters were troops going up to the front; all night long we could hear their continuous tramping; the roads were hydraulically jammed with cannons, ammunition trains, supplies and troops. They were going to Château-Thierry. They were retreating from the south it seemed, but why did they come to this side of the salient? Why not stop the Germans by a frontal defence?

In a few hours we knew why for on the night of the seventeenth, at nine o'clock we received orders from General DeGouttes of the French Army that the French Army, in connection with the First American Army Corps, would attack all the way from Soissons to Château-Thierry in an effort to flank the German advance and would continue at any and all costs until the Germans were forced to withdraw from the salient or face annihilation.

The attack was to start at daybreak on the following morning. Then I heard of Mitchell's flight and information. His recommendations had been concurred in by Marshal Foch and General Pershing. There was some activity in our headquarters. We got hold of our squadron and balloon commanders and ordered them to report immediately. By the time they all got there it was eleven thirty at night. Harwood was still up at the line where he had been all day in liaison with the line units. Brereton was over in conference with the corps commander, General Liggett. Lieutenant Mathis was busy getting out the necessary maps, so, I took the orders for the battle and, like a young Napoleon, I told the whole story and made the aerial dispositions for the first day. Fortunately the squadron and balloon units had already been assigned to the various line units and had made some arrangements.

Of course, the suddenness of the attack, and the short time we had been there, had caused many details to be incomplete. I told them that they would still have to go up to the lines that night and see the units to which they were assigned in order to be on the job at daybreak. This was absolutely necessary and yet it did not seem that they could possibly be able to get there due to the roads being packed with the on-marching troops. It was a great question, but it was the only way possible. Ben Harwood, our liaison officer, saved the day, for he came in just as I was about to dismiss them. Ben had shown his natural initiative and resourcefulness, and had already been to every American unit. He had gotten the big news while still at the front lines and had, very fortunately, obtained all the necessary liaison information. Harwood took over the meeting, explained everything he had learned from the line units, and by one-thirty o'clock all the squadron and balloon commanders were on their way back to their organizations to get out the necessary orders and to see that the planes were at the lines at zero hour.

The rain stopped just before daybreak. It seemed that even the heavens were effecting a close, immediate and personal liaison with us, as Harwood would say. When the barrage lifted and the boys went over the top in America's first big effort, they found there to cheer them and to assist them the drone of airplanes, upon the wings of which was painted the American cocarde. It was the real launching of American aviation—it was truly the beginning of the end.

We were tremendously handicapped by the shortage of pilots and observers and during the entire period of the offensive we were unable to get replacements for our casualties. In our office we were taking care of the transmission of every order pertaining to the Air Service, taking care of the aviation movements, issuing of instructions, getting out the necessary reports and information. Our office personnel consisted of Colonel Brereton, Lieutenant Harwood, Lieutenant Mathis and Sergeant "Spike" Marlin, of whom I cannot speak too highly for sticking to the job throughout that prolonged period. The boy was sick at the time, but knowing we had no one else, he stayed right with it and worked on the average of twenty hours a day for two weeks straight.

I might incidentally say that all of the rest did the same. In fact, our real activities began when the Germans made their attack on the fifteenth and with our shortage of personnel it was necessary that someone be on the job day and night. Our losses were terrible. It began to tell on me for I was losing all my dearest friends.

Tired and exhausted under this three days' strain, in which we had about two hours sleep nightly, on the third day of our own drive, namely, the twentieth of July, at about ten in the morning, it was deemed necessary by the American and French High Commanders that a long distance reconnaissance should be made immediately in order to determine as near as possible the intention of the enemy. The Americans did not have an Army Reconnaissance Squadron at Château-Thierry at the time so the mission came to us for proper action.

I talked it over with Brereton and we agreed that in order to do the mission properly with full justice to everyone concerned it would take not less than twenty-five planes and considering the distance of the mission, the time necessary in the air to complete it, and the supremacy of the air held by the Germans, based upon the average of our casualties, we decided we would lose not less than eight of these planes, with a minimum of sixteen officers.

But things were in a very peculiar situation. We had been temporarily stopped and it was necessary to find out whether the Germans intended to make a firm stand or whether their stand was only temporary, in order to give them time to withdraw their forces from the south. When we came to our decision we consulted the high command, telling them the number of planes it would take and what our minimum losses would be. We impressed upon them our already heavy casualties and how short we were of airplanes. The answer was that the importance of the mission would justify all losses should the desired information be gained.

At this answer I suddenly became a tactician and strategist. I hit Brereton with the suggestion that if we could find a pilot and an observer who were overloaded with "guts" and properly "hardboiled" and who did not care much for their lives, they might be able to get in fine by going very low and thus get the information. My idea was that if we went in with twenty-five, planes this would be such a force that the Germans would be able to concentrate practically their entire Richtofen circus against us before we would have had time to make the large circuit assigned and get out, while if one plane went in, extremely low, several favourable suppositions might be possible; namely, the German Chasse Patrols, high in the heavens above, seeing a plane so far behind the line, would not think that it could possibly be other than a friendly plane; and being by itself, the anti-aircraft and the command reporting it would not call out so much pursuit as they otherwise would; and, furthermore, being alone the pursuit planes would not have so much chance of finding it.

I agreed with Brereton that it was practically hopeless, but at the same time it was a long chance and as it was in the middle of the day, if this mission failed we could have another mission of the twenty-five planes required, in readiness to take off to perform the mission in compliance with the original plan. This large formation could leave as soon as definite news was obtained that the first plane had been shot down, or that it had failed to return after a reasonable time. Brereton laughed sarcastically and said, "That idea is just about as feasible as a single aviator trying to fly to Berlin, picking out the *Kaiser* from the rest of the squareheads and hitting him with a bomb."

I accused him of being arbitrary for not giving valid reasons against the plan whereupon he sprang to his feet and puckering up in his singular way, exclaimed, "I am running this Air Service, lieutenant, and I don't need any suggestions from first lieutenants."

Tired and exhausted from lack of sleep, a court martial didn't matter anymore to me than five cents does to a millionaire, and Brereton, who had suffered the same loss of sleep and, of course, more serious irritation on account of his responsibility, did not care anymore for a poor lieutenant than an elephant does for a fly. The dog's hair had been rubbed the wrong way for I reared up on my hind legs and began to paw air and it looked like the Corps Air Service was to have a slight disruption. I was so sore that I almost bawled. I hotly informed Brereton that if I was to hold the job of operations officer I intended to express my opinion, and if it wasn't approved, he had a right to say so in a military manner, and in no other.

Then came my downfall. I raved on, "I'm getting good and tired of this proposition of being stuck up on one of these bullet-proof jobs when all my buddies are flying two and three times a day and getting killed," and after a moment of silence, I continued, "I came over to be a fighter and I want to go to the squadron and take my chances with the rest of them."

Brereton was worn out and was in no mood to be irritated. "Well," he sharply and decisively replied, "if you want to go down to the squadron, go ahead, no one's holding you."

This made me more peevish than ever, for I had in some way or other acquired the idea that the Corps Air Service could not possibly exist without me. My pride was bruised forever. With even more irony he went on as if to leave no opportunity for a repetition of such bluffing on my part, "If you're so hardboiled and brave, why don't you tackle the mission you just outlined. Go ahead and win yourself the *Croix de Bois* (Cross of Wood)."

I was serious about the proposition; I was pretty sure of getting killed, but after that last sneering remark my decision was formed. Momentarily, I hated Lewis Hyde Brereton more than I ever hated any one in my life, but I knew his weakness, so, I was determined that we should die together.

"Well, why don't you go out" he hotly demanded.

It was up to me; I did not have the composure of a jack-rabbit, and I began to paw air again, pound the table and turn red, and said, "Well, Major L. H. Brereton, I'll go, you know that, and I'll get the information, but I can't pilot a plane. I am the observer. If you will order," and I accentuated "order," "a pilot for me, there will be no further delay."

I knew he would do it. He only needed to be brought to the psychological moment. I knew his big nature would not permit him to order any one on such a mission. Changing from his irritant, harsh and denouncing manner, his face registered the greatest possible human kindness and the merry twinkle in his eye told the world we were friends again.

"Well, Elmer," he said, in a sharply pitched voice, which, however, carried deepest respect and utmost conviction, "we have never asked anyone yet to do what we would not do ourselves. If you want to go on that mission, I'll go with you."

We hopped into Brereton's motorcar and were off to the airdrome. Mathis called the squadron and instructed them to have the command plane in readiness. On the way to the airdrome the trip was marked by a prolonged silence. We were not particularly fisty; at least, I was not, because I was beginning to realise the magnitude of our undertaking. It seemed to me that we were already making the flight. Just as a flyer keeps a cool and level head when actually engaged in a combat, even though at great odds, so, as we sped on, I did not feel any particular nervousness. It was not necessary to talk over the mission for Brereton knew as well as I what we were supposed to do, and the route we must take.

Arriving at the airdrome we found the plane ready. Only a few officers were on the field and to these we said nothing more than the ordinary greeting between flyers when leaving on a mission. We climbed into our places. Brereton played with the throttle for a few moments, then he turned around and in the usual way preparatory to taking off he asked, "All clear, Elmer?"

I looked around to see if any other planes were in the air, whose landing might interfere with our taking off; seeing none, I answered as cheerfully as possible, "All O.K., Sir." But he did not take off; he allowed the motor to idle away.

Suddenly he turned his head and in a tone that indicated profound sincerity, and at the same time extreme uncertainty, he said, "Elmer, we're a couple of boobs. We've got no business doing this job. If they do get us who in the devil is going to run this Air Service? Your darned hunch is all wrong this time."

Here was a thought that had not entered my mind for we alone were familiar with every detail of the organisation of the operations for the drive and our loss at that particular time would really have been felt. I personally felt it was too late then to change, but this was a question which I felt was up to the chief himself to decide, so after thinking it over a moment I said, "Use your own judgment. Sir."

He hesitated a few seconds, then shrugged his shoulders and turned loose, "Well, I guess Bill Mitchell can handle it all right, and as he made that flight the other day by himself, I guess we, together, can make this one." He pulled his goggles down over his eyes, hastily adjusted his helmet, motioned the mechanics to remove the blocks.

"All clear, Elmer?" he questioned.

"All clear. Sir," I replied.

He gave her the gun and we were off. We headed straight over Coulommiers, to La Ferte sous Jouarre, which was the headquarters of the 1st U. S. Army Corps, and followed the Marne on to Château-Thierry. We lost no time in climbing, but in a steady path like the crow flies we went directly over the lines. We were only nine hundred feet high and every feature on the ground seemed to stand out perfectly. Our course carried us straight north along the road from Château-Thierry to Roucourt; from here we branched off toward Fere-en-Tardenois, and from Fere-en-Tardenois we hovered along the road to Grandes Loges and St. Remy. Leaving St. Remy we clung to the road leading north and finally reached Soissons. Banking to the right we skimmed along the River Vesle, searching the roads on both banks to Misy-sur-Aisne. We followed the Vesle down to Braisne and Fismes. At Fismes we were thirty kilometres within the German lines, and had reached our farthest objective; it was now only necessary to get out without being caught.

I cannot remember the exact route we took in getting out I only remember that Brereton asked me at Fismes, which way home and I answered, "south with the wind." I remember that we crossed the Marne again at Dormans and headed toward La Ferte to drop our message of information. In fact on the trip out I was not concerned with the route particularly—I knew that south meant home and we already had the information wanted, so, to me, life and happiness meant home by the shortest possible route.

In undertaking such a mission as this, that is, in being so far behind the lines without protection, I fully realised the utter futility of trying to concentrate my attention on the sky in search of enemy planes and at the same time do justice to the importance of the mission which would require practically constant attention to the ground. I quite well know that if we were caught so far back we would have no possible chance to get away with our lives, so, in my mind, it was of no importance to watch the sky. My watching the heavens would not help us from being seen, but at the same time, as we were carried along, I was also carried off with a multitude and variety of thoughts. About the biggest question I was attempting to solve was just how long I would last after a German patrol started after me. Then, I figured myself falling in flames. It is strange the many thoughts that will play upon one's mind in similar circumstances.

The sudden pangs of regret that you ever left the airdrome and even more sincere sorrow that you ever got into the Air Service; the wondering what the boys in the squadron are doing, and how the folks back home are, and whether you will ever see them again, and what the preacher in the village church will say at your memorial services and whether the commander of the army will write your mother a nice letter of condolence and whether the girl who jilted you will be sorry; and you wonder what you would finally have turned out to be if you had not been killed, and other such trivial, little things; and the fact that you had wished you had burned all your letters before you left and a lot of little things you should have attended to before—for instance, on that flight I remembered that I was directed to call up the corps artillery squadron and relieve them from two flights during that day. I brooded over the thought that if that squadron went on with those flights and one of the flyers got killed how sorry I would be—how sorry I was that I had not attended to that before going out on this fool trip myself.

I was certainly thankful that I had $10,000 worth of government life insurance and was wondering how my mother would get along

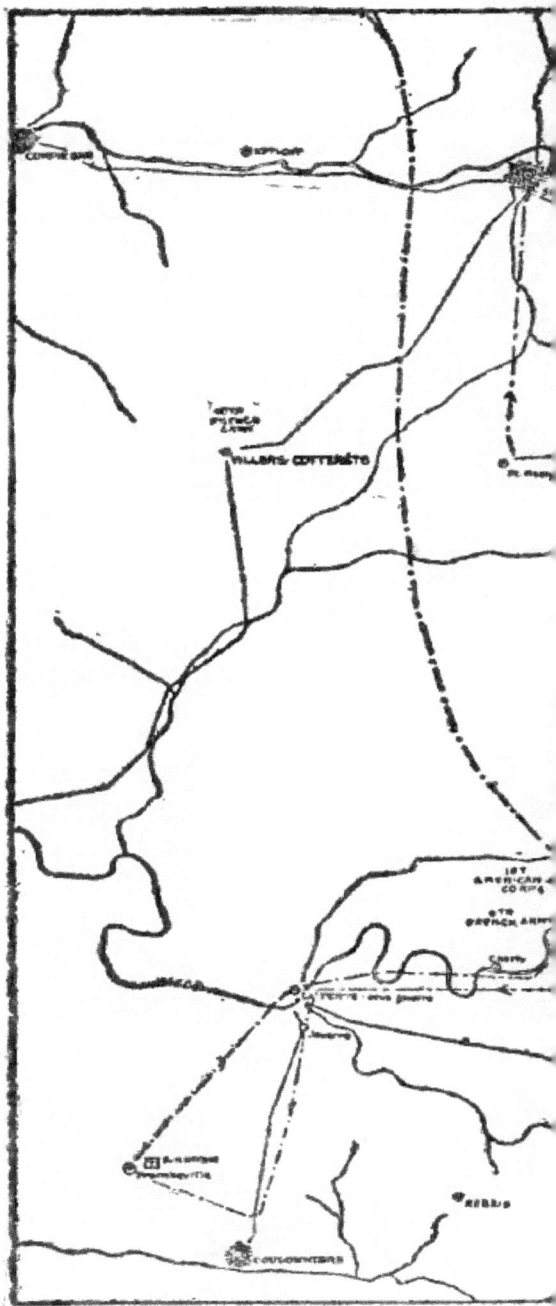

ROUTE-COVERED BY

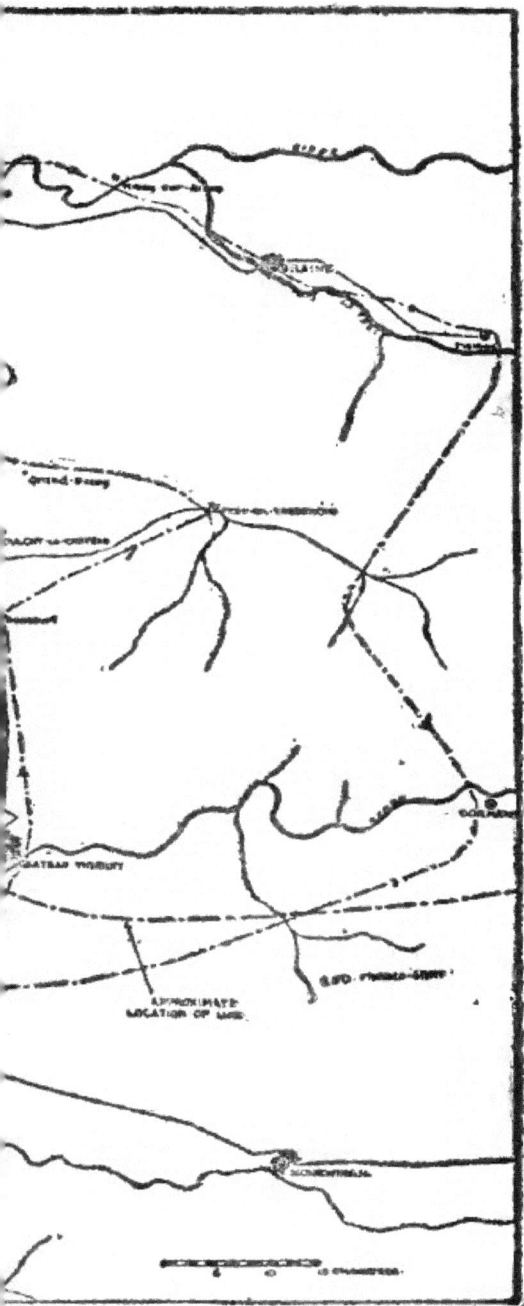

BRERETON'S FAMOUS FLIGHT

on $57.50 per month for twenty years, and I wished I had taken out $20,000 worth in private life insurance instead of spending two hundred dollars last month in Paris. All these more serious thoughts were going through my mind, having practically no one dependent upon me and with only the expendable rank of first lieutenant upon my shoulders, and then I thought of poor, old Brereton with a wife and two children, and a major's responsibility. Very shortly before this, Major Brown, in command of the 96th Squadron, had gotten lost in Germany and had landed with five other American planes and their crews, and this matter had occasioned unfavourable remarks as to his judgment. None of Brereton's friends would ever be able to explain why, in his responsible position, he ever even started out on such a hazardous mission as this.

Well, I came to the conclusion that one has two brains—one constructive and the other retrospective, for actually while I was thinking all of those things I was at the same time intently watching the ground and carefully noting the location of all my information.

That trip, from a standpoint of a war panorama, was a sight-seeing tour of wonder. Imagine the solid and continuous barrage of thousands and thousands of shells bursting in a line for miles and miles, the barking cannons on each side, like so many ferocious dogs spitting fire, roads filled with on-marching troops, coming up information from both sides, walking as it were, into that veritable valley of death and destruction; the air filled with hostile planes and our whole safety depending upon the supposition of being alone and so far behind the lines that the Germans would not realise the presence of an enemy plane.

We must have seen between a total of seventy-five and one hundred German airplanes during the entire flight, for do not think that we kept our eyes glued to the ground all the time; at least I did not; and in one place we were so near a Boche airdrome that we saw the German planes on the field milling around about ready to buzz up after us. Yet even at such a low altitude we were only fired at once or twice by machine guns from the ground. At the front the machine guns were busy firing forward and in the rear there did not seem to be any available.

Our mission had been a long one and one of the few in which the crew can use their own judgment. So, when he circled over La Ferte, the headquarters of the corps, and dropped our message, we had not only stated the facts as we had seen them, but also our conclusions, taking the whole aspect as it presented itself.

When we got back to the field Brereton circled the field twice before he could land. He was considerably discomposed—personally, I was the living "Wreck of the Hesperus." Brereton's car was waiting and we rushed up to headquarters. The boys on the field were still ignorant as to where we had been and what we had done. Neither Brereton nor I said very much about the mission for we didn't know whether we would be condemned for undertaking it or congratulated upon its successful completion. Of course, the line units around Corps Headquarters did not realise exactly the importance of such an undertaking, although I admit that Lieutenant Colonel Williams, whom we affectionately called "Houdini," and who was in charge of G-2 Information Group, stated that night, at the nine o'clock conference, that it was good dope and whoever got it, he certainly wanted to congratulate them. Brereton kept closed like a clam, while the position of my mouth was not unlike an oyster.

However, when the French Air Service commander, Commandant Gerard, heard of it, and he knew of it almost immediately, he came right over and offered his congratulations and was very profuse in his praise. Then we began to think we had really done something. The French told General Mitchell about it and he came right up to headquarters and patted me on the back. Brereton was out, but when General Mitchell did that I knew we had done something.

In a very short time came the famous order of the great French officer who commanded our army—General De Gouttes. It was as follows:

Secret

VIth Army   24 July 21h 50.
Telephone Order.
The enemy is in retreat on all our front. I give the order to march without stopping in such a way as to lay hands upon the enemy, to accelerate his retreat and not to lose contact with him under any pretext.

De Gouttes.

★★★★★★

136/G3   Headquarters 1st A. G.

24 July 1918.
Copy transmitted for your information and thorough compliance.

By Command of Major General Liggett:

Malin Craig,
Chief of Staff.

Hq. First Army Corps
Official
Operations Section

Afterwards, when we were around French Headquarters we were always pointed out as "*tres fort*" and "*tres brave*" and were treated with a great deal of consideration by the French, for they considered the flight as about the greatest thing they had seen pulled off for some time, especially since the information had been accurate and had been of great assistance. In fact, they thought it was so good that they did not hesitate to decorate Brereton with the Legion of Honour and the *Croix de Guerre*.

At that time I was only a lieutenant so I was decorated with the *Croix de Guerre* and, as Brereton expressed it, as long as I was with him I was in the Region of Honour. However, I received stacks of approbation that I feared for a while would be condemnation, but those are the chances one takes in undertaking any flight which is revolutionary in the form of tactics or strategy. In fact, if we had been shot down on the mission and had been unsuccessful we would probably have been referred to, even at this late date, as the participants in "Brereton's Famous Flight," only there would have been a different accent of insinuation on the word "Famous" than there now is in its common acceptance.

CHAPTER 5

Troubles on the Ground

Here is a story dedicated to the boys who fought the war on the ground, the holders of the famous "*Croix de Chair*," who were commonly known as swivel chair artists, or "Waffle Seaters." I was engaged in this duty myself at times and I know what it means. It is the most exacting and yet least appreciated task of the war. We used to call these staff officers "Waffle Seaters" for the reason that they sat so long on cane bottomed chairs that the seats of their trousers were beginning to take on the impression of a waffle.

There were troubles in the air and troubles on the ground. One of the reasons that made it extremely difficult to get a proper understanding between the units on the ground and the Air Service was that the ground units had never had an opportunity to work with the Air Service and they, therefore, could not understand the possibilities and the limitations of aviation. Neither the airman nor the ground soldier could be brought to realise that many of the troubles encountered were common to both. This lack of understanding and cooperation gradually was eliminated as the units became more experienced in working with each other.

However, for a long time the airman could not possibly comprehend how the same faults that bothered the flyer could also bother those on the ground. The contrary is also true—many on the ground thought the airman would not be bothered by the same elements that would hinder ground work.

An incident illustrating this occurred between a couple of air officers, a colonel who was in charge of American Balloons at the front, and a lieutenant, a balloon observer. This superior officer was a full-blooded German, born in Berlin. He spoke a German-American language that was mostly German. His name was Lieutenant Colonel

John Paegelow. Paegelow was a regular, and a regular fellow. We all liked him very much for he was very jovial and good natured. Anyway, his loyalty was unquestionable for he was about the worst Hun-Hater among us.

However, he had the Prussian idea of discipline and he took it out on the balloonatics whenever he felt they needed it. At Château-Thierry the balloons were under orders to remain in ascension day and night, and the personnel of the balloon companies had become noticeably fatigued from this prolonged vigilance; the balloon observers, especially, were worn out and naturally cross and irritable. It was a rainy night and Paegelow was standing on the ground holding the telephone in communication with the balloon observer two thousand feet above. This observer had been up for fourteen consecutive hours and was about all in, and the rain had made it a desolate and disagreeable night, adding considerable more woe to the occasion.

"Colonel," the young observer telephoned, in a very disgusted voice.

"*Vat?*" alertly answered Paegelow, thinking the lad had spied something.

"It's pitch dark up here, I can't see a damn thing and it's raining to beat Hell up here," spoke the observer.

"Iss dot up dare all de trouble you got?" said Paegelow, indicating his overruling of the demurrer.

"Well, what are you going to do about it?" demanded the exasperated lieutenant.

Paegelow hesitated a second, then replied, "*Veil*, vill you shut up and go on and vork. It iss pitch dark down here, *und* I can't see a damn ting down here either, und it iss raining to beat 'ell down here too."

When we started to work with new infantry and artillery units some were pleased and others did not want to have anything to do with us. It was at Château-Thierry that such lack of liaison became a serious matter and at the same time was the basis for several amusing incidents. The line units were prone to blame the Air Service for everything that went wrong. The reason was that they considered an airplane so experimental and uncertain in itself that that fact alone would preclude any argument as to the proper placing of blame for every failure.

One of the hardest things we had to contend with was impressing upon the line units the fact that the Corps Obseryation and the Corps Air Service commander had absolutely nothing to do with the Pursuit and Attack planes; that all these came directly under the French Army commander.

Several times I answered the telephone to receive the scathing denunciation that "the Hun was over shooting up some of our posts of command and that none of our d———d airplanes had been seen in the air all day." Whereupon we tried to explain that we did not control the pursuit planes; that it should have been reported to the Army Headquarters and that we, of course, would report it immediately. The ground units considered this rather poor tactics and a very unsatisfactory answer, for to their minds all planes were offensive fighters. Had the line units realised the actual number of planes we had on the front and the area they were patrolling they might have realised why our planes were not seen oftener. We did not have them to be seen.

One of the greatest difficulties we had was in teaching the doughboy to recognize the American insignia. Our publications were responsible for this, for every magazine published in the United States pictured the American airplane with a big star painted on its wings, while the insignia actually adopted was a cocarde—three circles of red, white and blue, within one another, the centre circle being white, the British centre circle being red, and the French centre circle being blue. As a matter of fact, the star in the air, at a reasonably long distance, looks exactly like the German Maltese Cross. In fact, a French airman once remarked that if the American had gone into combat with that much advertised star and the Germans failed to get him, a friendly airman, misjudging the star for a cross, certainly would have given a real battle.

Our doughboys actually thought that the American insignia was a huge star, for all the magazines had firmly implanted that on their minds. They didn't care about the insignia of any other nation outside of the American and German. To them one was a star and the other a cross, anything else was either friendly or enemy; and they would take a chance on it being enemy and fire at it.

One day before the Château-Thierry drive I was flying low along the lines and from my map I was quite sure which was our own territory, and which was that occupied by the Germans. I was well in the edge of our own territory when I heard machine guns firing at me from the ground. My first thought was that the Germans had advanced, so I directed the pilot to dive down to investigate. As we dived the machine gunners became convinced that we were going to fire upon them, so they turned loose upon us. As we flew on back, other gun crews having seen those machine guns firing at us, began firing too and although the pilot kept banking the plane up so that they might see our American cocarde, they kept on firing. About a half a kilometre back of the lines we began circling for altitude, and I kept hearing a few shots from a gun. Then, in a few seconds I saw a bullet go through the fuselage. Looking down on the edge of an old trench I saw about three lads with rifles firing at us, and they were good, old Yankee doughboys; I was sure of it.

I felt like turning loose a burst of about fifty rounds, aiming close to this group in order to give them a real scare, then I realised that there might be other troops around who might be grazed by a stray bullet, so I marked the place very definitely on my map, flew back to the airdrome and landed.

This was a serious matter, so I immediately made a trip up to the front to find out about it. I trudged around the trenches for an hour before any plane came in sight, then one of our own airplanes came along, flying very low. Suddenly I heard a rifle firing close by. I immediately ran in the direction of the shooting and I discovered a half-grown kid surrounded by a couple of his companions, coolly taking pot shots at this American airplane. In a rage I jumped on him with all fours.

"Don't you know that's an American plane?" I demanded in a manner neither affable nor pleasant. To my great surprise he responded that he knew it was an American plane.

"Well," I continued, speaking even more severely, "what do you mean by firing on an American plane?"

This doughboy casually continued chewing his tobacco and looking at the ground for some reason, apparently not from lack of composure, for he would take an occasional spit at an old, rusty helmet about six feet up the trench. The presence of an officer bothered him about as much as the presence of a king affects a Bolshevik.

"Well," I again asked, "where do you get that noise of firing at a friendly plane?"

This was just the opening he wanted, for he threw out his chest in all his independent dignity and said, "There ain't no friendly planes around here. I ain't seen any, no how. Them American planes ain't got no business being back this far from the lines and if them aviators ain't got nerve enough to go over there and scrap them Boche on their own ground, well force 'em over with our guns and put a little backbone in 'em."

Then the lad gave me a full explanation as to why they had fired upon these American planes and he claimed the American flyers always ran from the Boche; the Boche came over and shot up the dough-boys and he had never seen an American plane going over and shooting up the Boche. Then I asked him if he knew the functions of the airplanes. I wanted him to know that some planes had to stay behind the lines at times.

"Yep," he said, "they're all fighters, all of 'em, or supposed to be, but they don't fight. They stay back here; they're scared to go over."

Then I asked him if he had ever heard of an observation plane and if an observation plane shot a signal of six rockets to him what he would do. He replied that he did not know anything about observation planes and didn't want to know anything about them, but that several times large planes had flown back there and had fired fire rockets at the doughboys.

How many rockets did they fire?" I asked.

"Oh,"" he said, "lots of 'em. Sometimes three and six at one time."

I knew six rockets was the official signal from an airplane to the infantry, and that they were supposed to put out white pieces of cloth, their panels, to tell the airplane exactly where they were.

"Well, what did you do when the airplane fired six rockets at you?" I questioned in a more tolerating tone of voice.

"What did I do?" he answered as if surprised at such a silly question. "What do you think I'd a done? Why, I fired right back at 'em. There ain't nobody goin' to fire at me and get off with it without me firing back."

The other buddies backed him up absolutely and I spent a half hour explaining to them the real facts about the airplane game. They finally came to my way of thinking on every point except the courage of the American airman. They could not be dissuaded; they were convinced that most American flyers were cowards and "yellow."

I, of course, reported this firing on friendly airplanes to headquarters and an order was issued so as to acquaint the infantry with the Allied insignia. However, it was not until late in the Argonne offensive that this misapprehension of the doughboy was entirely cleared away. Time and time again when I would ask infantrymen, even officers, if they knew the American airplane insignia, they would say it was a "Star," but that they had never seen any American planes on the front. Perhaps it is for this reason that there are many doughboys who to-day declare they never saw an American airplane over the front. They undoubtedly saw many American planes, but they never saw any with the much-advertised star in the cocarde.

We had a great lot of trouble with wireless equipment in our artillery adjustments. When anything went wrong it was always blamed on the radio attached to the airplanes and we, of course, always attributed the fault to the artillery station on the ground because our wireless sets were always tested from the air to our own squadron station before starting on any mission. If the radio was not working, we always came down and fixed it. But this continual, unsatisfactory cooperation on radio communication was a serious affair all the way through and it was a bone of contention between the Air Service and the artillery in many instances. Finally radio officers were appointed to inspect the equipment on the airplane and the equipment on the ground and to determine where the fault lay. This helped some, but the trouble was never actually overcome. If the trouble was with the airmen, it was perhaps due to failure to throw in their switch.

An experience I had, led me to believe that the trouble was more with the personnel than the material. In each artillery regiment in trench warfare, there was one battery designated to fire upon a sudden call from the airplane. This battery was known as the fugitive target battery and the wireless crew was supposed to be constantly on duty from daybreak until nightfall so that when an airplane called, the designated battery could be immediately notified and the adjustment of artillery fire undertaken at once.

One day I decided to make a thorough reconnaissance of the front and to call the fugitive target battery to a certain regiment to make a rapid adjustment I crossed the line, found my target, which was a small convoy on the road within a forest. I was well within range of the fugitive target battery, so I immediately began to call the wireless station of the battery, I called it for fully twenty-five minutes but I could get no response. They did not put out any panel at all. I happened to know the location of the wireless station in the next regiment, which was also supposed to be looking out for fugitive target calls, so I called them and they immediately displayed their panel that they understood me. I was then certain that my wireless was O. K., so I flew back to my first battery and began to call them again. After another fifteen minutes I still received no response whatsoever. As the target had long since disappeared and being without the range of the alert battery of the next regiment, I flew home.

After making my report I called up the colonel of the regiment in which the battery was located. He, of course, being a very busy man, was not especially anxious to talk to a lieutenant, so he transferred me to his wireless officer, I told the wireless officer that I had called them for forty minutes and had gotten absolutely no response and that I was sure that my wireless was all right. He, in a very nice way, responded that he was quite sure that my wireless was not all right, because he was certain that the battalion concerned had their wireless in very good shape.

We got into quite an argument in which I told him that I called the designated battery of the next regiment and that they had answered and that I called my home station both on leaving and returning and that they answered, but the captain repeated that he didn't give a continental how many answered, he still knew his wireless stations were all right and he didn't want any argument over the telephone about it. Whereupon I mentally cussed the whole army, but merely said, "Yes, Sir," and hung up.

I immediately dispatched another plane to call the same battery and to keep on calling them until they answered. Then I got into the car and drove up to the battalion concerned. I paid my respects to the major commanding the battalion and told him the trouble—that we had called and had received no response. He was sort of peeved at the whole world so he said he was getting disgustingly tired of these airplanes hollering about the artillery's wireless; that his wireless was all right and it was the inefficient airplanes; that his wireless men were on duty and had been from daybreak until night. I told him I would like to go over, if I might, and look over his wireless station. He became very indignant and said, "Lieutenant, that is quite an unnecessary request. I know the efficient condition of my units and I know my wireless is listening now and I know that they have been listening in all day."

I was beginning to become accustomed to these rebuffs by this time so I smoothed it over the best I could and finally he agreed to take the time to walk over to the wireless station with me. The plane I had dispatched ahead was circling above and I knew he was calling. We went to the wireless station, which was a sort of improvised one down in a dugout. The place was deserted and there was not a person in sight. The major was sore, but apologetic. He remembered that Battery C was supposed to furnish the detail and that they were supposed to be on the job permanently. So we went over and found the captain of Battery C and the battalion signal officer, a second lieutenant, who were busily engaged in a poker game. The major, in a terrible voice, demanded, "Where in 'ell are those radio operators?" The poor lieutenant meekly gave the only answer he could think of. "Why, major," he said, "they are right over there at the station; they have been there all day."

The major calmly asked, "Lieutenant, have you inspected the radio unit today?"

Whereupon the lieutenant solemnly said, "No, Sir, I have not inspected it, but I am positive that the operators are right on the job," and he described definitely the place from which we had just come.

We asked him the name of his radio operators. They were all privates. With the captain and the radio officer we went over to the radio station. It was still deserted. The major began to tell the lieutenant in language that will not permit of repetition just what he thought of him. The lieutenant was speechless, and out of sympathy for him I made the suggestion that there was an airplane above which was probably calling them now and that it might be a good idea if we could get someone there at the station to listen in. The radio officer grasped the opportunity, jumped down and put the clickers to his ears, and the first thing he said was, "Q-P-R, Q-P-R—that's our call!" I felt like a million dollars, for this time the artillery was forced to concede that it was not the fault of the airplane. With the assistance of the major and the captain we manipulated the panels while the wireless officer took the calls and the lad in the airplane did the adjustment. Then we went back to find out where the radio operators were; that is, the three privates.

The captain dispatched an orderly to find the first sergeant. In about five minutes the sergeant was located and made his appearance. He was an old non-commissioned officer and was seasoned by experience in many climes and in dealing with many classes of men. He was rather heavy, and had not shaved for several days, which fact, in addition to his heavy, dishevelled moustache, gave him the appearance of a hardboiled bulldog.

"Sergeant," began the captain, "do you know where the radio operators are?"

"Yes, sir," grumbled the top soak, affirmatively nodding his head with self-satisfaction that he quite well knew where they were.

"Well," went on the captain, "I want to see them at once. If you will show me their quarters it will save time."

"They ain't in their quarters," came the reply. "They're in the kitchen."

We went to the kitchen and found the three expert radio operators—two were scrubbing big, black pans and the third was peeling spuds.

For moral effect, the captain called the top sergeant off to one side. The rest of us had to laugh.

"Why have you got these men in the kitchen?" hotly demanded the captain.

"Well, Sir," replied the sergeant, closing in his jaws firmly in determination, "there ain't no more reason why the rest of the battery should do K. P. and excuse the wireless men. I heard one of 'em say yesterday that he ain't never done no K. P. since he'd been in this man's army, and that kind er talk is bad for the morale of the battery, so I just stuck 'em all on fer a few days to show the fellers they ain't no favours played in this battery."

"Yes, but what about the radio?" asked the captain. "You should have left one of them on the job."

"Oh, well, captain," came back the "top" sergeant, "it ain't goin' to make no difference; these airplanes don't call the station more than once every two or three days and we ain't got enough men to waste on sitting around awaiting for 'em to call and they don't do nothing for us when they do call."

Thus I found one of the main reasons for this early lack of results. These old timers did not take the Air Service seriously. They had no faith in its present capabilities nor its future development. To them an army was composed of infantry, cavalry and artillery. Every other arm or service was experimental. I am glad to say, however, that later this battery, in fact the entire regiment of artillery, became very proficient in the work with the Air Service and the results were, indeed, satisfactory to all.

In the actual advance at Château-Thierry the ground liaison—that is, the communication by telephone, wireless telegraph and ground telegraph between the line units and the Air Service—became poorer and poorer as the troops advanced until it was really in a deplorable state. The area over which troops passed was all shell torn and it was impossible to move our flying fields farther up because we could not cease operations in order to make the move since we had no reserve Air units, and worse, we had no fields prepared and the Germans had destroyed theirs in the retreat.

As the days advanced conditions became more terrible. The entire corps headquarters had only one telephone wire and one ground telegraph line to the Corps Advance Headquarters and from there only one out to the various divisional posts of command and in front of those posts of command almost everything was done by runners. Our little force at the Corps Air Service Headquarters was all worked down. After the first few days the drive ceased to be exciting and it became purely drudgery and habit. We were all irritable and cross. We were over-worked and loss of sleep was showing very much in our dispositions.

This particular day things were getting pretty bad up the line. The German artillery was making a strong defence and all of our command posts were getting their full share of German artillery fire. At noon our radio operator told me that someone had been trying all morning to put through a message to us, but that we had been unable to receive it. Either the transmitting set at the line was not working or our receiving set was not At any rate, something was urgently wrong somewhere at the front or they would not have been so persistent About nine-thirty they started trying to call us and they kept on until eleven-thirty, but the operator could not get anything definite out of the sound. In addition, at about a quarter of twelve they succeeded in getting a telephone call through, but we could not hear. We tried to relay it, but that did not work. We worked an hour on that—until a quarter of one. Then they managed to get a priority call through on the ground telegraph, which telegram was dated at the post of command at one-thirty in the afternoon and was delivered to me at one-forty. The telegram read as follows:

> To Chief of Air Service. First Army Corps
> German artillery firing on my post of command. Stop it!
>
> ———
>
> General.

Of course, we all had a real laugh at the situation; that is, Mathis and I, for we were the only ones there, Brereton being away on business and Harwood being up at the front on liaison. Of course, such a request was obviously impossible. An airplane can spot certain batteries when firing, but when there are fifteen hundred different guns firing continuously on fifteen hundred different objectives one can imagine what possibility an airplane would have of picking out the particular battery that was firing on this particular post of command. At the same time, as it was signed in code by a general, it was imperative that something be done because that unit had not been any too friendly toward the Air Service, and, of course, the wishes of a general must always have immediate attention.

I knew there was no answer that I could send back over the wire that would quiet the situation, so we simply acknowledged the receipt of the message. At the same time I knew there was no use to send a special airplane for this request because we already maintained a plane over the front every hour of the day, the one duly of which was to report by wireless the location of any enemy batteries seen firing. I was mighty busy on a multitude of other things, but still the general must be answered, so I finally decided the best thing to do was to go up to the post of command and explain the entire situation, telling why it could not be done. After an hour and a half rough riding we finally approached the post of command concerned.

I left the car about a quarter of a mile away so as to not attract the attention of the German airplanes to the presence of a command post. all the way up I had been considering just what I would say, because, being a lieutenant, I wouldn't have much chance with a general, and yet I felt that since I had to do it I ought to have something worth saying. I had decided upon my whole speech—I would simply say that the mission was not only impossible but such a request was preposterous—an airplane was a great thing, but it had a limit of activity. At the same time I was in great fear of being laughed at and being balled out, because in a great many cases a lieutenant speaking with a general, with the slight difference in rank, is at a disadvantage. I knew I had to make some sort of a stab so, though I was determined on my speech, I really felt very much like a bashful schoolboy.

As to procedure I had it all fixed up that I would go in, click my heels together, salute smartly and explain to the general that I was the operations officer for the Corps Air Service, whereupon I thought he would certainly have some deference for me on account of the important position I was holding with such low rank. My greatest hope was that he would be reasonable and would take my statement regarding the situation as final and authoritative, without further argument. I concluded that the best way would be to impress him with the knowledge I had on the particular subject and not give him a chance to come back. To do this I must be absolutely firm and convincing in what I had to say, but at the same time, way down deep in my heart I felt it was a hopeless task, for these "higher ups" are inclined to consider nothing but results—and since we could not give him the results he wanted, he would conclude that the Air Service had failed, and as the line units had done on several other similar occasions, they would merely remark, "the same old story," shrug their shoulders and pass it up.

I, of course, expected to find the general down in his dugout, being heavily shelled, but I was determined to show him that I was a real hero by walking right through the shell-fire and calmly explaining to him why we couldn't help him. This last decision really required nerve on my part, for if there is any one thing I cannot stand, it is shell-fire on the ground. It did not worry me so much in the air, for there seemed to be such a good chance to dodge, but on the ground—well, I had been caught in it several times and, in each instance, I made the necessary distance to safety in considerable less than record time on the fastest tracks.

I picked up a stray doughboy to guide me to the post of command. To my absolute surprise I found that everything was apparently quiet However, the surroundings bore the unmistakable evidence that the region had undergone a very heavy and prolonged bombardment. I could not understand this; in fact, I was certain that we had come to the wrong post of command.

"Orderly," I said to a lad standing at the door, "is this the P. C. of General Blank?" using the proper code name.

"That's right, Sir," he smartly answered.

"When did the bombardment stop?" I demanded.

"About two o'clock, Sir," he replied.

"May I see the general?" I asked.

"What is the name, Sir?"

"Just tell the general or chief of staff that Lieutenant Haslett of the Air Service would like to see either of them at their convenience. There is nothing urgent."

The orderly stepped inside and almost immediately a lieutenant came out.

"I'm the general's *aide*," he said, extending his hand. "The general will see you at once. Come right in."

The door opened and I was ready with my speech. Out rushed the general and his chief of staff and the rest of his staff around him—none of them less in rank than a lieutenant colonel. Of course, I stood at attention, stiff as an iceberg, but they thawed me out by a cordial "Are you Haslett, the operations officer of the Air Service?"

I had never before in my life spoken to such a high ranking general and in a quivering, quick voice which indicated that I expected to be crucified at the next moment I said, "Yes, Sir."

The general advanced, put out his hand and said, " Lieutenant, I want to congratulate you. That is the first time we have ever had efficient service and cooperation from your airplane crowd. All morning while we tried to get you by wireless and we knew we had not succeeded, for you did not answer—they were firing upon us terribly; and then we tried to get you on the telephone, but I think the bursting shells around us was one of the reasons you could not hear; but when we got that telegram through at one-thirty and you acknowledged receiving it at a quarter of two—it was simply fine. We saw an airplane circle overhead promptly at two o'clock and that artillery stopped firing at exactly five minutes after two. Now that's what I call splendid work, and I am going to tell the corps commander about it."

For the moment I was completely nonplussed. There was nothing for me to say. I had a vision of a young hero with a Distinguished Service Cross and twenty-six and a half *Croix de Guerre*—I might not have been the Ace of Aces, but I certainly was the Deuce of Deuces. After a moment's hesitation I knew it was the time to act, so I shrugged my shoulders, casually lighted a cigarette and nonchalantly informed the general that I came to see that the airplane had satisfactorily completed its mission and to assure myself that he was satisfied and to tell him that any time he had any trouble we wanted him to feel that the Air Service was behind him, day and night; that if they only got the word to us, we would do our best.

Believe me, every one of the staff, from the lieutenant colonels up, shook my hand and individually thanked me for the efficient work we had done in stopping that artillery fire. This was the real case of having fortune thrust upon one. Perhaps I should have insisted upon explaining that we had nothing to do with stopping that artillery fire, but somehow I could not. It was a dream which was better undisturbed, for the German Heavy Artillery had certainly stopped of its own volition, not ours.

Forever afterwards that general and his entire staff were strong boosters for the Air Service, and when any one had anything to say against the Air Service, if there was a member of that staff around an argument was certain; and the general, I am told, still tells of how the wonderful American Air Service stopped the German Heavy Artillery on fifteen minutes' notice at Château-Thierry.

CHAPTER 6

The Wild Ride of a Greenhorn

One of the greatest experiences an observer can have is to take a new pilot over the lines for his first trip; in other words, "break him in." I had sort of specialized in this work in the early days in quiet sectors, but when I was sent up to the Argonne sector it was for an entirely different mission. I had long since gotten past this preliminary stage. The object of my being there was to carry on adjustments of artillery on the moving enemy targets, for I had been giving a great deal of attention to this special work all through our experiences at Château-Thierry and Saint Mihiel. At the opening of the Argonne drive on the 26th of September my position was that of Operations Officer for the Corps Observation Wing of the First Army.

It seemed that the development of artillery adjustments on fugitive targets had sort of been overlooked, so General Mitchell, who was then Chief of Air Service of the First Army, began to realise the importance of this work and decided that it should be given more attention. Of course, it was strictly a Corps Observation mission, and so he passed the order down to Brereton and Brereton, of course, passed the buck on to me, for the buck never passes up—it's always down.

It was an important matter, especially for the coming drive, and no satisfactory method of carrying on this work had yet been worked out, so I proposed to Brereton that I be authorised to visit each of the corps of the First Army during the drive in order to carry on this work; then I could compile the proper manual for future guidance of our observers. The big three, consisting of General Mitchell, Colonel Milling and Major Brereton, all approved, and so I went first to the 5th Corps, whose airdrome was at Foucoucourt, arriving there on September 25th, about six o'clock in the evening. The big Argonne-Meuse drive was to begin the next morning at daybreak.

The Corps Air Service commander, Colonel Arthur Christie, and the group commander, Major Joe McNarney, and I had a talk about the entire situation. They decided that I should work with the Hybrid Squadron, which consisted of a Flight of the 104th Squadron and a Flight of the 99th Squadron under the command of Lieutenant Jeff Davis. The Operations officer was Lieutenant Britton Polly, whom I knew quite well in the Observers' School, so I told Davis that I would like to take one of the first missions the next morning, in order that I might get an early start on my fugitive target ideas.

Polly told me the situation—they were up against it, as they had several new pilots who had never been over the front, so he wanted to know if I would help him out by taking one of the new ones over. Ordinarily there is not much opportunity to do real work when "breaking in" a green pilot, and although I knew this would detract from my chances for success, I agreed.

That night I worked quite late preparing a very complete chart, showing the location of all our batteries on the map, their radio call codes and a miniature picture of each battery's panels. I knew that the batteries would soon be on the move, and my scheme of adjustment had for its object the ability to call any battery which had halted temporarily, whether its location was permanent or not.

I got on the field about eight o'clock the next morning and walked over to the Operations Room of the 104th Squadron to find my pilot, who, for the purposes of this story, we will call "Lieutenant Greenhorn." Inside the hut I found a tall, slender, effeminate looking chap talking to Britton Polly. I was unnoticed by either. The lad was inquiring as to this new guy, Haslett, who was supposed to fly with him at nine o'clock. I heard him tell Polly that as it was his first trip over the lines he demanded an old and experienced observer to take him over. Since he didn't know me, he said, and had never seen me, he would rather have one of his own squadron go over with him, as he would have more confidence in someone whose experience he knew. Polly, who was a sort of hardboiled war horse, told him that he wouldn't find any observers in the American Service who were more experienced than Haslett and that he had better take me while the taking was good.

After "Greenhorn" left I had a good laugh over the matter with Polly and then I followed the lad to his room, went in, and disclosed my identity. He was noticeably nervous and made me a confession that he had had very little flying and that he really had no business being at the front; and, as this was his first trip over, he didn't want to stay long and wanted to know how it felt to be up there, and what to do when he was attacked, and what to do when the enemy anti-aircraft artillery shot him, what to do if his motor failed him over the lines, and a lot of such odd and foolish questions. My experience with Phil Schnurr on his first flight made me leary. I didn't object to taking a man over the lines for the first time so long as he knew how to fly well, but when a man did not even have confidence in his ability to fly—well, it was a very different matter. I was not seeking any thrills—observing had become a business with me, so I felt very much like refusing to fly with him, but on afterthought it came to me that perhaps this lad was not such a bad sort after all and maybe it was just his modesty and timidity that caused him to talk so disparagingly of his ability. At any rate, if he was going over, for his own good I would take a chance and try to start him right.

I proceeded with a story something like this (the same that I told all the new pilots I ever took over the lines for their first trip):

The pilot in an observation plane is, in one sense, the chauffeur. On account of the fact that communication between the pilot and the observer is ordinarily very poor, we refer to the pilot as the horsey for he must be guided, and for that reason we append to his arms directly under the armpits two pieces of twine, string or cord which we extend back to the observer. The observer holds the reins.

The observer is given the mission to perform and, while he expects the utmost voluntary cooperation of the pilot, when it comes to any matter of tactical decision the observer's word is final; for instance, in this flight, should we see five planes and decide to attack them, I would simply give the word and you would direct the plane toward them; or if we are attacked by them I would give the word whether to dive toward the ground and run from the enemy or stay and fight it out; or should I see a machine gun nest on the ground which was holding up our advancing troops, should I decide to go down and destroy that machine gun nest it is your duty to direct your plane down on the machine gun nest even though you know it is certain death. The observer points out the direction in which he wants to go, how long he wants to stay there, how long he wants to stay at the line, and, in fact, is the commander of the plane. As I said before, he is the holder of the reins.

Now, there is only one exception to this, and that is when something is mechanically wrong with the airplane. For instance, if the engine is failing or if a strut is broken, or if flying wires are destroyed—in such a case the pilot becomes responsible for the command of the plane. The fear of failing to hear clearly the directions given by the observer through the speaking tube is the reason we have the lines to guide the pilot like a horse, and when the observer wants to go up he points up and when he wants to go down he points down; and should he want to go to a certain place he would point to that place.

It is a sort of mental telepathy which is expressed in a sign language and is ordinarily easily understood, so don't worry—just pay close attention and don't lose your head and you will get along all rights for after all, flying over the front is not so full of thrills as one ordinarily is led to believe, and whether you live over your allotted twenty hours over the lines depends largely upon your ability and good luck and watchfulness.

"Greenhorn" took it all in and said he understood fully. After quite a little delay in getting a serviceable airplane we finally made a stab at getting off. I told Greenhorn to take me to a little town called Avocourt, which was in No-Man's-Land, and I carefully pointed it out to him on the map. Of course, Avocourt had been destroyed by shell fire and nothing remained but the ruins of the town, but they were plainly discernible from the air. I tested out my wireless and everything was O. K., so I motioned for him to head on up to the lines. I paid very little attention to the ground, intending to sort of take it easy until we got to Avocourt, thus getting a general idea of the lay of the country over which we were flying. I instructed him to let me know by shaking the plane when he came to Avocourt. He seemed to be flying along in good shape so I didn't concern myself with our location until he finally shook the plane. He pointed down to an extremely large city and motioned his lips " Avocourt." I looked down below me and recognised very well the historic city of Verdun, as I had flown over this sector one time with the French in the early days.

I shook my head and pointed toward Avocourt. "Greenhorn" had missed Avocourt only by about fifteen kilometres. However, the kid was insistent and nodded his head in affirmation of his own decision and he pointed to his map again and pointed down and said

"Avocourt." I swelled out my chest and pointed to myself to impress upon him the lesson that I was running the plane as per our previous conversation and that he was to go in the direction pointed without further argument He hastily acquiesced and turned the plane in that direction, and from that time on I used the cords attached to his arms to guide him. When we got over Avocourt I attracted his attention, pointed down and said "Avocourt."

He gazed down at the shattered ruins of what was once a town, but said nothing. However, his eyes and face expressed very well the fact that he would never have recognized Avocourt from her photograph. I couldn't blame him, for from the air a ruined town is highly deceptive and unless one had flown over that sector he could not realise that the effect of artillery destruction could be so complete. In a moment he gave some sort of a shrug of his shoulders to indicate that he was entirely lost, so I signalled to him and gave him his directions. Then, taking my map, I pointed north and said "Montfaucon," which is easily distinguished from the air for miles, being situated on the crest of a very high hill. "Greenhorn" immediately headed toward Montfaucon, thinking that perhaps I had pointed toward that town with the intention of going there. I did not have this in mind, but since one place was just about as good as another until we found a target I let him go.

Just over Montfaucon we were opened up on by the German anti-aircraft artillery. I heard a heavy thud under our tail and at once the plane began to side-slip and quiver. The "Greenhorn" was badly frightened and began looking in every direction. Then his eyes fell on me and I have never seen the equal of the expression on his face when he saw me laughing. He did not realise the significance until I pointed to the anti-aircraft bursts, which were fully three hundred yards behind us. I assured him that everything was O. K., and he had done well. That put him a little more at ease. After a while I spied a splendid target, so I started him back toward the line so that we could call our batteries. We then played over our own lines for about an hour, as we were having a great deal of trouble in getting any batteries to answer, since they had all started to move up farther to support the fast advancing doughboys. I didn't know whether "Greenhorn" appreciated that ride or not, but believe me, that sight was beautiful.

The heretofore impassable region known as No-Man's-Land was now converted to Every-Man's Land, for the whole shell riddled section was simply covered with the advancing American doughboys—in

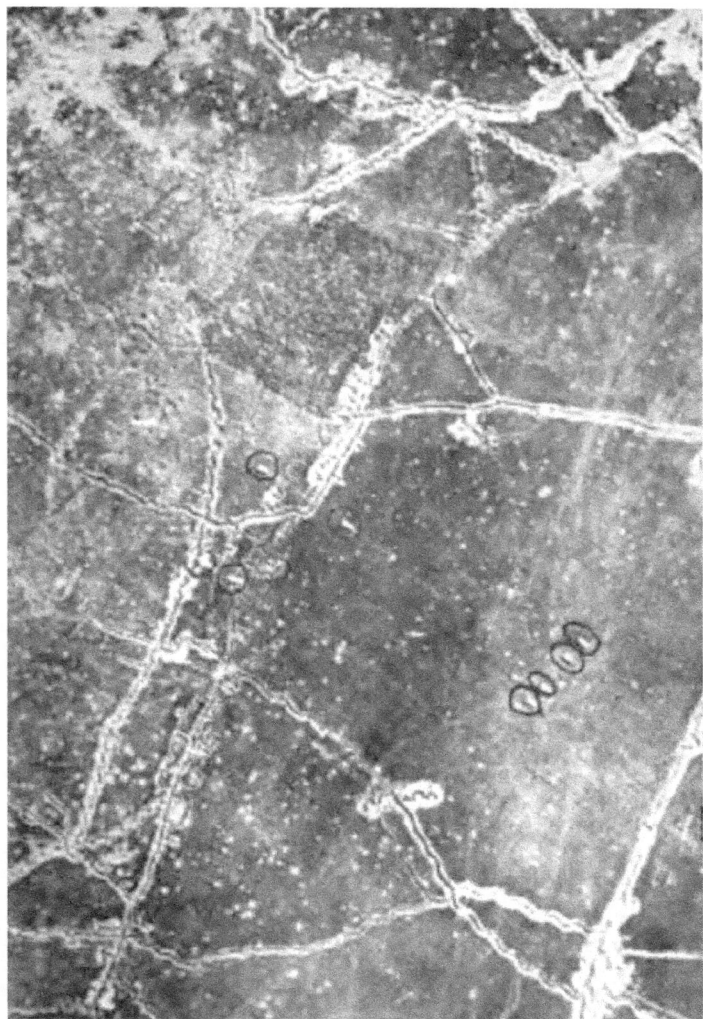

TANKS GOING INTO ACTION, AND THE TRACKS LEFT BY THEM

trenches, shell holes, everywhere. The mighty tanks were slowly plugging and lumbering along over the shell holes and we could easily see our most advanced lines, the troops deploying, the German machine gun crews at their nests vainly attempting to hold back the advancing infantry, and farther back we could see the retreating Germans, their supply trains, artillery and convoys. I marked down the location of our advance units, as this was important information, and told "Greenhorn" to fly north.

As we circled over Montfaucon to the west we drew a very heavy machine gun fire from the Bois de Beuges, which had put several holes in the plane, and since "Greenhorn" was getting more and more unsteady in his flying I thought it well for our own safety and comfort to get a little better altitude, so I motioned up and "Greenhorn" started a steep climb right off the bat. Of course, I did not intend for him to make such a steep climb, and as we started our ascent the machine practically stood still in the air in a stall. This gave the German machine gunners a chance to concentrate on us, and believe me, they certainly made the best of their opportunity. Fortunately, beginner's luck was with the boy and we got out of it after he finally heeded my frantic effort to get him to fly ahead for speed and not for altitude. I looked the plane over carefully when we were without the range of the German machine guns. Other than a few holes in the wings and the body of the plane I could find nothing wrong with it; at least, all the flying wires and struts were still good and the engine apparently was running perfectly. Upon getting more altitude, however, the "Greenhorn" started in the direction of home without any orders from me at all.

Suddenly I heard a faint, indistinct *put-put-put* and I began scouring the sky for the place from whence came the familiar and unmistakable sound. Away over to the right, north of Montfaucon, I saw a genuine scrap going on. There must have been fifteen planes and soon the faint *put-put* became a continuous rattle like the roll of an overtight snare drum. I could very easily tell by their manoeuvring that it was a dog fight and if we could only get over there in time we would undoubtedly get into it Maybe some of our boys needed help and sometimes the arrival of one additional plane can turn the balance of power in a scrap. So I shook the plane and called to him to head over that way as fast as he could. I expected some slight coercion would be necessary, but to my surprise "Greenhorn" immediately headed toward the show.

As we were speeding along like the assisting ambulance I decided to try out my guns to make sure they were in trim condition for a combat, so I pulled the triggers on both machine guns for a short burst, not thinking to warn the already irritated "Greenhorn." Instantaneous with the first report the plane began to go into a wild spiral. I dropped the guns and turned around to see "Greenhorn" twisting in every conceivable direction and manipulating the joy stick right to left, forward to rear, with the same cadence that the jazz orchestra leader handles his baton—while I was thrown around in the cockpit like the contents of a shaking highball. I had a similar trick played on me myself one time while flying with Brereton at San Mihiel. Brereton and I were alone on a mission photographing a difficult area behind the lines. Brereton, who was always a cautious flyer, ordinarily had a small mirror attached just above the edge of his cockpit in which my every movement was reflected. Thus he could tell when I was looking the sky over for enemy planes or watching the artillery or down in the pit operating the camera.

I used to stay down in the cockpit too long at one stretch to suit him. His idea was that the observer should spend most of the time searching the sky in order that the Hun could not pull a surprise attack. In this he was right, but it was extremely difficult to do this and at the same time do the mission well. Brereton had previously been accustomed to getting me out of the cockpit by shaking the plane, which merely consisted of gently vibrating the control lever from right to left. This day I was trying to get some very good photographs and I admit in so attempting I was staying down in the cockpit too long. Brereton shook the machine several times, but I didn't come out because I wanted to finish my set of pictures, taking my chances on an attack in the meantime.

Brereton was unusually irritable so he decided that I did not have the right way of doing things. He immediately turned loose his machine guns for a continuous burst of about twenty-five rounds, which sounded to me like two hundred and twenty-five. Believe me, I came out of that cockpit. I grabbed my machine guns and swung the tourrelle upon which the guns were mounted full around several times, up and down, under my tail; in fact, in every conceivable direction, for I was absolutely convinced that we were in a real scrap. Finally I got a glimpse of Brereton's beaming countenance. He was in a perfect uproar of laughter. The incident had its intended effect, for always afterward when Brereton would shake the plane, no matter how slightly,

I would come out of the cockpit right off, just as the ground squirrel comes out of his hole when you give him sufficient water, but with an uncomparable difference in rapidity.

So when I fired my guns poor "Greenhorn" was pitifully fussed. I could see he was losing his nerve, but I pointed in the direction of the fight and, obedient to my instructions, he headed the plane that way. It would never have done to have withdrawn after getting this far, for in so doing he would never again have been worth anything in the air.

We were still quite a distance from the show. I was looking over the top wing to get a line on the fight. They were still at it and it was just getting good. It seemed to be the ordinary aerial dog fight in which one allied plane is on the tail of the enemy plane and two of the enemy planes are on the allies' tails, and three of the allies on the tails of the two enemies, and so on—all going round and round, exactly like a dog chasing its own tail. Suddenly one of the planes dropped from the combat and, making a steep dive, it burst into flames and fell toward earth. I shook the plane violently and, pointing toward the falling plane, I joyously cried to the "Greenhorn," "Boche! Boche!" He was not so enthusiastic as might have been expected and I had no more than gotten the words out of my mouth when another plane started falling—also out of control.

At this point "Greenhorn" again suddenly headed his plane toward home. In a rage I shook the plane violently and with fury in my face I again pointed toward the fight. He shook his head. I became more infuriated and again pointed toward the fight, but the "Greenhorn" just as furiously shook his head and determinedly kept on going toward home.

This would never do—I would feel like a coward the rest of my life, so I reached over the cockpit and grabbed him by the shoulders and very affirmatively pointed toward the fight. He motioned for me to put on my speaking tube, and amid the pounding of the motor, in his high, squeaky, girlish voice I could hear him uttering something about "Motor bad. Mechanical trouble." It did not sound that way to me, so I doubtfully shook my head. He vigorously affirmed his statement, showing surprise that I should doubt his word or question his decision on mechanical matters. For the purpose of camouflage the plane kept rocking from side to side and the motor would become very strong and then suddenly die away. It was my belief that it was being controlled from the throttle. There was nothing I could do. I was not only disgusted with the "Greenhorn," but I was thoroughly ashamed of myself. I felt like a sneaking coward.

As we crossed the lines our anti-aircraft artillery suddenly began to fire violently and rapidly into the heavens. Then I picked up a lone enemy plane swiftly diving out of the clouds in order to attack our balloons. Here was our opportunity—I knew for a fact that a plane attacking balloons has not much chance to see any other plane approaching, so I shouted at the top of my voice, "See that plane there," and I pointed to it. "That is a Boche that's going to attack this first balloon. Then it's going over and attack the next one to the left. We won't have time to get him before he gets them both, but we will get him after he leaves the second balloon, for he won't see us. We'll get him sure. Here's our one chance to redeem ourselves. Nurse your motor along for we are on our own side of the lines anyway."

The man at the controls hesitated a moment and then started in the proper direction with full motor. I realised the danger of getting into a scrap with a plane that has for its object the burning of balloons, for they use nothing but incendiary bullets, and while I had no serious fear of being killed by a clean bullet, the idea of burning in midair was quite repulsive. Then, too, there was a green pilots but I actually craved in the worst way a chance to redeem our plane from its disgraceful conduct in the dog fight—here was the chance.

The balloon crews already were on the job and were frantically attempting to haul the balloons down to safety. No other planes were in sight. We were the only hope of saving the day. In a few moments I saw the observer of the first balloon jump with his parachute, saw the Boche empty his fire into the huge bag and then saw the balloon burst into flames. I do not know why it was, but for some reason at that particular minute our engine began to die and grow strong, then die again. I appeared not to notice the motor and excitedly pointed the "Greenhorn" to the direction in which we could meet the Boche most advantageously. His face registered a doubtful hope that he might be able to comply with my urgent request and then, as if his conclusion was drawn after a consultation with his better judgment, his expression changed to one of disappointed regret, for he again pointed to the motor and began to utter "Mechanical trouble."

He headed the plane toward home and away from the Boches. I knew what the people on the ground would think at our performance after we had once started after that Boche. They would be too ashamed of us to say anything. I was thoroughly disgusted and angered to the highest degree. Unmolested, except by local defences,

107

the Hun burned the second balloon and triumphantly flew back into Germany.

The "Greenhorn" was unbalanced by horrors he had seen. The morning had his goat, for he kept on looking back, time and time again, as if he were sure that he would be the next one to go down in flames.

That ride back to our airdrome was the wildest I ever got in my life as a flyer. The boy lost his head completely and I was absolutely helpless, not having a dual control, though I do not know much what I would have done at that time even if I had been fortunate enough to have had a dual control plane. We would take sudden jerks in which I would go half way out of the cockpit, nothing holding me in but my belt. I knew the boy was getting worse and I was figuring how I would look after the fall. When we got directly over our own airdrome, to my surprise he called back to me in a frantic voice, "I'm lost. Which way now?"

"Take it easy," I replied, "our airdrome is right beneath us."

The lad came down like a streak from the sky and I knew we were going to hit the ground in one grand smash. The "Greenhorn" tried to land and couldn't, so he gave her the gun again, circled the field, and in attempting to land almost hit one of the huge hangars with the tail. Death looked like a sure proposition to me. I felt like jumping—anything to get down to earth. In this second attempt he had a good chance to effect a good landing, but for some reason or other he kept on going. Then he foolishly did a vertical bank and came in with the wind, intending to land. To land with the wind is one of the most dangerous things a pilot can do, but it did not seem to affect our hero. Did he land with the wind? I'll say he did.

As we neared the ground I was sweating blood, for I knew what was sure to happen. Perspiration was flowing from my entire body with the freedom that it rolls from the winner of the fat man's race at the old county fair. We hit the field in the centre, took a two-storey bounce; the wind caught us and as the wheels hit again, S-P-L-0-W! We rolled over on our nose. Good fortune alone kept us from doing worse. We stopped, and I was up in the cockpit about twelve feet from the ground, though I expected to be found underneath the engine about ten feet underground—and the ambulance came rushing to pick up our remains.

They got me another plane ready and after considerable hard luck I finally got the mission completed with the help of a very wonderful pilot named Lieutenant Weeks. Late that afternoon the "Greenhorn" came around and asked me if I would mind going with him again to-morrow. I was forced to decline. He was relieved from further duty at the front. It was his first and only trip over. I don't think the "Kid" was a coward—he simply could not stand the gaff of air fighting.

There is nothing more nerve-racking or terrifying than a ride in an airplane with a pilot at the stick in whom you have no confidence, and especially so when at war and in an active sector where the enemy has control of the air. There are many times in my young and blame-less life in which I have been actually scared, but never one in which I have been carried in that state of fear and terror for such a long stretch as in that two hours, twenty-one minutes and eighteen seconds in a Salmson airplane in the Argonne Forest on September 26, 1918, with a green lieutenant, fictitiously named "Greenhorn."

Chapter 7

Eileen's Inspiration

Shortly after the great Argonne Offensive commenced, the Fifth Corps Air Service was visited by a small troop of Y. M. C. A. entertainers. I was at their airdrome at the time. In the party were two young ladies, one blonde and the other a brunette. As I was a sort of special boarder myself, I was very fortunately a guest at the Headquarters Mess, and at the head of the table sat Lieutenant Colonel A. R. Christie, who was the commander-in-chief of the Corps Air Service. I had heard early in the after-noon that these girls were coming, and it had been so long since I had seen a real American girl that my enthusiasm over their prospective arrival was not exceeded by a country lad's anticipation of his first circus.

As luck would have it, at the dinner table I was seated next to the brunette, which was just what I had wanted. I must say she was a "Queen." She had eyes that were all eyes, and when she smiled it seemed, as the poet would say, just like the flooding of a dark and desolate dungeon with the glorious light of day. She wore a daintily scented perfume that made it all seem to be just like the environment of a wonderful rose garden and this girl was the loveliest rose of them all.

I immediately felt my insignificance, for I was only a lieutenant, and around me were colonels, majors and captains, and on account of this sub-ordinance I knew my place demanded reticence rather than verbosity. Therefore, when introduced I merely told her quite formally how happy I was to know her and then I closed shop with all the good intentions of a huge, triple-locked, steel safe. However, Eileen, for this was her name, had the master combination for unlocking the deposit box of pent-up conversation. She started it, but after she had been going for two or three minutes, rank did not amount to anything to me, because I was quite sure, as I had been several times before and have been several times since, that this was the one girl God had made for Elmer. So to me Rank was business and Love was pleasure, and pleasure superseded business.

Versatility was this girl's middle name, and to my great surprise she even had a conversational knowledge of aerial observation, which is, indeed, unusual for a woman. Perhaps the reason she was so friendly to me was that I had some knowledge of aviation myself, and she wanted to learn more. She asked me no questions, however, simply volunteered her own information, so I felt she could not possibly be a spy, but whether she was or not it didn't matter to me, for I was thoroughly convinced that there never before had been a girl like this and there never could be another afterwards.

While dining, it developed that I was especially anxious to get a method for the rapid adjustment of artillery fire on moving targets. I explained to her that while it was no easy matter to make an adjustment on a moving target even in a quiet sector in closed warfare, the observer, at least, had the advantage of knowing where the battery was located, what the battery's signal panels would look like and what code signals both would use and what method of fire the battery would pursue. But in a war of movement in which we were engaged, our own batteries were constantly on the move and even if we did find a battery that was not moving there was no way of finding what code call it had been assigned, for the reason that they never displayed their panels as prescribed when taking a temporary position.

So I explained in a careless way just what difficulties I had to surmount before reaching a successful method satisfactory for all conditions. Perhaps I said a little more than I should, but I couldn't help it. I simply had to talk to this girl. She had the art of flattery well in hand, for she delighted me by demanding what business I had serving as an ordinary observer with my superior knowledge of things, whereupon I told her what a great man I really was—that I was the Operations officer for the Air Service of the entire wing, which consisted of six corps, and that I was only in this drive doing very special work. This sounded bigger than it really was, but it seemingly got by, for she seemed very sympathetic from the first I was quite sure I had won my happy home.

That night, upon an improvised stage in one of our huge airplane hangars, she sang. *Galli-Curci*, Breslau, Schumann-Heink or Farrar had nothing on her. She trilled and as she trilled, I thrilled. I even had wild

ideas of a little home in California and everything. After the performance was over I reported for duty and we started to walk back to the
main quarters together, she having spurned the proffer of one of my
superior officer's car. I had just made a grand and glorious spiel about
the beautiful night and the myriads of twinkling stars in the heavens,
and how wonderful it was to be walking along in the lovely delight
of it all with such a charming and entertaining companion, and how
I dreaded to think that in the morning I must go out to fly again and
might never come back to all these wonderful things.

I was raving and sputtering away, the enslaved victim of temperament, sentiment and ephemeral love. In brooding over the possible
tragedy of the next day I was, of course, fishing for sympathy, expecting her to say, "Oh, don't talk like that," or something similar to jolly
me along, but she evidently had had that line pulled on her before.

"You know, lieutenant," she smilingly said in a voice as welcome
as that of a dying aunt about to give you a hundred thousand dollars,
"I've been thinking of the wonderful work you are doing, and while I
was singing my first song tonight I looked down at you and I had an
inspiration which I think will help you."

This was the highest compliment I had ever been paid in my life.
I had disgusted people, displeased them, and even been repulsive to
some, but this was the first time I had ever been the cause of inspiring
any one. I thought it was the psychological moment to put the question. I had previously concluded that when a woman begins to talk
about inspiration she has fallen in love herself, so without inquiring
further about this particular inspiration, I turned to love.

" Eileen," I said, and my voice quivered, for I had not called her
that before—it had been Miss —— "do you know, I want to ask you
a question."

She said nothing, and I did not look, though I was certain that she
had modestly turned her head away from me, bashfully anticipating
the fatal question which was sure to come.

" Do you know, Eileen," I stammered on, nodding my head affirmatively in order to carry along with my words additional evidence
of my sincerity, "I have been wondering why you have paid this attention to me tonight and have been heedless of the pressing attentions
of the colonels, the majors and the captains. I don't like to talk like
this so soon, but you are leaving tomorrow and I might never have
another opportunity."

Then I thought of that song, "Just you, Dear, just you," and I knew quite well that she would say that she had been giving me all this attention amidst the jealous and envious looks of my superior officers because she, herself, individually wished to and because she liked or maybe loved me. Whereupon I was going to second the motion and say, "*Ditto*, I love you, Eileen," and all that sort of bunk and close the contract. I pictured myself enfolding her in my willing arms and making solemn vows such as I would stand on my ear for her, etc.; all of this, of course, being contingent upon her responding in the way I fully expected.

Smiling—her teeth reflected glory ui the moon-light—she demurely asked me, "Why, don't you know?" That would have been all right ordinarily, but it had a ringing inflection I failed to comprehend, and being a man of words instead of action, I said, "No, I don't know."

"Well," she went on rather surprised at my stupidity, "you see, our manager instructed us that the higher officers do not need the attention and encouragement of the young ladies because they do not have to undergo any hardships, so we have been instructed to pay as much attention as possible to the junior officers, and as you were about the most junior here—well—"

This was sufficient. I realised that I was on about the fifty-fourth floor of the Woolworth Building and had better catch the express elevator down, for it was going to be an awful fall. I had hit the mat and was already taking the count.

"I was telling you about the inspiration," she went on, and in a hollow voice I said, "Yes, Miss ——," swallowing many cubic feet of chagrin and remorse, yet still determined.

"I think I have a plan for adjusting your batteries. I got the idea while I was singing tonight. Of course, I know nothing about the practical part of it, but why wouldn't it work this way?" and she roughly described a scheme that seemed about as feasible as most military tactics that women conceive. I offered her no encouragement, but she asked me if I wouldn't try it out and I told her I would do anything for her. It would, at least, give me some excuse for keeping in touch with her, since I could inform her from time to time how her system was getting along, and I was firmly bent, in spite of the momentary rebuff I had just received, upon knowing this charming and bewitching damsel better.

As usual, the night gave me the opportunity to calm down considerably, so the next morning I took off quite early, the same old guy as before, with no domestic worries. Eileen was momentarily forgotten—my ardour was perhaps but a passing fantasy.

At a little village several miles north of Montfaucon there is quite a fork having two roads branching off to the south and over which the Germans were passing in their forced retreat. Flying in that direction the approaching roads were dotted with scattered German transports which consisted of many horses and very few motor vehicles as the Germans were short of gasoline and what they did have of this scarce article they used for their airplanes—their general transportation work was carried on largely by horses and a more extended use of their steam locomotives and railroads. But, coming from the south were several of these convoys trudging along as fast as they could, which, at best, was very slow. This was unusual for a retreat is generally done under cover of darkness, but, I suppose this material was such that it had to be moved at all costs.

Ah! I thought, this is a splendid target I'll put the artillery on. So, directing the pilot to go back to our own battery, I began to make furious attempts to get into communication with our artillery, by flying low and finding the location with the naked eye.

Again my theory of the previous day seemed to be all wrong, for in spite of all I could do I couldn't get an answer from any of our batteries. Finally, flying extremely low I found a couple of them and threw them messages. Neither of them would fire Why! I don't know. Perhaps they were about to move up again. However, I knew that of all of the batteries in our division there must a few that could work. Here was a wonderful target. I was to the last straw—there didn't seem to be anything else to do but go home, so, pretty well disgruntled I motioned the pilot to go on home. Thus, my mind being freed of the cares and responsibilities of the mission, it naturally began to turn toward the personal interests of life, and, naturally enough I thought of my recently acquired acquaintance, Eileen—and instantly I remembered her inspiration—that silly, tactical dream she had conceived the night before. I knew it was impossible to try it out as she had suggested it, but the principle had possibilities, and seemed to be worth taking a chance on. If it failed, it would do no harm, and, at least, I could give her some kind of a report.

Attracting the pilot's attention, I motioned him to turn around and although he gave me a look that indicated he had some doubt as to my mental balance, he followed the instructions. It was just a hunch at most. Instead of calling the particular batteries designated to fire on fugitive targets I calmly proceeded to call each and all of the twenty-four batteries assigned to the division. In about five minutes, to my extreme delight, I picked up a new panel from a battery. Consulting my chart I found its call. I immediately wired them a message and instantly they put out the panel "I got you" or "Understood." Communication was established. The inspiration was a success.

Over to my right, my eye caught another panel of another battery. Consulting my chart again I found that they were both Heavy Artillery—just what I wanted! The only fault with this method was that with so much wireless being flashed through the air it would very likely interfere with any other plane doing similar work in that sector. I knew of no other aerial adjustments going on just then, so, the chance was worth it.

Having gotten the two batteries ready to work I wired to every other battery I had called, sending them the code message, "I have no further need for you," this, in order that they would not, by any chance, hold up their firing on account of my previous message. "Well," I thought, "the nice thing about Eileen is that she is not only beautiful and can sing, but she is sane—she has a good bean." Even before I had done the work, which I felt sure I would be able to accomplish, I was formulating dreams of the way she would receive me when I told her of the great success of her inspiration.

I did not register these two batteries on the road fork, itself, for should the first few shells fall near the road fork it would give a preliminary warning and the Germans would, undoubtedly, stop their traffic and scatter. A few shells, even if they did happen to hit, would not serve the end I had in mind. I was thinking of something bigger—a few pot shots on the road would do more harm than good. So, selecting a point about a quarter of a mile, directly to the right of the road fork, I reported the location to the battery. Of course, consulting their maps, they could not find a legitimate reason for my desire to fire on this particular point; that is, from its natural location, but fortunately they did not question my decision and presently gave me the signal "O.K." I immediately wired them to fire.

On account of the hasty advances it had been necessary for these batteries to make, their firing data was considerably off, so, it took me almost an hour to get the two of them accurately placed on my temporary target. This accomplished, I began to again pay attention to the road fork. Our firing had not interrupted the traffic. Coming from the south about a quarter of a mile down, there seemed to be approaching quite a composite transport made up of wagons drawn by about four horses each, and coming from the north, approaching the same road fork, were a body of men and some horses. The men were not mounted, except in a few instances, and I should say there were almost a hundred men and about forty horses. To the best of my calculations, the head of the column coming from the south would pass this body of men with their horses at the road fork within a few minutes. With the road fork filled with passing troops and horses it would be all the more advantageous as a target.

The mathematical calculations and mechanical adjustments necessary for the batteries to correct a difference of a quarter of a mile in deflection, are considerable, I had been told, so, it was necessary that they know their new target immediately in order that they might fire immediately at my command I wired them to change their target three hundred meters to the left and then I specified the exact point by giving the coordinate location and last I told them to be prepared to go into a "zone fire" at signal. "Zone fire" is the deadliest of all destructive fire. It consists of firing the guns as rapidly as possible into an area, or zone, immediately adjacent to the target specified. The object of zone fire is that by the scattering of shells the target will certainly be hit by at least a few of the shells and if the target is large, as was the case here, the results would be disastrous.

To impress upon the batteries the urgency of speeding up their corrections I continually wired them in code, "Is battery ready?" "Is battery ready!" They put out the panels "Wait a few minutes," but I continued to wire, "Is battery ready?" We had no code for "Hurry up;" I wished many times we had, for the columns were fast approaching each other. In a few minutes it would be too late to get both columns. I realised those battery commanders had just cause to make use of an extended stream of profane language when I gave them that large correction of three hundred meters or a quarter of a mile after adjusting them to such a fine point, for, undoubtedly, they could not see the necessity for it. Fortunately they both had confidence and stayed with me. Just as the heads of the two columns began to pass each other, which was just a little north of the cross roads, the first battery put out a panel, "Battery is ready."

The airplane signal to fire was three long wireless emissions so it was only necessary now to press the key three times and the show would be on. I called the battery rapidly, but before I gave the fatal signal I thought of the warden of the penitentiary about to press the fatal buzzer that sends the doomed soul to his death. The simile naturally struck me for I had a hundred men and more horses directly in my trap. There was no way for them to escape. The deadly zone fire, with the speed of lightning, would soon crush them. I could imagine our men at their guns in the improvised battery pits, ready for the minutes of strenuous work before them, waiting for the radio buzzer to speak and command. As I looked down I could see the troops and transports were already passing each other—the road fork was filled—it was now time to act. I felt as if I simply could not bring myself to the point of pressing the key.

The men and the crushing out of their lives, the blighting of the hopes of many fond sweethearts, the wrecking of many homes and the grief of many mothers were strangely enough only passing thoughts, for it had to be done—"*C'est la Guerre*"—they were the enemies of my country. But there was another side of the story, the horses—for if there is any one thing in my life I have always loved it is a horse. Since I was a lad I have always picked up with the worst old skate in the town just out of sympathy, and to see a man abusing a horse would draw me into a fist fight quicker than anything else. The poor horses—dumb and senseless—they were not my enemies, except from a cold-blooded standpoint regarding them as war material of the enemy.

Looking back I found that the other battery had put out their panel "Battery is ready." It sternly called me back to my duty and the task before me for it was not the time to indulge in sentimental reveries—I must act! I hastily called the second battery and again repeated my call to the first, then directing my pilot to head toward home I took one last look at the slowly moving, unsuspecting columns—then, setting my face homeward, I firmly pressed the key— one, two, three times.

There was no doubt in my mind but that we should call it a day, so, we were homeward bound with that intention. From a strictly military stand-point we were proud enough of our performance and as we winged our way along I took things easy but kept casually looking about the sky to see that we were not taken unawares by any stray patrols. Looking ahead I saw the friendly captive balloons lolling along peaceably enough and my mind was centred pretty largely upon the seemingly monotonous existence of the men in the balloons who had to stay in one position for hour after hour, but I shuddered as I thought of being forced to jump from one of those bags in case of attack. After all, I was glad I was in an airplane instead of a balloon.

117

For quite a while it seemed that we were lower than the balloons, then suddenly the balloons seemed to be considerably below us. My impression was that we were gaining altitude, but upon consulting my altimeter I found that we were flying at a constant height. One thing was certain, the balloons were getting lower; they no longer lolled, but everything seemed taut. For some reason they were frantically being hauled down. I readily ascertained the reason,—four German Fokkers coming head-on from Hunland with the undeniable intention of either burning the balloons or burning me. I hesitated a moment; the Huns kept straight on and I heaved a big sigh of relief. They were not going to burn me; at least, not for the present.

The balloons seemed to be going down mighty slow, and the planes were coming fast. If the Huns could be stopped for only a half-minute the balloons would be safe. Here we were in a very happy position to divert the attack should we care to and also in a very unhappy position if we did not care to, for while it was not our duty to attack, yet indeed, in this case, it was our privilege. My mind was not made up what to do. If we turned to the right we would be directly in their path and above them. From instinct I shook the plane and motioned toward the four Fokkers and before I knew it, the pilot, thinking I intended to attack, started directly toward them.

Now there is a vast difference between manoeuvring for the purpose of diverting and manoeuvring for the purpose of attack, for had it been one or two planes I would not have hesitated to attack under the circumstances, but I want to say that I'll wait a long, long time before attacking four fast enemy Fokkers of my own accord under any circumstances.

It is surprising how rapidly two planes, when approaching each other from opposite directions, can come together, for before I had time to actually realise what was happening we were in the midst of a one-sided running fight in which we were doing the running and in which the Germans were peppering lead into us from all sides.

We had accomplished our mission for when the German planes attacked us, it guaranteed that they would not be able to attack the balloons, which would have plenty of time to be hauled down to a position of safely at their beds. While the diverting was successfully the diversion of diverting was not, for we still had to get ourselves out of the mess.

We were going in some direction, but which direction it was I didn't know and did not care. Right after us were these four Fokkers.

This was the first opportunity I had ever had to make a comparison of the Salmson plane, in a running fight. It was wonderful, for while the Germans were a little faster, it was hardly noticeable. The horrible truth of our predicament did not dawn upon me until, by some hunch, I looked at the ground during the fight and saw already considerably behind us, the village of Montfaucon, which is so clearly and unmistakably discernible from the air. I realised we had been completely outmanoeuvred, for we were headed straight and going farther and farther into Germany.

No wonder the Boche had not closed in on us. They were simply leading us to our slaughter on their own ground, or even worse, if we did survive we would be prisoners of war, a thought I had always dreaded much more than death, for once in flying over Pagny-sur-Meuse in the Saint Mihiel fight, I saw the thousands of Huns we had captured packed in bull pens like so many cattle. From this I preferred death to prison. Dropping my machine guns for the moment I violently pulled the cords that were tied to the pilot's arms and emphatically motioned him to turn completely around. He seemed to think that we were headed toward home and was extremely obstinate. The situation was serious; it was no time for discussion. I was sure of my direction. Reaching over the cockpit I frantically struck him on the shoulder and demanded that he turn around.

We turned and as we did the Germans realised that we had found ourselves and the battle royal ensued. The leader came first and behind him the three others in good formation, throwing two singing streams of fire from each plane, for in attacking balloons they used incendiary bullets. The leader, to my mind, was the only one that seemed to have had experience—he was, indeed, good—but the rest of them I thought were boobs—they did not seem to have the least bit of initiative, always waiting for the leader and doing exactly whatever he did first. Then they tried a formation I had never seen before. Climbing about two hundred feet above and on all sides of us, they kept making a series of short dives, each plane firing about twenty-five rounds at each dive. The object of this was undoubtedly to get our morale and if possible force us down without taking a chance on coming dose where machine gun fire could become effective. This was to our advantage for we were making time toward home and I only had one full magazine of ammunition left and it was all in my right gun.

Upon seeing that we were not falling for their cunning ruse the leader became unusually bully and came directly upon us. I let him

PAGNY-SUR-MEUSE, SHOWING PRISONERS CAPTURED BY THE AMERICANS AT ST. MIHIEL.

have it for a burst of about forty rounds which I knew went into his plane and at the end of which he had gone under my tail in a dive. It looked as if I had gotten him. With typical precision the other three came on. I deliberately aimed my gun upon the nearest, greatly encouraged in the belief that I had gotten the leader. Their bullets of fire were going into my plane, but with a most deliberate aim I again pulled the trigger. It would not fire. At most I had only sixty rounds left, but even in sixty rounds there was hope.

The gun was jammed and I could not get the magazine off to put it on the other gun. I was desperate. How close the three came I do not know, but seeing my predicament they realised my helplessness and pounced upon me like a toy target. Frantically I worked at the gun, my hands bruised and bleeding, hopelessly trying to unlock the jam for a last chance with life. If I only had something to fit in the cocking piece to give me enough leverage to clear that jam. In my mad desperation and hopelessness I looked around for something to hurl—anything to get them away. There was nothing to be done—it was all up with us. By chance I glanced into the bottom of the cockpit and on the floor my eyes caught sight of a Very pistol which had been left in the plane by the observer on the previous mission whose duty it had been to find the front line of our advanced troops.

A Very pistol is a gun resembling an ordinary pistol, except that it has a wide barrel. It is used to eject brilliant fixe rockets as a signal from the airplane to the infantry. These signals vary with the number of stars fired. For instance, a rocket of six stars means "Where are you? Show your panels," whereupon the infantry displays its white panels of cloth, while three rockets indicates "Understood" upon which the Infantry takes in its panels of white cloth.

I grabbed this Very pistol in a wild effort to throw it as a last means of defines, but the three had already passed under my tail, while to my disappointing surprise, I discovered that I had not gotten the leader as I had thought—he was coming up under my tail, already firing. The others seemed to be getting their formation behind him. As the leader came up under me in a final blow of death, I madly drew the pistol back in a position to hurl it at him when the sudden idea struck me that if it were loaded I would have a chance to set him afire. The cartridge was intact—it was ready to be fired. Amidst his volley of fire, I reached far over the cockpit and as the leader passed beneath me, I fired. The charge missed him completely, but directly behind him burst the signal—six flaming stars which brilliantly floated slowly on toward earth. My last chance had failed.

Suddenly resigned to my fate I awaited the onrush of the other three—I was sure it was only a matter of seconds—I had no defence. To my absolute surprise the first of the three violently tilted his plane, banked to the right, and the other two followed. I was at a loss to understand this move; then came another thought—there was still a chance. Rapidly ejecting the empty cardboard shell from the Very pistol I attempted to adjust the barrel to the cocking piece of my jammed machine gun. It fitted—here was the needed instrument of leverage—with all my force I jerked—something gave way and I fell to the other side of the cockpit—from the side of the gun there hung a mashed defective cartridge and the jam was cleared. With luck, there were fifty or sixty bullets left. Approaching me again was the leader, but where were the other three? I glanced back—they were still headed to the right—they had left the fight.

Calmly I waited his onslaught. Boldly coming up with the certain knowledge that I was still helpless and certainly his easy prey, he came, for nothing but wonderful luck on our part and rotten shooting on theirs had saved us so far. This time he did not fire until he had dead aim, nor did I fire until I had dead aim. Following his approach with extreme care and closest possible adjusted sights, I waited. When I was sure, I pulled the trigger—I don't know how many rounds he fired, but only a few, for my aim had been true—his guns suddenly stopped—his plane climbed steeply, even up beyond me, then tumbled over in a sort of half loop and began to swish away helplessly to one side and then to the other, like a falling leaf—at last it dived headlong and from its last dive it never recovered.

My ammunition was gone, but to the greatest of luck and horseshoes, I attributed the fact that the other three planes were also gone. In a few moments more we again passed over Montfaucon and crossed the lines. The balloons were just beginning to rise again. "Well," I thought as we passed them, "you seem to be safe enough this time, and I must say I admire you for going up again so soon after such a narrow escape, but for me—never again! I'm going to stay on the ground the rest of my life."

Of course, I often wondered why those other three Huns had left the fight. Here is the solution of the mystery. At Christmas time, three months later, I was in Coblenz, on the Rhine. The war was over and we were a part of the Army of Occupation. Under the terms of the Armistice the Germans had to turn over two hundred airplanes to the Americans and were to send twenty German flyers along to test the planes in the presence of competent American judges before they were accepted. Late in the evening, after a joyous Christmas dinner, at which wine and merriment abounded, an orderly came in and told us there were two German officers to report. We found that they were two of the flyers detailed by the German Government to turn over the planes.

One of them was a lad named Donhauser, who claimed to have shot down twenty-six allied planes, among them Quentin Roosevelt; the other was a lad named Teske, who also was an Ace. We invited them to join us, and during the conversation that followed it was interesting to note the many battle fronts over which we had fought against each other.

Upon discussing the Argonne it developed that Donhauser 's squadron was opposite the area in which I had this fight on the twenty-eighth of September, so, I took occasion to clear up the incomprehensible reason why these three had left the fight. I casually asked him if at a certain hour, at a certain place, on a certain date, he had a patrol, evidently bent upon attacking balloons, diverted by a bi-plane observation plane. He took out a little book from his pocket and after hastily scanning the well-kept notes, he looked up and said, "Was one of the Deutschen planes shot down?"

I answered "Yes."

"Do you know if it was the leader?" he inquired. I told him I thought it was. He again verified the time and the place and then opened up. This was his story:

> The leader, who was shot down, was an exceptionally good flyer and had several victories to his credit. There was something queer about it—in the squadron it was known as the 'Mystery Mission' for the reason that three of the German planes left the fight when the Observation Plane was absolutely helpless with jammed machine guns. They claimed that the German leader had fired a signal rocket to them, which was their signal for that day which meant for all the planes to leave the fight at once as larger allied patrols were approaching.

He explained that the German theory was that in obeying the signal the three German planes had left the fight, but the leader, being a very daring fighter, took a last chance, hoping to get away before the reinforcements arrived, and in attacking the observation plane alone, was shot down. He also said that this was the story the three had told, who all claimed to have seen the signal fired by their leader. Even at that they were threatened with court-martial for cowardice in leaving the combat and deserting their leader, and they were only saved by several German officers, who had also seen the same signal from the ground, testifying in their behalf.

Thus—the mystery was cleared—the Very pistol had saved the day. It was, after all, better that I had not set the leader afire with the flaming rockets. Indeed, they had served a greater use.

★★★★★★

What happened to Eileen? Naturally that should be explained. Well, it's this way: I had a lot to tell her, so, when I got to the airdrome I hastened across the field to the Headquarters to find her.

"Lad," I said to the orderly standing in front of the headquarters, "have the pretty girls of the Y. M. C. A. gone yet?"

"Yep," he replied, "that's them goin' down there now—to Souilly," and he pointed to a huge cloud of dust following the trail of an army auto a half mile down the road, and in that cloud of dust, seemingly rising into the sky, floated also my fond hopes and prospects of Eileen, for conditions, in a few days, made it impracticable for me to follow her movements for some time to come.

"Well," I said, sort of sorry like that they had gone, "they were sure pretty girls, weren't they?"

"Yep," he grinned.

"Especially the black-haired one," I went on.

"Yep, she's mine, lieutenant. She's been talking to me for a half an hour this morning," and he grinned sheepishly, until his grin almost became a smile, and we both looked longingly down the road where the car was fast disappearing from view.

I looked at the orderly and the orderly looked at me. "Talked to you half an hour, eh?" I questioned.

"Yep, fully that," was the proud reply.

I put my hands in my pockets and started to walk away muttering to myself "How do they do it! how do they do it?"—for this soldier was about the homeliest and most unattractive person I could imagine, yet he had evidently put my hopes to rout in quick order. Then came an idea: and I wheeled around and called to the soldier, "Hey, boy, what's your rank!"

"Ain't got no rank, Sir," he replied; "I'm a buck private."

Whistling a light tune I walked on. "I get it, I get it," was my soliloquy. "Eileen still following instructions on catering to the junior ranks. She's sour grapes." And thus she passed from my life—but I hope not forever.

CHAPTER 8

Down and Out and In

Eddie Rickenbacker told me a story while we were a part of the Army of Occupation which about expresses my idea of this narrative, the fact that I lived through it being what I consider my greatest accomplishment.

"Rick" had in his famous 94th Pursuit Squadron, a hair-lipped pilot with whom I was earlier associated in the equally prominent 12th Observation Squadron. This lad was one of the few of our many airmen who realised that the flyer at the front plays ninety *per cent* in luck and not on good judgment. His flying was dare-devilish and reckless, which, while it might be considered good form in pursuit work, was such that it involved entirely too great a risk for the two-place, or observation plane. So, the kid was transferred to Pursuit where he made good right off.

It was the day of the armistice. The boys were talking it all over, reminiscing and the like. Several of the famous pilots of the 94th had given accounts of some particular thrilling fight in which they had finally won, naming it—their greatest accomplishment of the war. So, as that was the topic of conversation, Eddie asked our friend what, after all, he considered his greatest accomplishment. The boys all listened attentively for the kid usually sprang something. The hairlipped lad puzzled for a moment, then answered with his inimitable impediment, "Well, Captain Rickenbacker, the war is now over, isn't it!"

"Yes," replied Eddie, hopeful that this was the correct reply.

"—which means no one else will get killed, doesn't it?" he added solemnly, and Rick solemnly attested to this fact.

"Well," the lad went on, "you see me; I'm still here."

"That's right!" said the great Ace of Aces. "What about it?"

"Well, Captain Rickenbacker," replied the boy with evident surprise at Eddie's apparent density. "Look me over, captain, I'm still alive. That is my greatest accomplishment."

And after all, I am sure that all of our fighting men who have done actual service at the front—going through its hazards and dangers for any length of time, will agree that their greatest accomplishment is the fact that they came out of the thing alive; for while the code of military ethics at the front taught that one's own life should be secondary to the accomplishment of one's mission, yet there could not help but be a justifiably selfish pride after the mission was accomplished, that the participant was also alive to tell the tale.

The 30th of September was a terrible day—there was very little flying, it was foggy and the clouds were low, irregular and uncertain, while the wind was almost a gale. We had no business going out—our over-anxiety, which the French say is the greatest fault of the American soldier, to get our work accomplished was the only justifiable reason for the trip.

But even at that on the morning of September 30th the Flying Corps had no reason for being in the air unless the mission was of grave urgency, and fortunately ours was urgent for I was still adjusting our artillery on important enemy moving targets. Here is how my greatest accomplishment happened:

I arrived at the hangars shortly after daybreak and found Davis, who was assigned to fly with me, ready and waiting. I had never flown with him before, but I had heard of him and his reputation, and it was a relief to know I was to get a genuine pilot, such as Lieutenant Raymond Davis, whom we called "Uncle Joe Davis, of Danville," since he hailed from the same well-known town as Uncle Joe Cannon.

At first, the weather was impossible, so, we had to wait for the atmosphere to clear a trifle and for the clouds to lift some, as a high ceiling in heavy artillery adjustments is not only advantageous but necessary. So, we hung around and hobnobbed and got acquainted. At about eight o'clock we decided we would try it—for the importance of impeding the retreat of the enemy as much as possible was imperative. The advance through the Argonne was proving itself to be a hard enough tussle for the doughboys, and we all felt that they certainly merited all the assistance it was possible for aviation to give them.

Luck was not our way, for it was not until after trying four different planes, all of which failed for one reason or another, that we found a bus that would buzz. It looked like an off-day, for the gale was so sweeping that we almost had a serious accident even in taking off.

There is safety in height, so, when we got up three or four hundred feet our morale also went up a trifle. The ground station signalled that my radio wireless was O.K., so I jokingly called to Davis, "All aboard for Hunland." He answered "Check," and we headed toward the line for our last mission of the great war.

I knew the wind was high, but I did not actually realise its true velocity until I happened to look toward the earth and to my surprise saw to our right the familiar ruins of the village of Montfaucon sitting high and distinct amid the surrounding ruins and desolations. I had never flown so fast, for a strong wind behind the airplane adds marvellous rapidity to its speed. We were swept along like a feather in a gale. In front, on the Bois de Beuges, there was raining a tremendous artillery barrage, which we knew extended all across the Argonne front. Almost instantly, it seemed, we were over Romange, which was Boche territory, and hastily I picked my target. We would again pile up the German traffic by adjusting our heavy artillery on their cross roads in front of our own 91st Division, whose batteries were around Epionville. We would repeat our previous successful adjustment and when the traffic was heaviest, would call for fire. Imparting this information to Davis, he turned the machine and we started back toward the line to call our batteries and start the fatal ball rolling.

A favourite trick of the Hun's anti-aircraft artillery, and our own, as far as that is concerned, is to allow the entrance of observation planes to a considerable depth within the lines without molesting them, closely following it all the time with finely adjusted sights, and just as the plane turns to go back toward the lines the artillery opens up with everything available.

I knew it was going to happen as soon as we turned into the wind and that in bucking the wind we would practically stand still in the air, making us an easy target, especially since we were skimming along low, heavy clouds upon which the artillery could easily get accurate data as to range and direction. It happened. The archies opened up. As luck would have it they realised our position and had us in their deadly bracket. One high-explosive shell burst directly under our tail, whereupon the plane reflexed like a bucking broncho.

The airman is bracketed when the archies have bursts on all sides of him, for in such a case he knows not what direction to go for one is about as bad as the other. One thing was certain, we did not dare to stand still in the air hanging on the propeller, as we were doing in fighting the wind. We must slip the deadly noose of the bracket and do it before it was too late.

Realising the necessity for quick action, Davis sharply slipped the plane into the wind, and amid a deafening applause of exploding shells, we plunged to momentary safety behind the curtain of the low, dark clouds with which the sky was filled. We were in the cloud, perhaps, for five minutes and the wind was with us. I knew we were covering a great deal of territory and in the wrong direction. So, when we emerged I quite well knew we were completely off our course. I asked Davis if he knew his location. He answered frankly that he did not—that it was away off his map. I was in the same predicament exactly as to the location, it being off my map as well, but fortunately I recognized the bomb-shattered town nearby as Dun-sur-Meuse, as I had many times studied it as a very prominent bombing objective.

"Head due south along the river," I cried through the communicating tube, "We've got to hit the lines sometime."

Dun-sur-Meuse had been bombed very heavily in the drive and I am sure the remaining inhabitants thought we too had that intention, for in heading south they certainly let us know we were not welcome. This time it was not only artillery, but machine guns in such a hail of fire that we would have been brought down with little effort had we attempted to fly a straight course. We didn't attempt it. We answered by sharp zigzags, and it was the master job of my life to keep up with the snaps, jerks, slips and dives of Davis', in dodging the archies; and to still keep our direction in mind. We attempted this for fully ten minutes, but we were making no appreciable headway. The firing was too heavy—we must get higher as we could not expect to live at nine hundred feet at a very long period. We had been lucky to survive this long.

Davis headed due south by his compass which was east by mine. It looked all wrong to me.

"Is your compass pointing south?" I asked feverishly, for it was a question of life and death.

"Yes, due south," he replied.

I knew one of the two was considerably off, but it might be mine as well as his, so I decided to try his. A constant mist of rifle fire and archies followed us in our ascent into the clouds, which fortunately was not long—thanks to the climbing power of the Salmson airplane. We were in and above the clouds for fully twenty-five minutes, and believe me, those twenty-five minutes were prayers that Davis's compass was unerring.

Finally, considering the wind velocity, our probable distance from the lines, and the speed of the motor, I was convinced that if the compass were true we should be well over the French lines, so, hoping to encourage Davis, I called, "Well, Davis, if that old pointer of yours is right we are in La Belle France again. Let's go down and see."

He put the boat into a dive and we came out of the clouds in a long, straight glide. In a jiffy I quite well knew we were not in France. A German balloon with the Iron Cross was directly beneath us firmly moored to its bed on the ground. Here we were at less than a thousand feet. The excitement around that balloon bed could easily be imagined when out of a cloud, in such terrible weather, a huge and awkward two-place enemy plane unexpectedly dropped. I have been on the ground at our balloon beds when they were attacked and know something of the awful fire the attacking plane goes through in attempting to burn the balloon even at the ordinary height, but it is many times worse when it is moored to its bed, for the lower the plane must come the greater the hazard. It is for this reason that most armies consider it a greater feat for an aviator to destroy a balloon than an airplane.

There we were like a great ghost suddenly manifesting itself, and take it from me, if the machine gunners were asleep on their work at our unannounced arrival, they mighty suddenly showed signs of speed for almost instantly, from every angle came the *put-put-p*ut, while we helplessly tried every conceivable manoeuvre to dodge the many guns which were firing upon us at full force. It is not strange that the airman does not worry much over the regular steel ammunition of the machine gun, for like other similar dangers, while they are the most fatal, they cannot be seen, so, he is oblivious to their presence; but when the guns are using tracer and incendiary bullets, the stream of fire is not unlike a miniature fire rocket and behind each of the pretty fire rackets comes two silent, fatal ball cartridges, for, indeed, the very object of "tracer" ammunition is to show the path the bullets are taking.

If there is anything that gets a flyer's wind up, it is tracer bullets from the ground. Our wind was up and had been up for some time. But, Davis did the right thing and again headed with the wind, while "tracers" saw us, met us and almost conquered us. It certainly is terrifying to watch them come up at you for the helpless part of it is that they come so fast you cannot even try to dodge them. They were all around us; our right wing was perfectly perforated with several accurate bursts and in the diving and slipping I had been thrown around in the cockpit like the dice in a dice-box. My seat had slipped from beneath me about three times, but the condition of my mind was such that I was positive that it had been shot from beneath me. The sharp taming with the wind left a wake of disheartening tracers in our trail. It resembled a billion small rockets for the flaming trajectories were easily followed.

The Fourth of July was not in it. I thought at the time that it was a sight well worth seeing, but dangerously unhealthful. Soon though as we shot along we were again greeted by the high explosive bursts of the artillery which was some relief for they were considerably behind us and we were at least away from the machine guns at the balloon bed.

The painful fact was that while we were going through the air at a terrific speed, that speed was carrying us farther and farther into Germany. The situation was becoming more and more serious. What could we now do? We could not possibly fight the wind below the clouds and make the long distance home, so I told Davis to go into the clouds again; at least, we would not be such an easy target This time we would try my compass, for while it might be slightly untrue, if we went long enough we surely could not fail reaching France at some point He started to climb and, well—those were long moments. The climbing greatly decreased our speed, while the machine guns again played upon us most cruelly.

But that climbing was a most wonderful piece of work; poor Davis twisted that boat in every conceivable manner, but the best part of it all was that he continued the climb at all costs. There was nothing so dear to me as those clouds—so near and yet so far. Anything to again get out of that constant and swarming beehive of fire bullets. Thai we penetrated the ceiling. My heart was again almost normal for a few seconds. Here was the supreme moment it seemed—truly to err was to die, or worse, to finally land from shortage of gasoline and be made prisoner. Hugging close to the compass, oblivious to all else, lest we deviate a jot from its true south reading, I slowly and distinctly called the directions.

For fully a half an hour we followed this procedure—sometimes above the clouds and most of the time in them, but never below them. At last I was absolutely certain that we were well over dear old France again; at least, somewhere between Paris and Nancy, so, after another three minutes to be sure, I called to Davis again.

"This time we have sure foxed the Hun," I said; "let's go down and look over the scenery."

We had climbed quite a lot farther in the clouds than we thought, and it took longer to come to light, so, in our anxiety to see France again he put it into a steeper dip and soon we emerged in almost a straight dive. Below us to the right was another balloon at its bed. It was our own balloon line, of course. It could be no other for my compass had been undoubtedly true and somehow the ground looked like France. Furthermore, we had not been fired upon.

"Davis," I said, "look out for a place to land and we'll find where we are, then after dinner we'll fly on home."

I had no more than gotten the words out of my mouth when a machine gun started to fire at us, again using tracer ammunition. I was convinced that it was all a mistake and that when they saw who we really were they would quit, so, I told Davis to tilt the plane and show the colours of our cocarde as the weather was not clear and any one might make a similar mistake.

Our own aviation never, under any circumstances, approached our balloons suddenly, for the reason that the Germans one time used some allied captured planes in the Château-Thierry offensive, and with the French colours on their cocarde, approached one of our balloons and, unmolested, burned it. Since then all balloons had adopted the policy of firing on any machine which came suddenly out of the clouds toward them. I was positive that this was the case here. Suddenly other guns vigorously began to take up the firing and by the time I saw the foreboding black, German Cross painted on the side of the sausage, the whole balloon machine gun crews had us well in hand.

When we went down on the first balloon I was pretty well convinced that it was all up with us, but this time there was no doubt about it, for we had lost far too many of our best pursuit pilots in attacking balloons at low altitudes for me to even hope otherwise, and our pursuit planes were smaller targets, were faster and more manoeuvrable. What chance in the world, I thought, has a lubberly, two-place observation plane in a hole like this when few of the pursuit planes even ever emerge with their lives?

Here I again hand it all to Davis, for with a bravery and grit that I have seldom seen equalled, and a skill that was uncanny, he did everything imaginable with that plane, but wisest of all he again headed with the wind, our only chance to get out of the mess. That second in banking into the wind was actually the longest of my life—the ground had surely anticipated it for we were truly the apex of the cone of lead and fire from the circular base of guns surrounding the balloon bed. The plane was almost a screen where so many bullets had perforated it. I heard a snap with a dismal twanging sound. One flying wire had been already cut by the barrage, but Davis kept right on twisting the boat as if nothing had happened.

We still had life—something for which I had almost ceased to hope. Like persecuted souls weak from exhaustion, but strong in determination, we went on, still with the wind unrelentlessly driving us farther into Germany. Already we had been up about two hours and the thought occurred to me that we would soon be out of gasoline. We could not take another chance. My calculation, which later turned out to be accurate, was that we were then about fifteen kilometres from the line.

The known splendid liaison of the Boche was already in action; this we well knew and undoubtedly several German planes were already up after us. The solution was simple. There were only two things we could possibly do. We knew the wind direction when we left France, so, we could pick up our direction from the smoke from locomotives, chimneys and the like and fly below the clouds toward the line. At best the condition of our plane would but permit elementary manoeuvring and at that we stood but little chance of getting through the continual machine gun fire at such constant low altitude. Then, too, it was certain that if we kept below the clouds on such a course we would soon have enemy planes hot on our trail, although, personally, I thought we would never get through two more minutes of the gun firing even with our plane in the best condition.

The alternative was to land, destroy the plane and try to escape. It all ran through my mind like a flash. I thought of Davis. I admit I thought of myself. One was justifiable life for the reason that the destruction of the plane, at least, would be guaranteed, while if we were shot down we would both die in the crash and the Boche would get the salvage and design of the plane. The impelling fighting chance of the second proposition was enough. There was no more hesitation.

"Davis," I shouted, "can you pick up the direction from the smoke on the ground!"

He looked around doubtfully.

"I'll try," he more doubtfully replied.

"All right, head into the wind again—beneath the clouds. This is our last chance. Fly straight into the wind. We will have to scrap for our lives, but luck is with us."

Nodding his head with characteristic determination, he swiftly steered the bus into the wind. For several minutes the combined fire of anti-aircraft artillery and machine guns played upon us. I will not attempt to describe the horrors of those minutes that seemed years— how we lived through it I do not know. A piece of my tourelle was shot away and my wireless reel was torn completely off. I could hear the plane whine in its flight, the broken wires even dolefully singing our requiem. Through it all the motor was not hurt—it was turning like a top. Indeed, it seemed just like the last moments of the poor fowl which, with its neck wrung, will continue to flop about. Veritably it seemed we were flopping—it was the wonderful Davis doing his best to dodge the myriads of deathly bullets coming at us from all angles.

Then suddenly all became quiet. The machine guns and the archies had for some reason stopped their firing. I had been there before—I knew. The time had come. Looking over to the right I saw what I expected—four German Fokkers had already taken off the field and were coming up after us. We could even see their airdrome and other planes ready to take off if necessary. It was a sad day. I had been in scraps before but such odds as these had not faced me. This was, indeed, foreign—ten miles from home, about out of gas, with a bunged-up plane and yet forced to stand there with hands on the guns and patiently await the seconds until they steadily climbed up to get us. I wanted to throw up the sponge in the worst way; it seemed but useless murder of the two of us, for there could be no possible chance to live through it. On the other hand, we might get one or even two of them, so it was the big game—the call of chance. We must give combat— now to break the word to Davis. I laughed hysterically.

"Davis," I called, "have you ever had a fight?"

Puzzled as to the significance of this question he turned around and answered, "No, Never."

"Well," and I again laughed for no reason in the world, "you are going to have one now." Of course, the airplane did a strange shimmy, after which I continued, "There are four Boche coming up to the right rear. Fly straight ahead, and don't worry. Only keep me in a position to fire."

Davis said nothing, but turning around he calmly eyed the oncoming Germans, then I saw his jaws set in fierce determination and without another sign of emotion he directed his attention to the damaged plane.

While the Huns were in formation and at twelve hundred feet, I levelled the guns and fired a burst of thirty rounds in order to scatter them for I have found that the Boche is not half so bold when he knows he is seen. It had the effect I wanted; they scattered and began firing at me from about one thousand feet, hoping to get us by a chance shot, or better, of frightening us into landing. They kept this position for several minutes. I did not fire another shot; I could ill afford to waste a single cartridge and ever hope to make the lines. Seeing that we intended to fight to a finish they separated; one plane came from the left, the other three from the right, and attempted to close in all at the same time

At nine hundred feet they again began to fire, and steadily close in. Still I did not pull the triggers. At my reticence they became bolder and when the right three got to about six hundred feet from me I carefully levelled my right gun and turned loose a well-directed burst of about fifty rounds. To me the real fight had now begun for soon they would be at close range where real fatalities occur. The lad at my left required my attention so I swung the tourelle and carefully laying the bead, I pulled the trigger. It did not fire. Thinking perhaps the locking mechanism had been caught by the sudden swinging of the guns, I reached down to pull it into place. The lock was O.K. It was nothing else than a plain jam. I did not feel so bad for I still had my other gun untried and there was sufficient ammunition yet for a good fight.

So, as the left plane closed in I aimed with unerring accuracy; and I was sure I had him unless something unusual happened. Something unusual did happen. The left gun fired about seven shots and stopped. It was no time for child's play—team work was the one thing necessary to save the situation. Davis realised it, for the moment the guns stopped firing he knew something was all wrong, and he took up the fight by a series of remarkable acrobatics, in a vain effort to get his own guns into play.

After many strenuous efforts, by brute force I succeeded in clearing the jam. At least, I thought I did, although things happened so fast from then on that the gun never had a chance. Amidst the violent jerking of the plane I frantically attempted to aim, then there was no more jerking—the plane seemed to be falling on its side toward earth and glancing forward I saw flames. There was only one solution— they had not only gotten Davis and we were rapidly falling to our death, but they had also set us afire. There were but the fractions of a second, and then the crash, for I was powerless—I did not know how to fly and, furthermore, the plane was not fitted with a dual control. A multiplicity of active and concrete thoughts took form in my brain in that short space of time from the beginning of the descent to the crash. I closed my eyes—the horror of it was too much for me. It was bad enough to face certain death, but the thought of burning to death closed the picture.

The plane struck and the next thing I knew we had stopped; at least, I thought I knew it. To be perfectly frank I was so scared I did not know whether I was dead or alive. But, looking out, I saw Davis already on the ground; Davis, who I was sure had been killed. This brought me to my real senses and in a second I was out of the plane and running top-speed toward the crest of a hill which was directly in front of us. Fifty feet to my left and running in the same direction was Davis, and swooping down from the skies, at an altitude of from thirty to fifty feet, the four Fokkers continued to fire upon us. This brought me still closer to the realisation that we were still very much alive, though how long we would be I did not know. I would run along about five yards and then fall on my stomach, then jump up and scramble on for another five yards and slide, the idea being that the planes, sweeping down, could very well judge our speed while running steadily, but when we stopped suddenly they could not quickly dive their planes to shoot straight down upon us, for in so doing they would crash headlong on the ground.

The hill was not steep, but at the same time it was not easy running. I think I beat Davis to the top, even at that. As I got there I will never forget the sight that met my eyes. Approaching us from the other side was the proverbial mob, coming out to get us. There were officers on horseback, officers on foot, soldiers, men, women and children with every means of conveyance, from artillery trucks on down to the antique oxen. There must have been five hundred of them. Of course, the fight had easily been followed from the ground and I suppose they were all anxious to come out to see what was left of us. Believe me, I had real stage fright when I saw that crowd, so, I turned around and as I started to run back down the hill to my surprise I saw that the airplane had not burned.

There is one hard and fast rule that all flyers are taught to follow and that is when shot down in enemy territory, their duty is to burn the plane at all costs, for otherwise the enemy not only gets the airplane itself, but also the latest designs, inventions and improvements which are a hundred times more valuable.

" Davis," I yelled at the top of my voice, as I started running toward the plane. Instantaneously he saw and followed. It was a bad trip back—the Fokkers, surmising our mission, came down to where they practically skimmed the ground, absolutely intent upon taking our lives.

When we finally reached the plane I was puffing like a steam engine, for my lungs were raw from exhaustion as I still had on this heavy flying suit which covered my entire body. The Fokkers were able to very well judge their shots for they made it extremely unpleasant.

"A match! A match! A match!" I kept calling, running around and not knowing what to do. Davis hauled forth a box with about eight in it. We had lost our heads absolutely for we were too excited to remember that we had such a thing as gasoline on board. Jumping around like a pair of ducks on a hot stove, we blindly tried to light the fabric on the wings which through the expenditure of a million dollars on experimentation had been made practically fireproof on-the surface by the application of non-inflammable varnish. We were too dense to take any cognizance of the fact that they continually failed to burn, so, we went ahead making repeated attempts to light the wings. In a minute the last match was gone. There was no hope. I felt like breaking down and crying like a baby. The right side under the motor was still smouldering from the flames in the air, which had been caused by an incendiary bullet striking the carburettor, but had been extinguished by the violent side-slipping of the plane, just as a match is smothered out by being swept through the air. Then Davis had a brilliant idea.

"Hell," he said, "We've got gasoline." And he jumped up into the pilot's pit and broke the main gasoline lead and in a second gasoline was spluttering all over the plane like a bubbling fountain.

"Look for another match!" I cried to Davis, and although he knew he had no more, he began to throw things out of his pockets right and left. Among these things there fell a smudge cigarette lighter. These instruments were devised by the French on account of their extreme shortage of matches. The gadget consists of a tiny steel wheel, which strikes a piece of flinty which in turn ignites the smudge. The only trouble with these things is that they do not always work. However, when this fell before me, it was Heaven itself, for I made a high dive and grasping it, began to strike the wheel. It would not ignite. Running back and forth, trying to get the smudge to burn, I began to strike it, pray over it, and do everything else. My kingdom, such as it was, for a light.

"Soak it in gas! Use your bean. Let me have it," cried Davis, and he snatched it out of my hand and soaked it with gas, but still it would not work. Disgusted, he threw it on the ground with a vehement oath, and took his spite out by trying to kick the rubber tire off one of the landing wheels. Snatching it up again I struck it sharply against a piece of the metal cowling on the motor with the hope that by some miracle this hasty remedy might help it. It was just luck, for something did the work. Whether it was hitting it on the metal or not, I do not guess, but when I gave it a brisk turn it bursted into flame, and my hands also being covered with gasoline, began to burn, too.

I dropped it like a piece of hot steel and Davis snatched it up and threw it into the gasoline soaked cockpit. Soon the $20,000 plane was a roaring furnace. It was like the last act of a big motion picture—the criminals at bay were fighting for time against the mob and like the hardboiled leader of the villains laughs in the face of his pursuers while he goes to his self-inflicted death rather than deliver himself, so I turned around, knowing there was no escape from the mob, determined to die in the wreckage. Already Davis was beating it across the field to the left, crying "Come on! Come on!" and so, while I did not have much pep left I started to run toward a sort of rude embankment over toward the left centre, which was not over two hundred yards away. Fortunately the burning plane momentarily threw the crowd back, for they knew if there were bombs aboard they would soon explode.

The heavy flying suit was causing me trouble, for I was stumbling through the mud like an intoxicated elephant, but even at that I am inclined, now, to think that I beat the intercollegiate record for the one hundred yards dash. As I rushed around this embankment, I hit something which landed me on the ground in a puddle of mud. What I hit was a horse, which was one of five being ridden by four officers and one sergeant, "who had come from another nearby village to get us. These horses stepped all over and around me, and I thought at the time how ironical it was to have endured and lived through the hardships of the morning, and have my life crushed out by a horse's hoofs. It was the same disgustingly disgraceful death that I have always feared since the war, namely of being hit by a Ford automobile on a quiet, country road after coming through the war in safety. However, the horses showed true horse sense and did not step directly upon me. Of course, I stopped. I was already stopped—if not by this sudden impetus, then surely from sheer exhaustion. I got up literally covered with mud.

The senior officer of the party was a true Hun, who had undoubtedly been drinking, for I do not believe otherwise anyone, regardless of nationality, could have been so cold-blooded and terrible. He could not recognize that I was American as my flying suit hid my uniform, so he spoke up in French:

"*Qui de vous a brûlé l'avion, et où est votre comrade?*" I quite well understood his French, but I felt it would be better policy to say nothing, so I looked absolutely blank. Again he demanded who burned the airplane and where was my comrade, which ultimatum he sharpened by a threatening "*Vite! Vite!*" I realised that something was necessary on my part, for deafness would be a very lame excuse for any flyer, so, I told him in English that I did not understand him.

"Ah," he smiled in delight, finding his prize had been even greater than he had expected, "then you are English or American. Which?"

He said this in perfect English, which upset my whole scheme of reticence, for it did not occur to me that he spoke still a third language. I said nothing, but looked at the ground, contemplating my reply.

"American or British?" he demanded.

I was proud of my nationality, so, looking up, I threw out my chest and exclaimed, "I'm American."

I expected him to immediately recognize the strength of my citizenship, just as the wise old Biblical character, whoever he was, got out of a tight hole by saying that he was a Roman. I had a surprise awaiting me, however, for he gave me a cynical laugh that gave him an opportunity to divert from the subject in mind.

"So you are an American, are you!" he sneeringly went on, "Well, I've lived in your America ten years, myself, and I know you all. You're a rotten bunch of lying hypocrites."

Strange as it may seem I did not see fit to take issue with him under the circumstances, so, he went on with another little round of abuse of the Americans that made my blood boil, but again I failed to go to the bat for my country. Thinking he had sufficiently riled me, he started on the subject of more vital importance.

"Now, which one of you burned that planet" he sharply demanded.

Again I said nothing, but I thought a lot, for since he was getting so individualistic about it, I was convinced that we were in a pretty serious situation; yet I knew I was going to have to answer that question. I was hoping that if Davis was caught he would say that he did it and I knew that Davis was human, and was hoping that I would say that I did it.

He interrupted my silent study. "Are you going to answer?" he growled.

What would I say to get by? I decided to spar.

"It burned itself," was my brilliant repartee.

"Don't lie to me," he hissed. "It might have been afire when you started down, but we saw you go back and burn it."

"Well, if you saw me go back and burn it, why did you ask me who did it?" I unthoughtedly retorted, and then I was sorry for if at first I thought him fierce, he had now become an irate demon.

"You did do it then, eh?" he said persuasively, as he slowly looked around to his companions in order that they might bear witness to my confession.

"What's the use," I thought to myself, so, I looked him squarely in the eyes and said, "Yes, I did it."

"Ah!" and he again looked around, shaking his head with intermingled scorn and pride that he, the Prussian, had been able to bulldoze an American. "Didn't you know that the moment that plane hit the ground, it became German property and that you wilfully destroyed German material!"

I most emphatically told him that I did not know it, for while I convicted myself on my previous confession, I didn't intend to sign my own decree of execution. He assumed a slightly conciliatory attitude.

"Now," he continued, "where is your partner, or comrade!" I told him that I did not know. "Oh, yes you do," he argued, coaxingly. After a little dickering dispute, I looked him squarely in the eyes and said, "I do not know."

Then he became fierce again. "Don't lie to me," he snarled in rage. "You do know and you are going to tell me."

I became pretty well convinced that my days were done for, so consequences momentarily did not matter. It was more than I could stand, for this was a matter that not only insulted my character as a soldier, but my integrity as a man—that he should call upon me to divulge the hiding place of my friend and my comrade-in-arms. In spite of the effort to control my temper, it flared up like a tyre-pressure indicator and in a daring attitude, I exclaimed, "I don't know and if I did know I would not tell you."

He flew into a white rage. "Is that so?" and he quickly reached back to his hip and pulled out a Luger, the most deadly German automatic pistol and with fiery eyes he put it right at my heart, the barrel even touching my clothing. I admit I inwardly swooned; in fact, I almost fainted for, while all the time I thought I was going eventually to be killed, I had no idea that there was going to be any snappy action like this. He meant business; there was no argument about that. His very attitude and the decisiveness with which he drew out the gun and the way he put his finger on the trigger convinced me that to spar was to die. If there was any chance at all, it lay in silence. He must have time to cool down or something else must intervene; so, like a weak sister I looked at him, just hoping.

"Are you going to talk or not?" he began quietly and I have never heard words uttered more decisively. I knew quite well that Davis had gone over to the left. One thing was certain, while above all things else I would not tell where he was, at the same time I was not exactly prepared to die. Since I was to die some time it could just as well be later, so, looking over to the right, in exactly the opposite direction in which Davis had gone, I noticed a clump of trees about three hundred yards away. In an attitude indicating that I was only telling to save my own life, I pointed to the clump and breathlessly whispered, "Over there."

He hastily gave some directions in German, and leaving me with one officer and the sergeant, he and the other two officers hurriedly galloped off toward the location I had pointed out. During this little entertainment quite a crowd had gathered around and as the tenseness was relieved, they immediately began ejaculating and mumbling in great fashion, completely surrounding me. Looking through the crowd my gaze was following the horses and surmising what my next move would be when they reached there and found I had deliberately lied.

When they were almost to the spot I had designated, we suddenly heard quite a noticeable scramble over to the left and looking over that way I saw that they had caught Davis and he was being escorted toward town, followed by a portion of the mob. Hearing the same noise, the arrogant Prussian stopped his steed and wheeling around, saw Davis had been caught in just exactly the opposite direction from that to which I had pointed. He knew instantly that I had deliberately pranked him at pistol's point. In Western cowboy fashion he gave his horse the spurs and drawing his Luger back over his shoulder came madly galloping toward me I knew what was going to happen. There was not a chance in the world; and the crowd around me also knew what was going to happen because they made a clearing just as the gamblers miraculously disappear when someone pulls a revolver in the game. Standing alone I awaited the inevitable.

As the fatal moment approached—suddenly there came from somewhere a sharp voice and from the crowd there rode forth another officer with a flowing purplish-gray cloak about him, the kind German officers sometimes wear when mounted, crying "*Halte! Halte!*" or something similar. It was a voice of command. The onrushing Prussian, riding past at his terrific momentum, dismounted and saluted. In a fast and furious manner this superior officer spoke to him in a well-modulated voice, but with a manner and expression, which, though I could not understand a word of German, I quite well knew was nothing else than a plain balling-out.

After about three minutes, in which our would-be assassin saluted ten or twelve times, he put his gun in its holster, remounted his horse and slinkingly rode away. Then this superior officer addressed something generally to the crowd, in reply to which one soldier stepped out, saluted smartly and after some directions by the officer, proceeded to explain to me, a broken English, that the officer wanted to apologise for the uncalled for conduct of the first German officer. After a little hesitation, I was surrounded by a proper German escort and marched over toward Davis—going where and for what I did not know—but trembling like a cur dog with *delirium tremens*—too afraid to be frightened.

CHAPTER 9

The Court of Inquiry

Like many other brazen Americans I felt throughout the war that in spite of the loss of my friends all about me, and the precautions repeatedly urged, that I was the one bird, who, alone, was exempt from mishap and misfortune. Undoubtedly the good fortune that always attended me caused me to adopt the viewpoint that my good luck was perpetual. Well, as a matter of fact, I still think that way today.

Such a thing as my ever becoming a prisoner of war in Germany was absolutely foreign to me. It had not even interested me, so, I had paid very little attention to the reports on the treatment of prisoner and I honestly did not know whether the prisoners were slowly starved to death or killed for some act which they had or had not individually committed, or what not. It was terrible at best. At any rate, I was convinced that it was bad enough that one could well afford to be desperate in taking chances to escape. So, when I finally, in spite of my confidence in my continued good luck, was taken prisoner on September 30, 1918, I immediately decided that I would escape no matter what the cost.

Upon being captured Davis and I were first marched down to a nearby airdrome—the den of our captors. There they dragged out a German automobile, which had steel, spring wheels. A very young and fat German boy, who, by the way, was an officer, climbed in first and told us to follow. Of course, we did; and soon we were off for somewhere. This youngster was a genuine pighead—he tried to be a Hun but did not know how and reminded me very much of a newly made second lieutenant. Like all other German officers he had the Iron Cross, which he wore complete and as he spoke a little English, I decided that the wisest move for me, was to find out just how much.

I had a hunch that the kid had probably just recently gotten his

Iron Cross and might be glad to make a few remarks at the proper opening. So, pointing to the cross and speaking rapidly, I asked, "What does that signify!"

He did not get me. His answer was a cool stare as if I had transgressed sacred laws. So, I again smiled and tried this time very slowly, "What is that?"

"*Ach*," and his flabby cheeks shook like a mould of jelly on a frosty morning, as we bounced along, "*dot iss der Deutschen Iron Cross.*"

"Oh, my! The Iron Cross," and I smiled with evident pride at our association. "You are very valiant" The youngster was flattered by my expression, though he did not grasp the words. This was what I was after. I could now converse safely with Davis, my pilot, if I spoke fast enough. So, turing to Davis I started to talk, but the kid rose up in all his dignity of rank and called a halt. In painful English he told us that communication between prisoners was absolutely "*verboten.*" We, of course, acquiesced most gracefully. I wanted to ask Davis especially if he had yet admitted burning the plane, because I already had admitted that I did it myself and if there was any one to be killed for the offense I could see no reason for both of us dying. This was information so vital that it had to be gotten to Davis in spite of any rulings of any school kid, German officer accompanying us.

At the same time it was not my intention to purposely antagonize our friend at this particular time, so with a very sweet smile I turned to this German and looking directly into his eyes as if speaking only to him, I rapidly, but convincingly orated:

"Davis, while I'm talking to this distinguished young Prussian, looking him straight in the eye, and I am talking so fast he has no idea what I'm saying, I want to ask you an important question and I want you to answer it right away and look at him as if you were speaking to him when you answer it, for he can speak about as much of our language as a clam. These Germans claimed that when that plane hit the ground it became German property and that in burning it, we have wilfully destroyed German property and the penalty is probably death. Now I've already admitted that I burned it, so, if they ask you who destroyed it you must say that I did it, in order that we may not both get stuck for the same offense."

Meanwhile I was making motions with my hands, shoulders, face, brow, mouth, nose, and ears, and looking directly at the German officer, as if I were performing for his benefit. The kid was dumb-founded—things were happening fast. Davis played his part like a trained actor and began to address this German, speaking very rapidly, and in a similar manner, while the poor German was shaking his head and hopelessly crying, "You are talking too fast; I do not hear you; I cannot understand what you say."

But Davis told me that I was a damned fool, that he had told them he had burned the plane and that if there was going to be any suffering done we would both do it together. Believe me, that boy's actions all through our experience endeared him to me forever, as a brave man and an honest, genuine fellow. However, when we got that one across our first custodian, I felt pretty much relieved for a great burden had been lifted from my mind. After all, I guess, there is a great deal of comfort in companionship even in trouble and misery.

We shot along those roads on that steel-wheeled bus at a remarkable speed. Quite soon we were at Montmedy, which was the headquarters of the 5th German Army. Undoubtedly here we were to be interviewed and sure enough we were taken into the large room in the front of the headquarters building, but, to our great surprise we were left for a few moments by ourselves as the force was out to lunch. I immediately threw off my flying "teddy bear" and hastily ran through my pockets and in spite of standing orders for flyers never to have written communications on their person, while flying over the lines, I found one order which would have given a great deal of aid and comfort to the enemy. I took this order, which was on very thin paper, and rapidly folding it, taking a match from the table I lighted a cigarette and then burned the order.

The few other things I had were not important, but at that I wanted to destroy everything, I had thrown my map in the burning plane, so my conscience was clear that I had done my duty all around as far as I was able. We were quite sure that the room had audiphones so we said nothing. As I was about to throw such other stuff as I had in the stove, the kid came in. I simply slipped my hand in my pocket and looked innocent. Then a very suave, English-speaking, German lieutenant came in and told us that he had been a prisoner of war in Russia and had just been released; that he felt sorry for all the prisoners of war, and wanted to tell us not to believe everything we had heard about the German atrocities and that since we were Americans we would be well taken care of, fed, etc., for Germany wanted America to feel that America and "*Deutschland*" were the best of friends.

His line was so smooth that I was sure that he told the same gag to everyone else, regardless of nationality. This intelligence officer was a very smooth article for instead of talking shop, he stated that if we would be so kind as to give him such things as we had in our pockets there would be no necessity to search us. By this time, he was welcome to everything I had on me. Then he told us that he wanted us to be his guests at tea that afternoon at five o'clock. We had no choice in the matter, so, told him we would be very pleased to accept his kind invitation.

It was about one o'clock then, and the kid took us in our steel-wheeled "lizzy" to the prison camp, which was to be our new home. I must say that ostensibly they treated us lovely in every way, and outside of the fact that our home was not in the same class with Riverside Drive or Orange Grove Avenue, it wasn't so bad. We were incarcerated without ceremony and the kid left us after many assurances of his kind offices. No one came in to attend to us, so, I finally pounded on the door until someone did come. It was the interpreter, who informed us that we were too late for anything to eat as only enough food was prepared for those on hand and they did not know we were coming, whereupon Davis and I sat down to wait until night for something real to eat, meanwhile anticipating, with a great deal of pleasure, our tea we were to have in the afternoon.

As I sat there on that old bench I really had my first opportunity for quiet reflection. In spite of the convincing environments I could not bring myself to believe that I was actually a prisoner of war.

This camp at Montmedy was some place. It was a rectangular affair, inclosing about an acre. Around this rectangle was a very heavy barbed-wire fence about twelve feet high, and about four feet within this was another big high fence and within this inclosure, at the four corners, were four separate buildings, each of which was surrounded by two huge wire fences, similar to those on the outside. In one of these houses lived the lord of the domain, the director of the prison camp, a sergeant in the German Army; in the second was the kitchen where they prepared the luscious food for the prisoners, and in which there was also located the quarters for the guards, where they lived, slept and smoked their German tobacco; in the third building there were bunks for enlisted men who were taken prisoners; and in the fourth were the non-commissioned and commissioned officers who were prisoners, and in this last named building were Davis and I.

We had been so down in the mouth upon actually entering this prison camp that we had little to say. Finally I arose from my old bench, shook myself like a dog after his nap, and in a graveyard tone of voice said, "Davis, we're prisoners of war," and we wept on each other's shoulders like sob sisters. When we got tired of that I walked to the door which was solid, turned the latch and, since no one interfered, walked on outside.

Walking about I took occasion to examine the heavy barbed wire surrounding us. There was nothing else to do, so, I kept walking along, glancing at the wire. It looked rather solid and was sunk rather deep in the ground. It was not encouraging. Then I had a real treat for as I walked along I saw a bunch of American doughboy prisoners, most of them privates, part of them barefooted, being escorted by the camp guard. Believe me, they looked good. I hollered to them and asked them how long they had been in and they answered they had been taken only a few days before, so, I told them I had been taken only that morning. In great eagerness, they demanded to know how the drive was coming along.

"Oh, boy," I yelled as they passed along, "we've sure got the Hun on the run."

About that time the German sergeant interpreter rushed out— "The Hell you have," he madly screamed. "Get inside." I took orders from a sergeant

He came after me and I didn't know whether he was going to browbeat me or not, but I had a strong hunch that it would be an advantageous idea to change the subject, so, I started to talk about what we were going to have to eat and he again surely informed me that we were too late, that they had not made any preparations for us and that we would not get anything to eat until that night. That subject apparently didn't interest him. I tried another.

"Where's the barber shop?" I asked

Here was a new field for him. He asked us if we would like to buy a razor and some soap and some cigarettes. The old boy liked a little money, that was clear. Here was a chance to eat perhaps, so, I encouraged his mercenary inclinations.

"No," I went on, "but I would gladly buy a ham sandwich."

He was taken back aghast at my not knowing it was impossible to obtain food for love or money, except as rationed by the government. So, I thought it would be a good idea to play up to the old boy, and smiling, I told him, "Sure, I'll buy a razor." We gave him some French money to get changed into German *marks* and after a while he brought our purchase—a very small piece of pure, lye soap, which we used for both shaving and washing, and which cost us exactly eighty-five cents. It was about the size of the individual cakes of soap you get in a hotel. I realised that the Germans must be quite short on soap for this stuff left our faces in about the same condition as one might expect from a massage with Dutch Cleanser—indeed, this was the real dutch cleanser.

In a little while an orderly came around and brought us our beds, which consisted of a couple of old blankets and one dilapidated mattress filled with wood shavings. Then he brought some wood and made a fire in the very heavy brick stove. We were so chilly that when he made the fire I kept on feeding it in order to get warm. It was not very long until the orderly came back again and we persuaded him to get us a little pack of cards, whereupon Davis and I sat down and played solitaire and casino, and meanwhile we took turns at getting up and putting another little stick of wood on the fire. By about four o'clock we had used up all the wood, so I went out and hollered to the orderly, but he did nothing but shake his head.

The sergeant came and I told him that we wanted some more wood. It did not concern him, for he said that we had used our allowance for twenty-four hours and could have no more until noon the next day. I began to swear and asked him why he had not told us that instead of freely putting it in there as if we could have all we wanted. He admitted it might have been more prudent to tell us, but at the same time he wouldn't give us any more wood. After all he wasn't a bad old duck, for he wasn't cruel—he was just overimbued with this old, German, military regime of austerity which believed in the letter of the law absolutely. In other words, it had his goat.

A little while later on the same steel-wheeled bus came rolling up and in it were three immaculately groomed officers with nice shoulder-straps, purplish-gray cloaks, and everything. All spoke perfect English, and as they were introduced they stood rigidly at attention and gave a snappy salute. The leader spoke up in the most elegant English and said perhaps we were not so unfortunate after all, as we would be well taken care of by the Germans; that they were German-Americans who had come to Germany at the outbreak of the war, long before America had entered, and since they had not heard from their folks for a long time they thought perhaps we might be from their section of the country and could give them some idea as to the welfare of their kinsmen.

This did not sound fishy to me; at least, not so far as I could see, so we did not lie to them—I told them that the German people as

A CAPTURED GERMAN PHOTOGRAPH SHOWING AMERICAN PRISONERS

a whole were being well taken care of in America, being interned in well-kept detention camps, and that no harshness was permitted by the government except in cases of spies or traitors, in which case they were arbitrarily shot I did not know whether that affected any of their kinsmen or not, but at the word "shot" they all looked at one another in a very sickly way.

After some remarks about the awful weather they started to leave, the leader remarking that they just wanted to come out and pay their respects and see that we were getting along all right, and that if at any time we wanted anything just to let them know. My mind was not on these empty formalities—it was on the fact that we had a chance to provide for our own welfare, so I took them at their word.

"That is so kind of you," I smiled. "There are several little things you might do for us now. We would like to have some wood to keep us warm for the rest of the night, we would like to have something to eat, we would like to have some better blankets to sleep on, we would like to have a better mattress and would like to have some fresh water, and if it would not be too much bother we would like to have that slop pan outside cleaned up so that it will not smell so bad—Oh, yes," I went on, "we would also like to have some exercise and some books or newspapers to read, and I, personally, would like to write a letter to my folks."

They looked somewhat dazed, so I ended my modest requests and said, "I think that is all we need right now."

They again looked at one another in a fanny manner, as if to indicate that I was not lacking in the power of expressing my wants. I thought their parting sympathy was all bunk, but surprisingly enough they gave instructions to the sergeant to give us some more wood and promised that they would send us some newspapers. When it came to eats, they balked.

"Food is something," they explained, "over which we have no control."

"But, as a matter of fact," the leader went on, "you really would not have time to eat anything, as you are soon to go to headquarters to meet the staff, and you will undoubtedly have tea there."

They left and after a while the tin-wheeled bus came again and under proper escort we went back to Montmedy. There we had "tea," which consisted of tea, about which the Germans constantly reminded us that it was exceedingly hard to get on account of the blockade, and that it was, indeed, a decided luxury and that we should appreciate that we were being served real tea. The rest of the "tea" was German war bread, which the intelligence officer admitted was bad for the stomach and was much better toasted, and then we had diminutive portions of confiture and butter, served individually, and as a finale we had cigarettes and sugar. They also offered us some liquor, which neither of us accepted, for we realised that the time of our interrogation was at hand, and since the usual trend of liquor is toward the tongue it was better not to imbibe, for we didn't want to talk any more than was absolutely necessary. They did not insist on our breaking the water wagon vows, and it's a good thing they didn't, for while I cannot speak for Davis, I, personally, know that my nervous and physical condition was such that I could not have withstood a great deal of persuasion on such sensitive subjects.

In the midst of our "tea bacchanal" the door opened and we saw standing before us a full-fledged German aviator, whose face was nicked and scarred from the great German pastime of fencing. Although wonderfully straight and well-built, with a face and jaw that spelled determination and strength, his eyes possessed all the hellishness and heinousness of a Hun. We were introduced, whereupon this young flying lieutenant clicked his heels together and gave us a salute almost as perfect as the world-famous salute of General Pershing.

After some sort of a framed-up conversation, the flyer sat down and the intelligence officer explained to us that the flyers and the anti-aircraft artillery and the machine gun crews had been in a controversy as to who should have the credit for bringing us down and that this lieutenant had contended that the squadron which he commanded was responsible; and he wanted to find out who it actually was that gained this victory. This did not seem to interest the other German-American officers present, so they excused themselves and left. The only remaining officer who spoke English was the intelligence officer; the young, battle-scarred lieutenant, to the best of our knowledge, did not. So when the intelligence officer stated that this lieutenant was in one of the four planes that was firing on us when we finally went down, Davis went to pieces and snapped out the impertinent question, "And was he one of the four who fired on us after we were already shot down."

The flyer conceded that all four of them fired at us, but that they were certainly not trying to kill us but were merely trying to keep us from escaping. This was too sad an excuse to get by. Davis told him that he didn't care a hang who got the credit for shooting us down—

we were down and that was all there was to that subject—but that in the American Army it was considered mighty poor to strike a man when he was already down. The intelligence officer was surprised and scornfully asked me if the Americans did not do exactly the same thing.

Davis reared back like a rattlesnake about to strike and with eyes flashing fire of indignation and contempt told them that if an American aviator was caught doing a thing like that—firing on the enemy when he was already down—that the Americans, themselves, would take their own countryman out and, without giving him the pleasure of being shot to death, would tar and feather him and hang him, for to an American, when a fellow was down he was down, and whether we were fighting a war or not, we wouldn't stand for murdering anyone in cold blood. I saw we were getting in Dutch, right off, and so did Davis, for as the intelligence officer explained it to the high-spirited flyer we could see his temples throb and his eyes quiver from anger; and his jaws closed with hatefulness and scorn. The intelligence officer, realising that the conversation was getting into deeper channels than was especially desired for the occasion, told the German aviator something and without saluting or otherwise rendering military courtesy, he left the room.

There remained only the intelligence officer, Davis and myself. The court of inquiry was in session—the suave Prussian on the bench and two obstinate American jailbirds in the pit. The German told us to help ourselves to the cigarettes, and believe me, we realised that it might be the last time we would have such a liberal invitation for, maybe, many months to come. We accepted. Take it from me, we certainly smoked—rapidly, but at the same time languidly. We consumed those cigarettes like a vacuum cleaner takes up dust. When we had depleted the supply of twenty the Intelligence Officer produced twenty more.

As a hard and fast rule a prisoner should never talk. In this way it is certain that no information will be given out. Once in a great while a prisoner can do some good by talking—I am sure that no American ever told, deliberately, any true information, either voluntarily or under pressure or even threat of execution; but a great deal of dope was gained through subterfuge, or from the ordinary man who foolishly tried to spar against the keen mind of the officer who has made a life study of that particular work. Thus our case was different, for as an operations officer of an army I also was versed in intelligence work.

At least, I had an equal chance.

As usual, the first ruse of the German was to find the location of our airdrome, for, since they found an identification tag on Davis, they knew his squadron was the 104th. Of course, I didn't belong to that squadron, but I said nothing, for the reason that it would serve no useful purpose to dispute this presumption. He showed us some absolutely marvellous photographs of our airdrome taken by German cameras at extremely high altitudes and also pictures of other airdromes close by. I recognized them all right, but, believe me, I gave no signs of it.

After about thirty-five minutes of dickering with those photographs in which he tried by every possible manner and means to catch a clue as to the location of our airdrome, he pulled the very subtle change in conversation from airdromes to the general feeling about the war. He wanted to know what schools we had attended and what subjects we had taken, and what Americans did for diversion in their colleges, whether or not they fenced, and then he nicely asked us to explain a little about football; in other words, perfectly harmless questions. We gladly talked football, but kept on the alert lest we be taken unawares. Suddenly in the midst of these immaterial questions and discussions about our schools, customs and life in general, from a clear sky and in a very nonchalant manner, came a new surprise.

"Oh, about your relatives and friends," he remarked sympathetically—"they will be very worried to hear that you have been reported missing in action." We both agreed to that, of course. "Well," he went on as if he had been inspired by a solution, "if you wish to write a little note to some of your friends back in the squadron the German flyers will very gladly drop the messages over the lines on the next patrol, which will be tonight. You see," and he cleared his throat by way of emphasis, "by this method your parents and your friends will not worry; otherwise, they may think you have been killed."

I was surprised, really, at this ostensible kindness–it was attractive enough to bear investigating. As a matter of fact, the recent illness of my mother convinced me that she could not withstand the shock of my reported casualty. I immediately decided that if it was possible to adopt this expedient news service, provided I did not have to give any military information, I would do so. Like every boy, I knew that the one person in the world who loved me most was my mother. She had a right to know. So, accepting his pencil, I wrote very rapidly:

To Any Allied Officer or Man:
Kindly notify American General Headquarters that Lieutenants
Raymond Davis and Elmer Haslett, Air Service, are safe prison-
ers of war in Germany.

He took it, read it, and in a business-like manner wrote something
over it by way of endorsement, which, he explained, meant "Cen-
sored," and handing it back to me I read what I had written to Davis.
Calling a man, who like all the other Germans we had seen so far, gave
a smart salute upon entering, the officer handed him the note and
muttered something in German, then hypocritically smiling, he assured us that he was sending the message direct to the airdrome to be
dropped over the lines by the next patrol. His matter-of-fact attitude
led us to believe that everything was a matter of course, and the incident was closed. However, after the soldier had been gone a few seconds the officer jumped up, hastened to the door and called him back.
The man handed him our note and, hastily glancing at the address,
the lieutenant said smilingly, "Oh, you know, you neglected to write
on the note where you want it dropped," and handing me a pencil he
continued quite concernedly, "Lucky I thought of it, wasn't it?"

I began to see the gleam and colour of the snake in the grass. So
I wrote on it "France." I knew he expected to see the name of our
airdrome on there, so after a cynical laugh he tried to look serious,
although he well realised that he was being out-manoeuvred.

"Oh, you know," he explained, "you must make it more definite
than that. Where are your friends? That would be the place to drop
it."

Whereupon I told him to write upon it "Paris."

"Oh!" and he manifested complete surprise, "you have come from
Paris?"

I laughingly told him that I had been there, and then he grew serious, but did not show any anger.

"Now really," and he looked directly at Davis, as if to solicit some
aid from him, "you should tell us your airdrome, for instance, which
would be the best place to drop it."

Davis told him that we really did not know the name of our airdrome, or its location. This was a good hunch, and backing Davis up
with our mutual ignorance, I told him that if he dropped the message
anywhere over the lines it would certainly be found, and while we,
ourselves, were not very well known in France, having been there

154

only a very short time, the American General Headquarters was well known and our names were on record at headquarters. He was nonplussed, for his last card had been played and the location of our airdrome had not yet been divulged.

The Germans were, of course, anxious to find out the location of our airdrome for the reason that if by collaboration of information they found that several squadrons had been moved from other places to airdromes opposite their own front they would know that the forces were concentrating at a particular point and that something was likely to pop. Thus, it gave them the opportunity to distribute their own strength accordingly. He had failed on this, so he started out on new tasks.

"How do you like Rickenbacker?" he said very casually, by way of changing the subject.

"Who?" I questioned disinterestedly.

" Rickenbacker, your greatest flyer—Squadron 94," he added in surprise at my ignorance, and corresponding pride at his own intelligence.

"New one on me—never heard of it," I replied.

"Never heard of the 94th?" he ejaculated, even more surprised. "Well, the 94th is your best chasse squadron and," he continued, by way of demonstrating his superior knowledge, "the 12th is your best observation squadron, the 96th is your best bombing squadron and the 91st is your best surveillance squadron. As a matter of fact, by following the movements of these four organizations we pretty well know where your main body of aviation is concentrated."

A hasty reflection taught me that the old boy had the situation pretty well sized up, for, indeed, he had accurately named our most famous-squadrons in their particular work.

However, I still professed ignorance.

"So you don't know Rickenbacker?" he proceeded. "I can also tell you something about him." Where-upon he enlightened me by the statement that Eddie was a German, born in Germany and educated while a boy in German schools—all of which he pointed out as the reasons for Rickenbacker's superior skill and efficiency. But the Fatherland was completely off with "Rick" in spite of their proud—but, by the way, unfounded—claim of nationality. The intelligence officer told me that they considered him as absolute traitor to the Fatherland.

Another potent reason, he explained, was that they emphatically believed that Rickenbacker's tactics of burning balloons at night was inhuman, since the poor balloon observers did not even have a chance to get away with their lives. It was at this time that Lieutenant Frank Luke was at the height of his marvellous success of burning German balloons at night, but they had blamed it all on "Rick." In fact, it could easily be gathered from what he said that Luke had the German balloonists' goat so well haltered that many of them refused to go up for night observation, and naturally the command was worried.

As I told Rickenbacker afterward, there certainly would have been a crowd around the fire if he had been shot down in Germany, for he was the one man for whom they were all looking, for more reasons than one.

After again emphatically denouncing "Rick" for his "inhuman tactics" he changed the conversation and asked me how many Americans we had in France.

"That is a matter we do not care to discuss," I said in a manner indicating that while we knew positively the exact number we wished to sidetrack the issue.

He momentarily permitted it.

"Your losses by our submarines must have been appalling," he said, not forcing the subject

I told him that our losses by their submarines had not been nearly so great as their losses by their own submarines. This was Greek to him, so he asked me that I meant, and I explained to him that while their submarines were causing us some damage all right, and a lot of worry, yet they were also responsible for our being in France and that if the American Army had not already caused them all the losses and all the worry they could possibly withstand that it soon would. He was very anxious to impress upon us that he believed that the policy of Von Tirpitz was all wrong and he admitted that Germany realised that she could not win with America in the war. "To Germany," he said, "it is now a proposition of defence."

Then Davis calmly proceeded to tell him that 'if Germany ever wanted to save herself she had better throw up her hands quick, because in 1920 the Allies were certainly going to give her a walloping blow from Switzerland to the sea.

"Ah," he said, "1920 is a long way off. How many Americans will you have here in 1920?"

I looked at Davis, hesitated a second as if calculating, then said, "Let's see—we have three million five hundred thousand here now;

we ought to have seven million by that time." Then I assumed a sheep-ish-looking attitude, as if I had said something which should have been kept secret. He looked at me a moment in amazement, then laughingly said:

"You are joking. You have not three million five hundred thousand here now."

I nodded my head affirmatively, while Davis chirped up, "That's right."

"In France?" he gasped.

"Yes, in France," I repeated.

"Oh, no. It is not possible. How do you know?" he exclaimed.

With a perfectly straight face I told him that the only way I knew was that every man who came across was given a number as he sailed, and that I had been in France only two weeks, and that my number was 3,246,807, and I was quite sure that the difference had been made up. If he had asked me to repeat those figures I couldn't have done it to save my life. He looked thoughtfully at the floor, which gave Davis and me the opportunity to smile and wink at our little joke.

"How long do you think the war will last!"

I bowed my head and rubbed along my temples as if in deep thought, then suddenly looking up at him as if some muse had given me a correct solution of the problem, I told him that while it was very hard to tell accurately, most Americans felt that it would be not less than three years and not over five. The officer threw back his hands in utter horror like a spinster at her first view of a t. b. m. production.

"Three years more of this Hell?" he said. "Ugh! It will be not more than three months."

I agreed with him entirely, although I did not say so.

"Three months?" I said in surprise. "Do you think you will win this war in three months?"

"No, Germany will not win the war," he sighed in apparent regret, "but we will quit, for we cannot win. We lost our last chance when he failed to get to Paris in July."

Seeing that we were evidently interested, he thought that it was the proper time to get down to the real subject of "intelligence," but we, too, were prepared.

"Do your aviators know everything that is taking place!" he asked.

"Yes," answered Davis, "our aviators are very intelligent. The command has great confidence in them;" "and," I added, "in fact, aviators see a copy of every army order issued."

"You knew, then," he continued, "that you had attacked from Verdun to Rheims and the French from Rheims to Soissons and the British from Soissons to the sea."

"Yes," I said, "I know that the Allies have attacked all along." And, as a matter of fact, I did, but most of our flyers did not, and it was only on account of the nature of my work that I knew this information. But I also knew that for some time past Marshal Foch had been pulling a big, strategic fake down in the Vosges mountains from Luneville to the Swiss border, a very quiet sector, by displaying an unusual amount of activity in the parading of empty motor trucks back and forth to the front, which, of course, could not have been unnoticed by the Germans and necessarily caused them much concern.

As a matter of fact, I knew that those trucks were empty and were being paraded only to create the impression that the Allies were getting ready to attack in that sector. Intelligence reports that I had read previous to my capture stated that the Germans were looking forward to this attack and that some of the newspapers had even mentioned it. So, when he fired his next question I, too, had my little pop-gun all ready, cleaned, oiled, primed, bored, trigger pulled, cocked, aimed, set and loaded to the brim with T.N.T., triple forced dynamite, and I let him have it.

"Ah, if you are attacking all along here," he said as he pointed to the battle area on the map on the table, "you are pushing us north. Now, you must attack from Verdun east or you are leaving your right flank unprotected, so unless you do attack toward the east we will flank and annihilate you." Sweeping his hand over the big, broad map of France, he assumed the air of a Napoleon.

I wasn't worried about that flanking movement, for I was all fixed for that; in fact, I was way ahead of him. I was doing my best to figure out my location and the way to the lines so that if there was any chance of my escaping I would know, at least, the general direction in which to go.

"Oh," I said, apparently without thought, "you haven't the latest reports, have you! Well, since it's out I'll tell you. Our latest *communiqués* this morning stated that we had attacked in the Vosges, had surprised the Germans, and our troops will have taken Mulhausen by tomorrow morning."

I have never seen a man so happy as this intelligence officer—he was all smiles. He had made certain a conjecture, for he had found out that we were really going to attack in the Vosges, and he knew that it had not yet taken place. I could see the gleam in his eyes as he visioned the honour, prestige and the like he would reap as the reward for his wonderful discovery. He apparently could not wait to get the news to headquarters. Abruptly closing the conversation, he shook hands with us, rang the bell and turned us over to a couple of officers who took us out to the camp in our tin-wheeled bus, and in a few minutes we were again in jail, where, relieved from the presence of German officers, we threw off the cloak of dignified propriety and, giving vent to stored-up jollity, we laughed heartily and long.

Indeed, we felt sure by the very affable manner in which we had been released that the duck had been royally fixed. I do not know how true it is, but I afterwards heard that this intelligence officer was so convinced and enthusiastic over his discovery that the general was also convinced, and in turn reported it to the Gros Headquarters at Treves, and that the supreme command issued preliminary orders to take two divisions away from the Argonne Reserve for duty in the Vosges. This may or may not be so, though I am inclined to think it is not, but it does not particularly matter. I do know, however, that afterward, for some reason or other, when I was transported by rail through Germany I was honoured with extra guards, who had in their possession a descriptive card which honoured me to the extent of remarking that I was a very dangerous character, a clever liar, and was to be especially well watched.

CHAPTER 10

Becoming Kultured

I was born in a small town, and I'm a small town guy. A small town always gets the fall advantage of propaganda, and as people in small towns do not have a great variety of subjects to talk about when they once get a good one it has a long season. The folks around the towns where I had lived in the West and Middle West had been led to believe that while the ideal environment for the ground work of stability of character was to be found in the broad, open atmosphere of the country west of the Mississippi, yet for further polish and refinement it was necessary to seek the Eastern States, or better, to sojourn a while in England or France. There was some discussion as to which was the better of these two places.

However, for the final graduation in culture, it was an entirely different story—there were no two sides to the argument at all that the post graduate course in refinement could be obtained but at one place in the whole wide world. There was no alternative. It was thoroughly agreed that if one aspired to become a finished product with the proper veneer, that person must beat it to Germany and become *kultured*. Perhaps this feeling was the result of well-directed German propaganda; at any rate, it was a firmly established belief where I lived, at least.

This *"kultur"* bunk had never interested me, for I always had felt that the United States was good enough. A man who had good tips on the horse races was a hundred times more interesting to me than a much vaunted German count who came from the wonderful country of Wagner, Goethe and Schiller. At that, though, I had studied German a couple of years in preparatory school, but I want to say here and now that the only reason for my it was because the only other choice was Latin, was entirely beyond the possibilities of my mind. So when I finished the laborious German course at school I promptly proceeded to forget it.

Now fortune had thrust upon me the opportunity for which many Americans before the war had vainly wished—namely, a sojourn in Germany and a course in *kultur*, for, indeed, was I not being entertained as a guest of the German Government—or was it the jest of the German Government?t

Thus in spite of the fact that I never aspired to become *kultured*, it was certain that I was going to get it whether I wished it or not. It was like the compulsory inoculations and vaccinations in the army—there was no choice in the matter for the poor guy who's getting it.

Perhaps the condition of my appetite had something to do with the shaping of my observations as to the actual working of German Kultur, for I was hungry when I was made prisoner and that empty feeling never left me from the time I was shot down until several weeks after I was released.

All during the first day of our imprisonment we had nothing to eat, except the dainty "tea of bribery" at the session of the court of inquiry in the afternoon, and the only effect of that tea was to whet our already cutting appetites. So, having been returned from the session of court, we sat down on a rude bench in our dingy abode at the Montmedy prison camp to brood over our misfortune and to settle down for that course in *kultur*. We were thoroughly blue, for the only joys in life during that day had been the facts that we had successfully lied to the German intelligence officer and so far we had not divulged any military information.

And here is a point that I noticed all through Germany from the officers on down—with rare exceptions. A German will promise you anything in order to appear affable and pleasant. It is commonly done, and they get off with it for a certain time. From these continued observations of unfulfilled promises I formed a definition of "*kultur*." In my mind it is that superficial and subtle form of hypocrisy practised by the German race and commonly accepted by them as justifiable and necessary in their state of affairs, which permits of the affording of temporary satisfaction in meeting the emergency in hand by giving indiscriminate promises—which promises are never fulfilled nor intended to be fulfilled at the time of making; and which further permits and justifies the explanation of nonfulfilment of promises by the giving of more and similar empty and insincere promises.

Our room was rather chilly, for in our absence the fire had gone out. With the wood we had coerced from the sergeant the orderly finally came in and built us a little fire. We used French economy, for we were quite sure that it was going to be cold before the night was over, with the limited covering they had given us.

I was getting as hungry as the snake which sleeps all winter, or summer, whichever it is. So I put it up to the orderly, who politely told us he would bring our food at once. I am sure we waited a full hour and a half for that food and I was experiencing all sorts of sensations as to whether slow starvation was about to begin. I remembered reading that starving people were sometimes sustained by chewing shoe leather, so I was wondering how long my poor shoes would last at a ration of a square inch of leather to chew each day. This hunger was getting my goat. I had heard of walking off intoxication and seasickness so I decided to try walking off hunger.

I opened the door and walked into the surrounding bone-yard, which was hemmed in by several high fences of barbed wire. While most prison camps are well lighted at night in order that there will be little possibility of any one escaping without being seen by one of the many guards, this was different, in that it seemed totally dark. Perhaps the reason for this was its proximity to the lines, or it might have been that it was too early for lights. I was just milling around aimlessly when suddenly from somewhere without the darkness came a voice in German and so gruffly that it almost took me off my feet.

I realised that I was being addressed individually, and while the words meant nothing to me, the tone of voice in which they were spoken convinced me that it could be nothing else than the familiar old "Halt! Who goes there?" Not being well versed in the number of times a German sentry calls his challenge before he fires, I took a chance on one of the few words I knew and quickly answered "*Freund*," for, as I figured it, "Friend" is a harmless word any way you take it. The old squarehead only answered "*Ja*" and quite unconcernedly walked on.

"Well," I thought, "this is easy." So, continuing my tour, I got around to the side where I found that during the day some prisoners had been working, probably digging weeds, for to my pleasant surprise I discovered, perhaps for their own purposes, they had left their tools, including a couple of spades. Such luck, for with those spades, on such a dark night it would be easily possible to tunnel out. The big rub was that the orderly told us that the door to the hut would be locked at nine o'clock and that we could not go out of the house until seven o'clock the next morning.

It was then about a quarter of nine, so I went in and told Davis, and he, of course, agreed to attempt to escape that night. The big point first was to manage to get out of the house, which could only be effected by crawling through a window. Davis was just in the act of testing the strength of the window when the door opened and the orderly came in with our sumptuous repast In ravenous anxiety we sized up the banquet—it consisted of a piece of hard, mealy, black bread, dimensions two inches by three inches by three inches, and in a pot was the rest of the dinner, which consisted of soup.

I never did like soup, but I'll say this much in favour of it: I have never enjoyed a meal in my life like I enjoyed that soup. We had two nice tin pans in which to serve our soup. We put the pot on the stove to keep it warm while I proceeded to dish it out, spoonful by spoonful, the liquid coming first: then we divided the remaining vegetables—two dilapidated looking spuds and three little samples of hard, gritty, grimy meat. I gave Davis one piece and I took the other, then we matched three times to see who would get the other piece. We matched, and the first time I won; the next flip Davis won. Believe me, small and insignificant as that piece of meat was, I was too hungry to lose it, so I got cold feet

"Davis," I suggested, "this is damned foolishness. We'll cut that meat in two pieces. I'm scared I'm going to lose."

As Davis was cutting it this hard, gritty, grimy, little piece of meat slipped and fell into a pail of water which we had just lifted off the stove. Like two South Sea Islanders diving for coins thrown by the generous tourist from shipboard, we rescued the meat by diving into the water with both hands, making a beautiful splash all over the floor. Davis showed himself to be a religions sort of a guy, for he suggested that since we had been so lucky in escaping with our lives that we make a burnt offering of this meat. I didn't know whether he was joking or not about the burnt offering, so I took no chance on his not being serious and told him we had already made one burnt offering that day in burning up that airplane. Without further argument we sliced the meat into two pieces and each had his portion.

I had eaten about half of my bread and was still so hungry that I could have eaten puckery persimmons with considerable relish when I realised that if we intended trying to escape that night we had best lay off mincing that bread, for we would certainly need it the next day. We talked it over, then viewed it from every angle, but since we were in occupied French territory we decided that I could speak enough French, and with Davis's pathetic eyes we could sure win enough favour with the "froggies" to get by, although they probably had barely enough to eat themselves.

We crawled into our bunks without removing our clothes for the reason that it was too cold to sleep without them and we also intended to get out during the night. About two o'clock, after continued tossing and tumbling, wondering just what process we would follow in the attempt, I got up and awakened Davis; then I crept to the window. After a good twenty minutes of tinkering with that window, cautiously moving it an eighth of an inch at a time, I finally got it open to such a point that we could get out—at least, so I thought. Directly in front of us was one of those little houses so commonly used at garrisons in France and Germany, known as sentry boxes.

I figured the old boy would be in there all right, but he would be fast asleep, so I stuck my head out, gave a little spring, and as I brought my stomach up on the sill like a flash from out the sentry box stepped this hardboiled Boche. He had a huge flashlight and immediately I was in the spotlight. The window was the stage and I the star. There is some humour in the situation, now as I look back upon it, but believe me, there was none then. For when that German began to excitedly ejaculate "*Loze! Loze!*" whatever that is, I took my head to cover just like a tortoise draws his protruding physiognomy into the secret confines of his shell.

"It's all right," I called as we hit for our bunk, "we've got to have a little air."

That night we almost froze to death, for we didn't dare to close the window, for we did not know the extent of the German sentry's memory of foreign expressions, and the fact that we left the window open all night would be a good alibi for opening the window in that we did need air. It was a hard result, but since it was our story we shivered and stuck to it. Take it from me, we were icebergs the next morning.

Fortunately they served us an early breakfast, which consisted of some hot German Ersatz coffee, which is no coffee at all. It is made from acorns and it doesn't go well as a substitute. In fact, you must train your appetite and taste for Ersatz just as you do for olives. They brought us a little confiture, which was also imitation and it didn't have any more consistency than a marshmallow. The orderly started to walk away and simultaneously Davis bawled out, "Where is our bread?" The orderly explained that they had given us our allowance last night for twenty-four hours.

If this was to be our regular ration I could see ourselves starving to death by degrees. It was useless to say that they had not given us enough, for that line does not appeal to the German. If each of us received a piece of bread, that settled the argument, but if the allowance for both of us was brought in one piece there was room for discussion. The orderly claimed he had brought two pieces of bread, but I claimed that he had brought only one piece, so how did we know it was supposed to be for the both of us. Finally I said that I was going to tell an officer. This got results, for after conferences between the sergeant of the camp, the corporal of the guard, the orderly, the cook and the keeper of the official storehouse they brought us in another little piece of bread.

The next night they brought in a French pilot, who was supposed to have been shot down the night before on a bombing raid. We suspected right off that he was a German spy trying to gain our confidence, for the first thing he did was to tell us in French how much he hated the Germans and to give us addresses of people who could help us to escape when we got to Karlsruhe, which, he said, was the place they sent all prisoners. He said he could speak but little English and knew no German at all.

After venturing a lot of information about the number of his squadron and its location he asked me the number of my squadron. I told him the number of my squadron was "2106" but that I had forgotten the name of the airdrome, as we had only flown up there. Then he began to suggest some of our prominent airdromes to assist my memory. I did not bite at his bait, but rapidly changed the subject. Then he began to play solitaire with our cards, at the same time paying very keen attention to our conversation.

I decided to justify my suspicion that he was a German spy, so I made the suggestion that since I was a prisoner it might help to know more German, so as Davis had studied it more recently than I, I asked him to give me a German lesson, as I especially wanted to learn some words that might come in handy. So as I would ask Davis for the German words for a number of ordinary objects he would give me the word and his pronunciation of it. We worked hard for fully half an hour. The Frenchman had said nothing, and as I noticed he was not paying very close attention I indicated to Davis not to tell me the next word. Davis did well, and I repeated, "Dog—dog—dog," several times.

Davis said he did not know, and then the Frenchman, seeing us both puzzled, spoke up and said, "*Dog. Qu'est que ce 'Dog'?*" which in French means "What do you mean 'Dog'?" I told him in French that I wanted the word for dog in German, and just as natural as could be he instantaneously replied, "*Der Hund.*" He had fallen into our trap and we knew quite well then that he was a German. It was too apparent for argument. After that Davis and I said absolutely nothing. In fact, we had nothing to do with him whatsoever and later that night the sergeant of the guard came in and told him that he had been ordered to proceed to Karlsruhe, but that the orders for us to be moved had not come. We afterwards found that this same gag of French friendship had been pulled on several other prisoners, some of whom were, unfortunately, unsuspecting.

In a couple of days we were taken over to Montmedy, or rather we walked over, for after having once gotten our supposed information there was no reason to be courteous enough to furnish us transportation. At Montmedy we were to take the train for the big prisoners' concentration camp at Karlsruhe. Before we left we were given our travelling rations, which consisted of some boiled meat and bread, and this was supposed to last two days.

On the trip and at the station at Montmedy I noticed that the morale of the German Army must have failed a good deal, for the discipline was not what I had always supposed it to be. The proud Prussian officers carried their own trunks while the enlisted men stood around, and I actually saw a crowd of enlisted men push aside an officer who was trying to get into the train ahead of them. I realised then that the statement of the German intelligence officer that it was a proposition of not more than three months was actually more accurate than I had been inclined to allow myself to believe.

There was one real character on the train—a hard-boiled *feldwebel*, which was the German name for sergeant-major, and corresponding pretty largely to our first sergeant of the line. He was in charge of our party.

Feldwebels are actually the backbone of the German Army. They are well trained and highly efficient. This man had many decorations and physically was a superman. He tried his best to be affable, and though he did not speak good English he tried hard enough and we tried our best to supplement his deficiencies with our rather scant knowledge of German. With great pride he told us of all the battles he had been in since the beginning of the war, and I must say he would be entitled to many bronze stars on his service ribbon.

Finally the conversation drifted to the relative fighting qualities of each army. He said he was quite sure that the American doughboy was the nerviest fighter on the front, although he was seriously handicapped by lack of experience. He, himself, had specialized in bayonet fighting and proudly stated that he was one of the best bayonet fighters in the whole German Army, to which fact all the others agreed. He said that with his blade he had whipped four Russians single handed; that unassisted he had cleaned up on four Italians, and he pointed to a coveted ribbon as a recognition of his feat; that at Arras he had gotten the better of three Englishmen, and he pointed to still another ribbon; and that at Verdun, in the early days, he had even bested three Frenchmen in a deadly bayonet combat; and he had individual bayonet victories galore; "but," he said, throwing up his hands and laughing good naturedly, "an American gave me this—a negro," and he showed me a bronze button that he wore for having been wounded in defence of the Fatherland. He opened his blouse and shirt collar and showed us a long scar along his neck and shoulder.

I had heard conflicting stories as to the fighting qualities of the American negro, so I asked him to explain how it happened. He said it was during a raid near Verdun; the negroes were, undoubtedly, in training with the French Foreign Legion in that sector. It started with a regular bayonet fight in which he quickly knocked the bayonet and rifle from the negro's hands, but as the *feldwebel* was just about to give the final fatal stab the negro pulled out the proverbial razor from somewhere. The scar was the final result. He dramatically summed it up by telling us that he would willingly fight the Russians, the Italians, the Englishmen and the Frenchmen at unequal odds, at any time or place, but he was absolutely through with all Americans because they were crazy; they didn't care whether they got killed or not.

"The coloured troops, as a whole, are poor fighters,'" he said, in words to that effect, "but the American negro is the exception—he fights, and fights dirty."

After a more or less monotonous journey we arrived at Karlsruhe and were just leaving the station when we heard a big brass band coming down the street, followed by great crowds, and then a detachment of German soldiers swung into view, doing their famous goose step. As they passed we could see that they were just youngsters who did not look over sixteen years of age. Clinging fondly to them and showering flowers in their path were their mothers, sisters and other relatives. There might have been sweethearts, but the boys looked too young for that I was convinced that Germany was getting into pretty hard straits when she had to send that class of men. It seemed to me that the flower of her male population had withered and that there were now only the upstarts and old men left.

At Karlsruhe we were taken to an old hotel which had been converted into a detention camp, and were put into confinement for a while. I was fortunate enough to be put into a room with several Britishers who had just been released from German hospitals. These lads had some food that had been sent them from home while in the hospital. They were wonderful fellows and if I had ever had any previous misgivings as to the sportsmanship of the British they certainly were removed in short order by the splendid and generous conduct of these boys.

The second day at Karlsruhe we were again called before an intelligence officer and again interrogated. This time I gave more beautiful demonstrations in the art of prevarication, for there were more cigarettes at stake. The examination here was confined to technical matters, while before it had been tactical. I became so interested in the subject in hand that I told him about our new combination sound and vibration recorder which did many things for us, even accurately indicating the moment that the German airplanes took off from their airdromes, what direction they were going, their altitude and the number of planes. By this instrument we were able to follow their planes and shoot them down very easily. It might have been a scientist's dream, but I blandly explained it all to him, while I rapidly smoked his costly cigarettes, and the old boy took notes of my misinformation. But before I left this camp he had also found out that I was a liar, so he too tacked his little report to my already shattered reputation for truth and veracity.

After a week at the temporary detention camp we were marched up, *en masse*, about fifty prisoners in all, including British, French, Italian, Portuguese and American, to the main prison camp at Karlsruhe.

We had to have all our money changed into German prison money at a terrible discount. I'll say those Germans are thorough. For the fifth time we were searched. They even made one English captain take off his wooden leg to insure that he did not have a compass or anything like that hidden within it. They searched every stitch of clothing on us, and finally tried to make us sign a little statement saying that we were not taking anything in there that was forbidden and that we had read the rules of war and would be guided thereby or pay the penalty. The solemn word of an Allied officer did not mean any more to the German than the ordinary word of a German meant to us.

Our money was exchanged at the rate of five hundred *francs* for three hundred *marks* in prisoners" money, which was really worth about one hundred *marks*.

To search us they took us into a separate room, two at a time. As rumours will naturally leak out of the most secret chambers, we soon found that they were confiscating all leather goods, so in one accord everybody began to cut their leather goods into bits rather than turn it over to the Germans. I had my Sam Browne belt next to my skin and then my under-shirt, then a woollen O. D. shirt, and then my blouse. In addition I had a pair of leather gloves. I intended to save them both and, if absolutely necessary, to give them up only after a good fight.

Finally my turn came to go in. I took off my blouse and my woollen shirt. The searcher demanded that I also take off my undershirt. I didn't have a lot of choice in the matter, so without argument I proceeded to remove my undershirt, and of course he found my belt. He motioned for me to take it off, for he spoke nothing but German. I balked and told him in English that the belt was mine. We argued for two or three minutes, but I refused to budge. He got real peeved at my stubbornness and called an interpreter.

The interpreter explained that all leather goods were being confiscated on account of the shortage of leather in Germany and that I would have to give my belt up. I told him to tell the German that I had paid for that Sam Browne belt out of my own money and it wasn't government property and was just as much mine as my trousers or my blouse. He told this to the guy who was searching me, but he merely shrugged his shoulders and mumbled something, so the interpreter told me that it was ordered and not to talk so much and hand over the belt.

I calmly proceeded to put on my undershirt, but the searcher began to lay hands on me, saying to the interpreter, "*Nicht, nein, verboten,*" etc. The interpreter asked me to wait, he would request an officer to come down. In quick order an officer arrived to find out about the near riot. He spoke good English and explained to me that it was a ruling of the German Government that all leather goods were to be confiscated.

This officer was very rushed and didn't have the time nor inclination to explain much, for explanations were not often made in Germany in those days, and especially not to prisoners. He told me it was an order and therefore had to be done and there was no use arguing about it. I politely told him the only kind of orders I took were in writing, and I had a right to see the written orders. I expected to see him order the belt off of me by force, but to my surprise he sent up to the headquarters and got an order; at least, it looked like an order, for I could not read it after he got it—so, after palavering around for about five minutes I finally decided that the order was O. K. and I would have to give up the belt.

The officer immediately sent the order back and I then demanded a receipt for the belt. We had another argument over this and I insisted that the order had said that a paper receipt would be given for all leather confiscated. I was trying to stall, but, true to the traditions of German efficiency, they sent for the order again. Hastily looking it over as if I read German perfectly, I begged his pardon gracefully and told him that I guessed I had read it so rapidly the first time that I had mistaken a similar word for receipt. In considerable disgust at this uncalled for delay the officer left.

I put on my clothes and started out, taking my gloves with me. The searcher came after me, calling, "*Nein, nein,*" and attempted to take my gloves. Going back into the searching room, I told the interpreter that they did me out of my belt, but they couldn't have my gloves, for they were not flying gloves—they were nice gloves, dress gloves, riding gloves—and I had paid for them myself, and that while they could take my belt under the provisions of the order, yet the order had not said anything about gloves and if they wanted the gloves they would have to send for that officer again and get those orders and show me. The searcher was getting pretty indignant because there were a lot of others waiting to be searched and if they overheard our conversation it would set a bad precedent for the others, so far as he was concerned.

So he dispatched a soldier immediately to get the order for the third time. After about a half hour it did not come and I was just sticking around making a general nuisance of myself when along came the officer I had previously dealt with.

"Why are you still here?" he demanded.

I explained to him that we were waiting for the order to see if it said gloves when they were privately purchased, dress gloves. He must have had a sense of humour, for he laughed outright and said, "Keep your damned old gloves and get out of here." Whereupon I walked out of the room with a pair of big, black, leather gloves which came in mighty handy on several occasions afterward and which I carried without further trouble throughout my trip through German Prison Camps on the strength of the precedent that they had been passed O. K. by the searchers at Karlsruhe. The only trouble about retaining those gloves was that I had a terrible time convincing the rest of the guys that I really was not a German spy, for they could not otherwise account for ostensible favouritism.

CHAPTER 11

Escaped Almost

I have little sympathy for any prisoner who, having been so unfortunate as to have been taken by the enemy, allowed himself to settle down to prison discipline, practically a subject of the enemy, without standing up like a man and at least trying to escape.

Around a prison camp one hears many, many big ideas of escaping, but there are comparatively few actual attempts. In fact, this boasting habit got on one man to such an extent that he was known as "Wild Fugitive Bill," for the reason that he was always concocting some new and novel means of escape and yet never had the nerve himself to put it through. Always at the last moment he would get cold feet and give up.

The real test of courage comes when mental plans end and physical action begins. Some prisoners have even prided themselves upon being model prisoners. I have even heard a captain of infantry call the Americans together and suggest that some of us quit raising so much hell during roll call as our actions were counted against all the Americans. I pride myself on the fact that I "raised hell" at every opportunity from the time I was made prisoner until I was released. The more trouble the prisoners of war caused the enemy the more men the enemy must keep away from the battle line to guard the disturbers. Not many prisoners considered this a point, but I believe that as long as there is war the enemy should be fought and embarrassed—inside and outside.

Karlsruhe seemed to be my ultimate destination, so after a few days to allow me to catch up on food which was more plentiful here on account of the remarkable contribution of the American Red Cross, I again began to set my mind to escaping.

I talked it over with all the old prisoners and they said that no one had yet been able to escape from Karlsruhe, so, in order to get the advantage of experience I talked it over with everyone who had ever tried it. It seemed that the camp was only for concentration, and as statistics showed that the majority of escapes were attempted by newly made prisoners, this camp was especially guarded in order to challenge all comers and to discourage them early in the game. I looked over where every previous attempt had been made and was told just how it had failed to materialize.

The entire camp was certainly well guarded. It had one inner, high fence of barbed wire and one outside fence constructed of wood, about twelve feet high and on top of it was a quarter arc of steel extending inward, heavily covered with barbed wire. They had several guards on the inside and quite a large number on the outside, and both the inside and outside fences were well illuminated with electric lights.

At one place along the high, back fence the guards had constructed a sort of chicken house, which threw a shadow against the fence, making it possible, providing enough assistance was rendered, to construct a small tunnel. The bunch, which consisted of Oscar Mandel of New Jersey, a couple of other birds and myself, got together right after the evening meal and talked it over. After full deliberation we decided to try. It was our intention to have it as secret as could be, and we planned there would be only four of us in that escape—and no more; so, after we pledged to one another that we would tell absolutely no one else about it, we shook hands and started right away to make the preparations for the dirty work. Of course, the big job at first was to construct that tunnel for the man who should draw that job would get the real lemon. The beat of one of the guards took him about every three minutes to within about ten feet of the place, and of course, directly on the outside was another guard whose movements would have to be largely guessed at.

The approved plan was to put the "tunnel man" over the barbed wire fence; station another man on the inside, walking back and forth, whistling or something of the like to give the proper signals; then put the other two men at different corners near the buildings close by in order to signal the movements of the watchman to the man walking back and forth. Stepping into the light we got a deck of cards and made the agreement that the man who got the lowest card would go over the fence and dig the tunnel and the man who got the next would do the signalling. Mandel shuffled and Blackie, a little English doughboy, drew the first card. It was a Two of Diamonds. Mack, the second lad, drew a Queen. Mandel, whom we called Mendelssohn as he was a wonderful musician and also a past master in the art of escaping, picked an Eight of Clubs. I had a good chance for I didn't think it likely that I could get a lower card than Blackie's "Two," so I snapped out a card just as unconcerned as could be and hastily looked at it—it was the Ace of Hearts.

Now the question was whether the Ace was high or low. I had lots of queer sensations. We had made no agreement about it before drawing, so, I said nothing until the other two boys spoke up and said it seemed to them that Ace should be high. Mandel suggested that in order to be fair that we draw over again, it being agreed that the Ace would be high. This time I drew first in order that all the high cards would not get away. I picked a winner—the Three Spot of something—just what didn't worry me for I knew the thing was settled and that I would have to go and dig that tunnel. I was picturing myself out there getting shot at when Blackie again saved the day by pulling his same Two of Diamonds. Several sighs of relief were registered by my heaving lungs for my draw assigned me as outer watchman where I had to give Blackie signals all the time. It was quite different than being between two fences, guns all around me and no place to hide.

We agreed to start at once, so, instead of putting Mandel and Mack at the outer comers of the house nearest the scene of operations, we decided to station them at different windows in the house, so as not to cause suspicion by having too many outside. All the blinds were drawn on account of air raids. so we arranged that as the boys walked back and forth in front of the door, that they should quietly keep me informed as to the exact location of the guards.

My signals to Blackie were very simple: Whenever I whistled a tune that sounded like rag-time he was to lay off; when I whistled a tune that sounded melancholy he was to work for all he was worth.

"Do you understand thoroughly, old man?" I asked before he left to crawl over the first fence.

"Sure, you don't think I'm deaf, do you?" he answered in his incomparable English cockney, as he shook my hand and started for the fence.

Blackie got over the first wire fence with remarkable agility, but he was hardly over when he remarked he had forgotten his little coal shovel which was the only tool we had. Finally we found this for him and as soon as I returned to my post Mandel gave me the signal that all was clear, so I began whistling the army funeral march, and I heard Blackie plugging away. In a few minutes when the boys signalled that the guard was again approaching, I began to whistle "In the Good Old Summer Time," but to my amazement I heard Blackie still working away. Then, to get something real raggy I whistled "Alexander's Bag Time Band," but still Blackie worked on. The guard was fast approaching. Something had to be done for if he kept on working he would sure be caught, so, stepping right out in front of the guard, who, of course, could not speak English, I began to sing a very sad and mournful tune, with my own lyrics.

"Blackie," I sang, "this guard is right behind me and for the Love of Mike, lay off."

Blackie stopped; I kept on singing, and the old guard walked right on by. When he was on the other side of the building I rushed up to Blackie.

"Blackie, you damn fool," I softly exclaimed, "can't you tell ragtime from a classic?"

"Ragtime," he said in barely audible cockney English, "Why ragtime's the name of a song, and by the way, old fellow, if you don't like the way I'm digging this tunnel, come and try a hand at it yourself. It's beastly, you know."

"Go ahead," I argued, "but from now on I'll whistle only when he is coming. Get me?"

The next time the guard came around the corner of the building I began to whistle. To my surprise Blackie kept on working. I began to whistle louder than ever, but he kept right on, so, as the guard approached me, I stopped whistling and instantly Blackie quit working. As the guard passed on I again went over to Blackie and said,

"Hey, you poor fish! Didn't you hear me say to quit work when I whistled?"

"Oh, you're wrong, old chap," he insisted. "You said very plainly to work only when you whistled."

I began to think Blackie had to have it impressed upon him, so, I said, "All right, now. Forget it all and let's start over. Next time remember that when I whistle you work. See, when I whistle, I work; and when I whistle, you work, too."

He understood this illustration pretty well and we kept this going successfully until about roll call, which was at nine o'clock. Then I asked Blackie if the tunnel was dug plenty deep enough. He was quite sure it was deep enough to get through, so, he crawled over the wire fence again, and we all beat it to our quarters to pack up our few belongings with the agreement that we would meet just outside the assembly shack right after roll call had finished.

This escape, as I have stated, was to be between four of us and no more; but I would swear, there were a hundred eyes on me at roll call. And afterwards, not more than fifteen guys came around and wished me luck.

"Luck on what?" I asked one fellow.

"Why," he said inquiringly at my question, "you're going to try to escape, aren't you?"

So, my well-wishing friends all began to talk about how they wished they had an opportunity to get away too, and all that bunk. I have concluded that a bunch of prisoners are the worst gossipers in the world anyway. Tell one and you tell all. This first experience taught me at a dear cost, one of the most valuable lessons of my life. When you are going to escape, or, in fact, try anything else which from its nature requires secrecy, never, under any circumstances, take anyone into your confidence, and at most, if ever, only one trusted pal. I had heard the same bluff before, so, I told them if they wanted to get out after we had gotten away, to go ahead, they knew where the hole was, but not to go around and cackle about it like a bunch of old hens; either to get their clothes ready and try to escape or else to go to bed and let someone else try it

In escaping, the first man to try has not only the greatest opportunity to escape, but also takes the greatest hazards in that if the plot is discovered beforehand, the guards will be on the job waiting for him, while if it is not discovered he has the best chance to get farthest away before the hounds are given the trail.

It was the same old test of passing from words to action, and, so with that bunch of twelve or fifteen who said they wanted to escape. When it came down to the courage of action their wishes were merely words. Of that number, including the four original conspirators, only two went ahead with it. The other fellow who kept faith with me was Oscar Mandel.

Most of the rest of the men all beat it to their different bunks; some hung around to see the fun, while Mandel and I stayed on the job. I took all of my insignia off of my coat in order that there might be nothing to reflect any rays of light that might strike us. Then, we mixed some mud and blacked our faces and hands in order that they would not stand out against the blackness of the night.

Mandel and I matched and it was decreed that I should go first and that I would wait across the road for him. If I got caught I was to make a lot of noise and, if he was also unfortunate, he would do the same.

An electric tram line ran right along by the camp and we felt that by following this road we would, at least, get out of the town. So, with a fond farewell to the camp, as the Guard went around his beat, I slunk along in the shadows of the building. In the death-like stillness could be heard beyond the other fence, the steady beat of the outer watchman. Over to my right the guard of the inner camp was just stepping out of sight. Could ever opportunity be better than this? The time had arrived. I stepped up to the first wire fence, and threw my little sack over, then getting near a post I began to climb over. I cut my hands a lot on the barbed wire, but that was only incidental, and did not bother me. I weighed too much to get over like Blackie. It seemed to me that every wire I stepped on squeaked like the high "E" string of a toy violin.

I dropped myself within the enclosure and ran along, slinking in the shadows of the fence, until I came to the tunnel. Here was a disappointment. I could no more get through it than an elephant would have a chance of entering a doll house. It might have been O.K. for Blackie, but he miscalculated for me. It was not large enough for my shoulders, so, peeping out I saw the other German sentry, not over twenty feet away, and in his apparent unsuspecting demeanour I also saw my first step toward liberty.

I realised it would be necessary to make the tunnel considerably larger if I ever expected to get through it. Blackie had made a bum job of it and worse, he had taken the shovel with him, and I had no implements whatsoever, except an unusually large jack-knife. Whipping loose the big blade I began to cut the frozen ground, taking a look around and then chipping away like a beaver at a dam. I felt like a real criminal and every motion picture play I had ever seen, of escaping prisoners, played vividly on my mind. I was working frantically and getting along pretty well, too, in spite of my rude implement, when all of a sudden I heard a tremendous noise that made me think that I was knocking on the door of Hades—it was a big siren blowing a warning for an air raid.

Our Allied bombers were coming over to pay a visit to Karlsruhe. Believe me, I was for them. The reverberation of that siren was deafening, but I was certainly taking advantage of its tremendous noise by chugging away with all my might, when suddenly, not over a hundred and twenty-five feet from me a huge 107 calibre anti-aircraft gun exploded. I leaped like a squirrel against that fence for I felt sure that the gun had been aimed at me, and furthermore, that I had been hit. Pulling myself together I realised that it was heavy artillery instead of a short-barrelled shotgun.

Immediately other huge guns began to fire and for a few minutes there was a real bombardment going on around there—the whole earth was shaking. I kept right on digging away for it was the chance of my life. Of course, all the guards were frightened and confused and were chasing back and forth, crying out strange ejaculations and perfectly good German words of profanity, mixed with earnest prayers from "*Gott Mitt Uns*" to "*Teufel Strafe 'em*," for, believe me, they were acquainted with the variety of bombs dropped by the Allies.

About this time everyone was out of the huts looking for the airplanes in the sky, and the inner guards were making a big rumpus and causing them to close the doors so the lights would not show, which, of course, would give away the presence of the "enemy."

In all this confusion and excitement I thought it was a good time to duck, for while I did not feel that the hole was quite big enough, yet I would try it anyhow because I probably would never have such an opportunity again. So, I started out. After considerable grunting and labour I got my head and shoulders through, and then my coat caught on a nail on the bottom of the fence and in spite of every imaginable manoeuvre from a wiggle to a "shimmie," I simply could not pull through. In twisting and squirming I shook the fence, whereupon the excited guard on the outside noticing me, came running up at full speed ahead and with a pointed bayonet he frothed, "*Loze! Lozel Vass is Dass?*"

He was more excited over me than he was the prospect of a bomb dropping on the both of us. He thought that Gehenna had surely been transferred to Karlsruhe and that the whole camp was on the march. I thought he was going to take me for a practice dummy and judging from his speed I decided that he could not possibly stop until he had put that bayonet completely through me. He must have realised that if he captured me alive he would get more credit for it. Exasperated like a sick infant with the mumps, excited like a schoolgirl at her graduation, and worked up like a Hebrew at a bargain, he cried out, "*Commen sie aus! Commen sie aus!*" making all sorts of ejaculations and motions, indicating clearly that he wanted me to come on out. He was making more noise than the archies.

About this time I began to feel my leg being violently kicked and someone beating against the fence from the inside, also crying out, "*Commen sie in!*" This old boy on whose beat I had escaped had real cause for concern, for he knew that he would be placed in jail for allowing me to get away should I get the rest of the way out. No wonder he had an interest in the matter.

In a jiffy the two guards were in a dog fight over a bone—yours truly being the bone and the bone of contention—one was kicking me and the other pulling me—one anxious to get the bonus for capturing me and the other trying to save himself from jail. I was not only under the fence, but I was on both sides of it. I was afraid if I went on out the guard on the inside would shoot me, and if I backed in I knew I would be punished and I did not know but that the guard on the outside might become real excited and stick me. So, while they were fighting between themselves, one pulling and the other tugging at me, I decided that if I did go on out I might have a chance to hit this other guy on the bean and take a run for liberty.

The guns were firing all the time and things were getting good and hot around there. The boy on the inside was about as scared of the guns as he was of my escaping, so, I began to tug and with the help of the other sentry was pulling myself through. Then the old boy on the inside administered his trusty bayonet blade to my leg, and while I cannot describe the particular motion through which he went, I can certainly testify that he gave me one mighty persuasive jab. For believe me, I sure did back in at the rate of a mile a minute, for I had no further inclination whatsoever to go on out. I realised that duty called me at the camp, and while it had taken me fully five minutes to get my anatomy that far out—well, this little flying machine had a reversible propeller, that's all.

The old boy on the inside was terribly sore, because in climbing the fence after me he had torn his nice, new, green pants, yet he was over-delighted that he had saved himself from jail. As we walked up to the fence I attempted to climb the wire first, whereupon the old boy said, "*Nicht! Nein!*" and menaced me again with his bayonet. Needless to say—I unhesitatingly obeyed. I had hoped, should I have gotten over the fence first, to ran immediately to my bunk and fool the foxy old boy, but when he flashed that bayonet on me it was the halt sign of my new fraternity. A little blood was beginning to trickle down my leg and I began to feel pretty much like a stuck pig, so, in courtesy, I let the old boy climb over first and I went after him.

On the way to headquarters, I realised that I had a compass and a map and knowing what it would mean if these were found on me, as we walked along, I carefully slipped my hand in my pocket and crumpled up the map. I then began to cough violently, whereupon I took out my handkerchief with my left hand and put it over my mouth, and in so doing I managed to put the tiny map in my mouth; then I chewed it up and swallowed it. I didn't know what gag to pull with that compass, and I didn't dare to swallow it. The old German who was taking me along didn't feel any sympathy for me, but kept poking me along in spite of my overemphasized limping. Finally I deliberately stumbled and fell, but as I fell I threw that compass a good twenty yards away, and into a section of the lot where it was not likely to be found. Then after considerable moral persuasion, I got up and went over to the headquarters with the feeling that in spite of the worst I had saved myself, at least, two weeks in jail.

In a very cold room, at headquarters, they summoned the commander of the camp, the officer of the night, and the officer of the guard, and all the sergeants and corporals at the camp. Then the joint board was in session. They gathered around and proceeded to cause me a good deal of embarrassment because they took off all of my clothes and did not leave me enough in which to feel modest. Like a poor, belated, half-soaked, blind owl, after an April shower, naked from head to foot, with my face and hands covered with mud, I stood there waiting for them to finish searching my clothes, before I could once more become a respectable looking German prisoner. I also was patiently awaiting the announcement of my penalty. It was my first attempt and I expected almost anything from shooting to hanging.

Chapter 12

The Privileges of Prisoners

A serious old philosopher once said that every man had his price. That may be true but I don't agree with it in principle. My early training taught me that the man who offers a bribe is a lower parasite than the man who accepts it and experience has not altered my views. But, a more serious old philosopher came forth expounding the doctrine that everything is fair in love and in war. According to my way of thinking this second boy was on the right track.

So, when my German captors took me down and with a lot of ceremony, deposited me in the camp calaboose, a hasty examination of the barred windows and the tremendous lock on the door almost convinced me that my only hope was to experiment with that philosophy of price, as my biggest asset happened to be a pocket full of prison money, which, if acceptable at all, would have to be disposed of at a discount. At any rate, I was determined to get out—the means might require bribery and it might require lies. Whatever was necessary to effect my state of freedom, so long as it was honourable, was in my mind the privilege of the prisoner—for it was fair in war.

The cell was not so bad; in fact, it was much better than the quarters I had in camp, except that I was alone. I had a German orderly who took care of me, which convenience was something foreign in the regular camp. First appearances were so attractive that I thought it unfortunate I hadn't discovered it before. In the morning the interpreter came around to see how things were going along. I told him "Fine, except that I wanted something to eat," an habitual complaint among prisoners. There was the rub, for he informed me that when in solitary imprisonment in jail you only receive a portion of German food and that under no circumstances are you allowed any supplemental food from the Red Cross.

So, about nine o'clock this orderly brought me my breakfast which consisted of a bowl of Ersatz coffee and that was all. Believe me, the scarcity left a funny empty feeling in my stomach that decided the question at once—bribery it would be.

In the afternoon, when one of the calaboose corporals came around on his hourly inspection, I figured that he was a pretty good guy to play up to, so I knocked the old boy sick by offering him a pipeful of my real, American tobacco, which had been given me by a fellow prisoner. Lieutenant Shea of the 26th Division, who handled the Red Cross supplies at Karlsruhe. Shea was a real guy; he was fearless and while under very strict German regulations, he always allowed his staunch Americanism to be seen by Germans and Americans indiscriminately. This German corporal had a whopper of a pipe for he made a big hole in my already slim sack and tobacco was as scarce as desert icebergs. How his eyes sparkled when he lighted it. These Germans had been smoking ground cabbage leaves for almost four years and were getting mighty tired of it.

"*Sehr gut, sehr gut*," he ejaculated many times, sniffing the old time aroma.

Then, he warmed up and we got to talking. It finally dwindled from the war generally to our own family histories. He was in great distress. He had lost four sons in the war, and what he considered much worse, his two daughters would probably never be able to get husbands, for so many men had been killed. I thoroughly sympathized with him and agreed that it was all wrong to require such a sacrifice of him. Then he told me what his army pay was—it was very small—and he said he had been in the war five years. I told him how much the American soldiers received, which surprised him very much and seemed fabulous.

His understanding was that only the poor people had gone to war for America—the sons of the rich men stayed at home; and further, that practically all Americans of German descent had absolutely refused to take up arms against the Fatherland. I refuted this latter remark as well as the first—I told him that both my father and mother were German, having both been born in Berlin, and that my father was a very wealthy man, but I had to go into the service because all the young men had to become soldiers—the rich and poor alike had gone into the war and it didn't make any difference whether they were German-Americans, or just plain Americans, they had all gone. So, he asked me what I did before the war, and being a pretender for the purpose I had in mind, I assumed a thoroughly shocked attitude at such a question, and informed him that before the war, my father being very rich, I didn't do anything except go to college as "dad" came across with twenty thousand marks a year for spending money alone. The old boy's eyes popped open to the size of an owl's. He thought such an allowance fabulous and criminally extravagant. I filled him full of a lot of this hot air about the war, and especially my own financial stability, for I expected to sooner or later establish my credit with him.

We parted the very best of friends and to cinch it I gave him another pipeful of tobacco. The next morning the rather expected happened; he came to talk some more and to further test my depleted supply of Red Cross tobacco. Our second conversation ended with my parting with seventy-five *marks* cash, and a promissory note for seven thousand five hundred *marks*, payable three months after the war, in consideration for which the old boy was to leave the outer latch open that night and slip me a screw driver with which to manipulate the inner latch, and, at my request, he arranged a guard and that afternoon I went out and took my first exercise.

The guard was a measly, withered-up shrimp, who spoke quite a little English, as he had been in America. His knowledge of American people and of American customs gave me a new field of activity. He told me that he was on guard that night around this same area, about eleven o'clock, so I cautiously sounded him out as to whether he was particularly scrupulous or whether he might accept a little bribe. Laughingly, he told me that like all other men in the world he supposed that he had his price, but that it was high enough that it could not possibly interest me.

"Well," I said, manifesting surprise, "you've heard of my father, haven't you, since you've been in America?"

"No," he said.

"What!" I ejaculated. "Oh, you certainly have heard of J. P. Morgan, Haslett & Co., of Wall Street."

Of course, he understood the first and last parts and the old boy stood still in his amazement, for that "J. P. Morgan" and my connection therewith had simply hypnotized him. Suddenly he became cordial to the extreme. After blushing in honest modesty I got down to business.

"You've been in America long enough to know what notes are, haven't you? If you give your note it's as good as gold, any time, any place, anywhere."

"*Ja*," he affirmed, nodding his head. "I know that."

"Well," I went on, "all that is necessary is a little cash consideration given with a note and it is good. Just like a contract."

He agreed perfectly.

"Well," I said, feeling like a street-corner politician, "name your own price."

After considerable hemming and hawing around about it, he surprised me by naming five thousand *marks*, which then was about one thousand dollars, one hundred *marks* to be in cash, and my note for the remainder.

He agreed to buy me a map and compass, to bring them in, and leave them wrapped in an old rag at the foot of an iron post which he pointed out; and he agreed that as he was to be on duty that night about eleven o'clock he would not see me as I went over the fence on his post. He told me the exact spot where he would be standing between eleven and eleven ten, so that I could avoid him.

As to the financial arrangements he was to take me to the jail and then go over to the canteen at my request to buy me some paper, which purchase was approved. In the meanwhile I was to prepare the note and dig up the coin.

As he came in the corporal came with him as no one was supposed to enter the room without the corporal, but just as he laid my purchase on the table the telephone rang and the Corporal had to step away temporarily, which gave me the opportunity I needed. I handed the guard the piece of I.O.U. paper and a hundred *marks* in prisoners' money. The deal was closed.

All the remainder of the afternoon I carefully laid my plans. This time it looked like a clean get-away, but there is always something to take the joy out of living, for about four o'clock the interpreter came around with the prison paymaster, who told me to turn in all my money for which they wrote me out a receipt. I decided that I had been double-crossed by the corporal; the other guard would not have had time since the act.

"You had more than this the morning after we had you searched," the paymaster said after perusing a big ledger.

"Yes," I stumbled, "but I sent some of it back to one of my friends to whom I owed some money."

Then they put all my fears to rout by telling me that I was leaving at five o'clock with a transport of prisoners, going to a permanent camp. This was simply hard luck, because as I figured it, it was absolutely impossible for either the other corporal or the weazened-up old guard to give this plan of mine away. Furthermore, they would not have dared.

Well, that was finished for me, so, I asked the interpreter where we were going, and about my sentence. Like all other Germans he pulled the *kultur* stuff by telling me that I was being sent to a fine, big camp and that my penalty here was finished. So, he and the officer left and the door was locked behind.

Immediately it was again unlocked; the old German corporal came in, highly excited because he thought the visit of the officer meant that they had gotten something on him. I told him I was going to leave at once for a permanent camp.

"Oh," he whispered, really surprised, "then you will not escape tonight."

Upon affirming this statement that I was really leaving, the old fellow, to my utter surprise, looked around to see that no one was looking in the window, then closed and bolted the door behind him and handed me back my money and my note. Here was a real, decent old guy. I believed in his sincerity, and German or not, if I ever have a chance to do anything for that old fellow I'd do my best to do it, for he was absolutely honest, no matter what one might say as to his patriotism. I gladly gave the old fellow the last bit of tobacco I had and when I left we parted real friends.

But, the other old fossil—of course, I didn't have a chance to see him, and my one hundred marks, together with my large note, was gone to the devil. Of course, I didn't worry about the note; I never intended to pay that any way, if for no other reason than the fact that it would bankrupt me even though the mark is not now worth much at all.

I marched down to the train with the rest of the transport, and here again they sent a tag along with me, telling of my bad record. They honoured me with several guards personally assigned, while the rest of the party had about one guard for every four prisoners. We travelled for about thirty-six hours in third-class coaches and were, indeed, tired and worn out and sleepy. But, in spite of German efficiency and secret service, within a few hours after starting we all knew by well founded rumours that we were going by way of Munich to a place called "Landshut."

At Munich we were taken off of the train and given some food, which consisted of powerful limburger cheese and a little piece of dog sausage, with a hunk of dainty potato bread. In spite of their intense hunger, some of the boys could not possibly go that cheese so, showing resourcefulness, I made a collection of it for I thought it might come in handy, later on. I gathered so much that I was a human cheese factory; I had that cheese stuck in my pockets, I was carrying it in my hands and I even had some of it securely put away in my blouse, and all the way from Munich to Landshut, Bavaria, as I had nothing else to do, I ate cheese. Believe me, people knew I was coming a mile away. When that stuff began to get a little tepid, I was a man hated among men; extremely unpopular for a strong reason.

We were turned over to a new set of guards at the Landshut station and I noticed that they had lost my identity since I was not being given special attention, so, I mixed right in with the rest of the prisoners; that is, until they got a good whiff. The new sergeant, after lining us up, walked along the lines calling the names and checking up the prisoners.

Standing directly in front of me, with his face about two inches from mine, he gruffly called, "Oberleutnant Haslett."

"Here!" I bellowed, whereupon the German, getting the full benefit of the cheese, staggered and moved on.

I went up to the old abandoned estate known as "Traunitz," which was a very beautiful and historic old court. However, we did not live in the castle. I think it was the servants' quarters we had, for there were twenty-five of us in one room.

Landshut, itself, was a lovely little town; in fact, one of the most beautiful I have ever seen. The feature was the variety of church bells. They were ringing day and night, and the sounds ranged several octaves.

At this camp they took away our American uniforms and gave us old Russian prisoners' clothes, with a big yellow stripe down the back of the blue uniform. I don't know whether that "yellow streak" was supposed to have any real significance or not, but anyhow it was there.

At Landshut was imprisoned Captain Jimmy Hall, the James Norman Hall who was prominent for his *Kitchener's Mob* and other books, and a very famous member of the Lafayette Escadrille. "Jimmy" was quite a character as he hobbled around the place—we all liked his wonderful democracy

We had only been there a day or so when they began to inoculate us for, I think, every known disease. A big, fat, German Major stood there and in apparent delight, pumped serum into us like a baker fills creampuffs. The worst part was that he stuck us right in the chest. He was a good natured old duck who didn't seem to take things seriously. Not only did he vaccinate us for smallpox, but he gave us shots of typhoid, para-typhoid, triple typhoid, typhus, tetanus and cholera, and what else I do not know.

We were to have five jabs of the stuff, but when I took my first one I decided then and there that when I took the next it would be when I was held and given it by force. I never received another jab, for every time afterwards I went in with the in-going line, and after my chest had been painted with iodine by the assistant to the doctor, as the old boy would turn around to fill his needle for the next man, I would quietly step over in the out-going line, and with many apparent indications of pain, passed to my bunk,

Immediately after this first jab was given and before the pain and fever had a chance to take effect I was mixing around with the boys, having a good time, when in came a sergeant who, amidst considerable pomp and display, stated that the captain commanding the camp wanted to see Oberleutnant Haslett at once, I asked him what the officer wanted to see me about, but he didn't know and I'm sure I didn't, although I had a good strong hunch. As I still had my yellow-striped uniform, I put it on and went over. On the way over the Sergeant sympathetically ventured to tell me for fear that I did not know it, that the German officers were terrible men, very strict and stem and it was to my advantage to be very careful and to be absolutely military and courteous.

After considerable palavering around, the sergeant ushered me in. Seated there at his desk was this potentate, the commander of the camp. I hardly knew how to figure him for he was a hard looking customer with the squinty eyes of a Chinaman, the pugnacious pug nose of a bull dog, and the mouth and jaws of an ape. However, he was groomed to the extreme. Take it from me, he was some little fashion plate all of his own. This was a combination, to my mind, extremely difficult to tackle. To be perfectly frank, he almost had my goat to start with. The thing that bothered me most was the charge.

I was a soldier the day war was declared. The day before I had been a hard plugging law senior in the University of Southern California— just counting the days until I could realise my life's ambition—to stand before a court and plead a righteous cause. While like all other young

Americans I was happy to serve my country, yet at the declaration of hostiliies the thing that hurt me most was the fact that my perfectly good legal education had all gone to the rocks for, as a soldier, I could not see where my law could possibly serve any useful purpose.

It was Lincoln, I think, who said to be prepared for the opportunity so when it knocked it could be accepted. Well, regardless of who said it, my life's ambition was before me. I had always wanted to plead a righteous cause before a court—but I had never calculated that the righteous cause would be my own. This was nothing more than a court and I was to be the culprit appearing in my own behalf.

The proceedings had all the environment of a rural police court with the solemnity and dignity of the Supreme Court of the United States. So much pomp and red tape I never saw before in my life. The sergeant went in, clicked his heels together, saluted smartly and proceeded to babble away in German. The Prussian officer looked up from his desk and snarled, whereupon the sergeant saluted again. Then he faced about, walked four paces toward me, saluted and said with great feeling, "The captain commanding the camp commands your presence." I wasn't a soldier in the true sense of the word. I was an aviator. I was a real snappy soldier once, having been graduated from the New Mexico Military Institute; and, having had some training in the line on the border and in the early training camps.

Since my judge seemed so strong on display, I decided to compete for the prize, so I drew my shoulders back, put my chest out and pulled my tummy in. As if by command and, by the numbers, I marched four paces forward, clicked my heels together and in perfect cadence brought my hand forward in a salute. Instead of bringing it down in the ordinary manner, I pushed it straight forward and let it slap loudly against my trousers. It sounded like the snapping of a champion boot-black's cloth as he finishes the job. The captain stood, sainted and immediately sat down.

I thought he would ask me to have a chair, but it wasn't being done by the Prussians in those days so I stood there strictly at attention looking directly at him like a tiger ready to spring. In a few moments he got up again, holding a document long and engrossed. Clearing his throat like a chief justice about to render an opinion, he proceeded to babble, "*Der Deutschen*, etc." After one mouthful, he turned to the sergeant and the Sergeant stiffened up even more rigidly and began to interpret. I cannot repeat it *verbatim*, of course, but it went something like this, not vouching for the accuracy of the names:

Whereas, I, Antonio Mark Snicklefritz, Captain of the Imperial German Army, duly appointed and ordained by the Imperial German Government through Wilhelm, Emperor of Germany and Poland, in his own name, am entrusted with the command of and authority over this prison camp at Landshut, Bavaria, including all allied prisoners of war there-in, do officially, on behalf of the Imperial German Government, inform you, Oberleutnant Elmer Haslett, *Amerikaner*, an officer of the Air Service, that the general of the Imperial German Army, Otto von Beetpots, commanding the 37th Army Corps of the Interior, has decreed, ordered, directed and commanded that you have at Karlsruhe, Baden, on or about the fifteenth of October, at night, disobeyed, disregarded and broken all rules pertaining to prisoners of war in that you did wilfully, maliciously, deliberately, and with malice aforethought, attempt to escape the confines of the prison camp of the Imperial German Government; and that in so doing you wilfully and maliciously destroyed and otherwise damaged official property of the Imperial German Government in that you dug or otherwise excavated earth from the confines of the prison camp of the Imperial German Government.

Whereupon, for these acts you were duly sentenced to serve a period of solitary imprisonment, upon which imprisonment you entered and which sentence and imprisonment have not been completed. Therefore, the General von Beetpots, commanding the forces of the Imperial German Government, and of the 37th German Army Corps of the Interior, commands that you immediately, without delay, be placed in solitary imprisonment for the unfulfilled period of your sentence.

This was interpreted in twenty different relays and I swallowed it all and was getting pretty tired of standing at attention, so, as the officer spieled, I would stand on one foot and rest but when the sergeant started to talk, I would stiffen up and look directly at him for the judge had his eyes focused on none other than the prisoner. During this entire ceremony, the Justice of the Peace did not make one gesture with his hand, simply holding the documents in his hands, standing constantly at attention. He was more like a marble statue holding a scroll.

Then, like most other courts, came the question, "Have you anything to say?" My inoculation was beginning to take effect; my lips were hot and my brow feverish, but, best, my brain was stimulated. I didn't intend to go to jail without a fight so I pitched my voice as low as possible and sounded off slow and deliberately for I was not talking for time. Indeed it was more than that. The sound of my voice gave me the moral courage I needed. Looking straight at the Prussian and attempting to improvise a proper form for my defence, I threw out my chest an extra inch and I started out with something on this order:

I Elmer Haslett, First Lieutenant Air Service, Army of the Democratic Republic of the United States of America, having been entrusted as an officer of the Democratic Republic of the United States of America with the duties, rights and responsibilities of an accredited officer am, of course, entitled to all the reciprocal courtesies of captured officers of belligerent nations; and, therefore, as the officially authorized and duly accredited representative of the Democratic Republic of the United States of America I have the honour to submit to the Captain as the officially authorized and duly accredited representative of the Imperial German Government, the following answer to the matter he has just officially communicated to me:

That I, Elmer Haslett, First Lieutenant, United States Air Service, do admit that part of the facts of the case stated by the general commanding the 37th Army Corps of the Interior are true, especially in that I was captured in the act of escaping and had dug a tunnel, thereby indirectly destroying the property of the Imperial German Government, for which I was imprisoned at Karlsruhe. That during this imprisonment, the officially authorized and duly accredited representative of the Imperial German Government was a *feldwebel* named Schneider whom I, of course, had the right to presume was vested with the authority of the Imperial German Government for he had given me commands in the name of the Imperial German Government which I, of course, did not hesitate to obey; he had given me privileges which I did not hesitate to accept and when he made any statements or promises, I took them as authorized and final statements and promises of the Imperial German Government.

Now, may it please the captain commanding the camp to know that on leaving Karlsruhe for this camp, this same *feldwebel* of-

190

ficially informed me that I was leaving for a new camp and, furthermore, that my penalty was complete for the reason that misdemeanours against prison camps are local, which, in law is known in Latin as the *lex loci*, and since my offense had only been an offense against the prison camp at Karlsruhe, the penalty could not be imposed or served in any other camp; therefore, the penalty for my offense was absolutely completed.

Therefore, since I, as the representative of the United States of America, had dealt with no one officially except this one representative of the Imperial German Government, I had just as much authority for going to jail at his command as I had for leaving for this new camp at his command and just as much right to believe that no other sentence could be imposed for the misdemeanour committed. Now, may it please the captain, in view of these statements made to me, if any other penalty is now imposed upon me, it will have to be for acts against the German Government which I have committed at this camp and unless the captain representing the forces of the German Government can point out the offense I have committed at Landshut, under his jurisdiction, which warrants my further imprisonment, I, Elmner Haslett, as the duly accredited representative of the Democratic Government of the United States of America, do consider the imprisonment as being without cause and, therefore, absolutely illegal.

Therefore, if the captain as representative of the Imperial German Government cares to imprison me under these circumstances, I here and now protest very firmly before him and request that an opportunity be given me to use the kind offices of the high plenipotentiary minister of Switzerland, the high plenipotentiary minister of Holland, the high plenipotentiary minister of Spain, or other neutral representation in order that efforts may be exercised in my behalf before Wilhelm, the Emperor of the Imperial German Government.

And here and now, I request to be put on record before this court that I have claimed these rights under Article 26, Geneva Convention, Article 23, London Agreement, Article 88, Hague War Clause and Section 41, Article 12 of the International Treaty of Paris, all respecting the rights and privileges of prisoners of war. This concludes my answer and I wish to thank the captain for his kind courtesy in hearing this official protest.

The old boy was taken off his feet. I couldn't have pulled an improvised spiel like that in ten years had I not been keyed up with the high, raging fever and when I finished the reaction left me weak. But I was sure that the captain commanding the camp was fully convinced that I knew what I was talking about. In fact, I felt that I could see it in his very attitude. The sergeant then told me that the captain would consider the proposition and let me know his decision. Of course, I could not wait to get back and tell the boys how I had foxed the Germans. I was just in the act of repeating and acting my long spiel to them when the door opened and in came the sergeant again.

"Well," I thought, "the old boy has come to tell me that I do not need to serve my penalty."

"Oberleutnant Haslett," he called before everybody, "the captain commanding the camp has decided that you will go to jail at once."

Well, believe me, I could have been knocked over with a hair of a feather. The boys gave me the merry titter and the royal ha! ha! I tried to argue with the sergeant but he evidently had my number. "Come on, pack up," he said, "and don't try to pull your line on me. I'm acting under orders." So amidst considerable personal embarrassment, I picked up my few belongings, which consisted of a note book, a wooden back toothbrush and a quarter loaf of bread, and the sergeant walked me over to the guard house. Here he assigned me a hard looking guard who, menacingly, loaded up his rifle right before me which, admittedly, had the moral effect intended; and then, followed by every Boche youngster in the whole town, I was in military fashion marched down through the old village and lodged in the town jail.

It was a whopper of a jail for a small town. We went up to the third floor back, after locking three steel partitions behind us. We finally came to the cell rooms and the guard rang for the key. After a time, a hoary relic of the Napoleonic days shuffled in and with great ceremony produced the fatal steel and turned the lock. Whereupon I entered and automatically the door was closed behind me. This cell was about five feet wide and eight feet long. The bed, or rather the bunk, folded up against the wall and was locked. It couldn't be opened, although I tried many times. The walls were blank and bare and at the rear was a high barred window with a slanting projection which made it even impossible to look out. The door was massive steel and one look at it convinced me that I was in a real cell in a real jail and I was a real jail bird.

Not having had a great deal of experience with jails, I naturally thought it was a horrible place, although I am told it was really a very nice jail, as far as jails are concerned, but at that, it was damp, musty and cold. At the door was an electric push button and since there were no telephones or servants in attendance. I naturally supposed this was to call the attendant. Practically exhausted from my fever and the long walk, I sat down on a wobbly old stool and stared at the wall, gradually getting physically weaker, but seemingly mentally more alert. In a moment I began to chill and I realised that I would have to lie down. The bed was locked. The cold stone floor was not inviting so I tried to ring the buzzer and I buzzed intermittently for about five minutes. There was no response. It was a desperate situation. I had to lie down and still I must have some covers, so I wedged a match in the buzzer in order that it would keep on buzzing until someone answered.

Then from sheer exhaustion and faintness I fell to the floor. This continued buzzing soon brought the attendant up and, believe me, he was very, very peeved. He came in, snatched the match from the push button and began to swear and make some furious ejaculations which I couldn't understand and it wouldn't have made much difference anyway. In reply to my insistent demands that he unlock the bed at once, he did nothing but say, "*Nein, nein, seben heur*," that is, "No, not until seven o'clock." I asked him to send for the prison officer but he insisted that the officer would not come up. I told him that I was an officer myself and that I was sick and had a right to see an officer. He did nothing but slam the door in my face. Something told me I was on my last 1eg and I must soon get out of that place or something would happen that I would never remember.

So summoning every ounce of my remaining strength, shivering and chilly, I took my notebook and wrote an official protest couched in language not proper for publication, addressing it to the Spanish minister. It was a last hunch. When I finished, I again put a match in the buzzer. This time the old boy was certainly fierce but he had nothing on me. I was in the same condition myself. Like two tigers we came together. He cautiously opened the door for he knew from my previous attitude that I was liable to make a jump at his throat. Reaching his hand back to his hip so that if I started anything he could draw his gun, he demanded to know what I meant by ringing the buzzer again.

Insane with rage and raging fever, I shook my fist in his face and said, "For the officer," whereupon I madly slapped myself on the chest and said, "*Ich bin ein officeres Amerikaner*," which, if correct, is to say, "I am an American officer and must be treated as such." Reluctantly and disgustedly, he took the paper and started to pull the door shut again. I staggered forward to impress upon him the fact that I needed medical attention at once. Too late, the door was closed. Whether from pure anger or from actual exhaustion, I don't know, but for some reason I simply went down to take the count.

I was awakened by someone shaking me. Dazed, I got up. Three hours had elapsed. With head swimming, I looked around. Before me was the prison attendant, the sergeant interpreter of the camp and the commanding officer of the camp with whom I had had the set-to that morning. It was another court but this time the ceremony on my part was lacking for I sat on the stool. The captain straightened and again stood stiffly at attention, while the sergeant interpreted:

I, Antonio Marie Snicklefritz, captain commanding the prison camp at Landshut, am directed by the general commanding the German Military District of Munich to inform you, Elmer Haslett, Oberleutnant, Air Service, American Army, that the general has decreed that you be released from solitary imprisonment until further orders.

As expected, the "further orders" never came.

CHAPTER 13

"Coming Out"

The modern *débutante* looks forward with no little anxiety to her "Coming Out." It is naturally quite an event for, veritably, she is imprisoned, as it were, by the conventions which do not permit her to take her place among the friends of the inner circle until she has been formally presented by her "coming out."

So, the prisoners of war, even after the armistice, were withheld from their friends until the "coming out," which consisted of the formalities of turning the prisoners over to their friends. Naturally, it was quite an event. But, believe me, no *débutante* could possibly anticipate her "coming out" with the keenness and anxiety that the American prisoners of war could theirs. We, too, had planned it all—of course, not so much as to the clothes we would wear, but more especially as to the things we would eat.

Several days previous to the signing of the armistice, we heard that the people of Bavaria had revolted, and that the will of the "Soldiers and Workmen" was paramount. Although locked in the confines of a prison camp, the proverbial little bird told us that something was in the air—indeed, one felt it in the atmosphere—for, if a new republic was formed, they were certainly not the enemies of the United States, so we would indeed soon be "coming out."

The regulation cap of the German officer and soldier is adorned by two buttons in the front centre—the top and larger button having the colours of the Imperial German Government in the form of a miniature cocarde, while the lower and smaller button is made up of the colours of the German State from which the officer or soldier hails. Thus, all the soldiers at our camp had the large German button and the smaller one of green and white, the colours of the State of Bavaria.

One day, around the first of November, we noticed that all the officers and soldiers of the camp, including the hardboiled Prussian captain, had taken off the prominent German button. Then there was a definite certainty that the revolution was on. We did not know how loyal to the new government the soldiers were going to be, and we were rather concerned as to what the attitude of the new Bavarian Republic would be toward us, for we had heard nothing about our release. All sorts of rumours began floating around that camp—some to the effect that the soldiers and workmen were coming up to mob us for being Americans, others, more popular, that they were coming up to release us, others that we were going to die of slow starvation on account of the shortage of food, and still others that we were going to be sent to Switzerland for protection.

With all these things before us, a vigilance committee was formed, and we all got together and had a meeting. "Jimmy" Hall, being the senior officer present, automatically became chairman. So, the big question was "For whom would we declare?"—the old German *régime* or the new Bavarian revolutionary party. Naturally, on such a momentous subject, we had quite a number of bursts of oratory, and a lot of arguments were laid down on both sides of the question, but, at the same time, neither of us knew anything about either of them. We viewed it from an economical and military phase, but most of all, for the present at least, we looked at it from the standpoint of "things to eat."

But judged by the solemnity and seriousness of the conference, the destiny of the world was seemingly at stake, so we asked one bird, who was sort of a jay, what he thought about it. "Mr. Chairman,'" he said seriously, "I make a resolution that we declare that we are for the party that gets us out of Germany the fastest, and we don't give a damn which one it is. " At that, the meeting almost ended in a riot, though in my mind the jay had absolutely the correct solution. Finally, it was decided that we would leave our fate to the council of three—the three most influential prisoners in camp, the controllers of the food supply, namely, the Red Cross Committee.

Shortly, conditions began to get real tense around there, and we actually didn't know what was going to happen for, about our camp, the prison authorities had hoisted the red flag of Socialism. The few days during which that flag stayed there were the only days of my life that I have not been a Republican—I was a Socialist like all the rest of our boys, from force of circumstances.

Amid all this excitement, we were summoned together, and the official representative of the new revolutionary party came up to address us. Amid the quietness of death, the great man announced to us that he was now the great representative of the Great Revolutionary Party, and that the Great People of the Greater State of Bavaria had had a greatest revolution—not a bloody revolution like the Russians, but a quiet, orderly revolution, for realising that the old government had failed to take care of the needs of the common people, the soldiers and the workmen of Bavaria had gotten together and had overthrown the monarchy. The outcome had been the ideal democratic form of government—a Republic—and the revolution had been entirely successful, for the soldiers and workmen were in complete authority and command and the old regime had been entirely displaced. "Indeed," he said, "everybody realised the inevitable and made no attempt to stop the onward movement, and such a thing as mob violence or shooting has been unheard of."

He had just started on his next sentence when, down in the town, a machine gun sputtered. We had been hearing pot shots occasionally for some time. So we all began to laugh. It was a rather embarrassing situation, and the old boy immediately modified his statement to the effect that in rare instances there had been a little shooting. Then he went on and blabbered about fifteen minutes more as to the aims of the new government, what it had in mind, how it wished especially to be the friend of America and the good things it was going to do for the prisoners, and, as a Republic, the prisoners would, of course, be released. Here was the one thing that interested us, so, at this with one voice the prisoner colony responded, as if to a yell leader, "When!" The great man was almost taken off his feet by the anxious debutantes anticipating the "coming out"

"Of course," he went on graciously, "those arc details that will have to be arranged later." Our release may have been simply regarded as a detail to him, but we held it much more important. In fact, the situation looked so serious to us that only the continual talk of the general armistice kept the bunch from attempting a wholesale "coming out"

Finally, the armistice came, and that day was the greatest of my whole life—not so much for the reason that I would soon be released, but because I was in a position to observe the Germans in absolute misery. I have heard a lot of people say that their arrogance was not affected by the armistice, but that is all bunk. They were humiliated to the extreme—they whined around like a pen of stuck pigs—they thought the terms of the armistice were terrible, inhumane, and impossible. As usual, they blamed it all on England. I could have stayed there for months just enjoying their misery in crying over the terrible terms laid down.

I was getting good and sick of the Germans, as such, for they had worked some good gags on us at that camp at Landshut. They took all our clothes, including shoes, to have them fumigated in order, as they said, to safeguard the health of the camp, and, as a substitute, they issued us old Russian prisoner uniforms. For shoes, they gave us some toy paper bedroom slippers, which could be bought in an American novelty store for a dime. To our surprise, in a few days these clothes were returned to us, unfumigated, in fact, untouched except thoroughly searched. It was the typical shell game under the guise of *kultur*, for, at the end of the month, we found that we had been charged three dollars for the said shoes, and, since the Germans controlled the prisoners' exchequer, the transaction would not permit of any argument.

Another time, I was soaked outright. The officer at my previous prison camp at Karlsruhe gave me a receipt for my fast dwindling purse. When I presented this receipt at Landshut, the authorities stated that they had no record of it, but that, if I would turn over this receipt to them, they would send it to Karlsruhe for verification. Like a boob, I turned the receipt over, and I have never seen it or the money since. I demanded the money several times afterwards, but demands, when a prisoner, do not carry a great deal of pull.

Shortly after the armistice, the orders came for us to be taken to another camp, preparatory to our "coming out." Our Red Cross food supply had been running short for some time, and, just the way things always happen, a carload of food arrived for us the day we started for the new camp. On our trip, they sent the customary number of boards along, including the sergeant interpreter of the camp, whose name was Kapp, and who was in charge of the party. The railways were congested, as they usually were in Germany, so Herr Kapp sat in our compartment, and his presence eliminated the necessity of the objectionable guards.

Herr Kapp was a well-to-do German of the middle class, an artist by profession, well educated, and about forty years old. The only objection I had to Kapp was that, like most other Germans, he was an habitual liar. However, he tried to be a good fellow, which was decidedly in his favour, and there was one other good thing about him—his unusually good sense of humour.

Realising the uniqueness of our position, which happens only once in a couple of centuries, namely, being a member of the victorious army about to pass from the hands of the enemy, I sought to engage Herr Kapp in honest, frank conversation, since there could now be no reason for deceptions. After a while, he opened up, so I asked him when he considered the German cause was at its best. He said that it was undoubtedly in the early part of the war, when the Germans were at the gates of Paris. I asked him when he thought the tide had turned, and he said that the German people realised, on July 18, 1918, when the Allies attacked between Château-Thierry and Soissons, that thereafter Germany was fighting the war on the defensive.

"What," I asked, "was the attitude of the German people toward their prospects of victory when America entered the war?"

"Well," he calmly replied, "to a large number of the common people who, of course, read the governmental propaganda, they only considered it as a big bluff, for they reasoned that it would be impossible for America to transport her army overseas. You see," he went on, "the reports of the sinking of allied ships by our submarines had been greatly exaggerated, and the general public honestly thought that America could do no more harm as a belligerent than she could as a neutral, for she was so unprepared that, before she could possibly raise an army, the Von Tirpitz U-boat warfare would have brought the Allies to their knees.

"But," he continued emphatically, "to us educated and thinking Germans, we quite well knew that, when America declared war, it was all over for us unless we succeeded in capturing Paris, which, of course, would paralyze the French Railway System, and cut off the Allies' means of transportation and supply to the front. This was the reason for our big spring drive. It was a last hope, and we banked everything on its success. America won the war for the Allies." "Herr Kapp," I said, "do the German people realise that America entered the war from purely unselfish reasons—only as a matter of principle—and that they expect to gain nothing materially?"

"Oh," he laughed sarcastically, "how could any nation make the sacrifice that America was prepared to make and yet expect to gain nothing material from it. That is not to be expected. But," he continued, "the truth of the matter is this. Your President had made us so many promises, so many speeches in which he stated that he was the friend of the German people that, when it came to the worst, we took him up—for the German people expected that he would make good on some of his utterances, but, when the terms of the armistice were made public, they knew that either Wilson had been overruled, or that the German people had been a bunch of suckers and had bitten the wrong bait."

"But at that," he emphasized, "the Germans fed no natural animosity toward the Americans, but they hate the French and despise the English."

Kapp told us that our destination was Villingen, which was a prison camp in the State of Baden. The journey was very slow on account of the congestion, so the day before we arrived there, as we were sidetracked at one town, Kapp left us to call Landshut on the long distance. When he returned, we knew that something was terribly wrong—he was as pale as a ghost. Poor old Kapp! I never saw a man so nervous and upset. He acted like a rooky after being bawled out by a drill sergeant, and he fidgeted and twisted like an old maid about to say the words "I do." Finally, I summoned enough courage to ask him what it was all about, for I thought perhaps that hostilities had been resumed.

"Anything wrong, Herr Kapp?" I asked.

"Wrong!" he ejaculated bitterly. "Hell, everything's wrong!"

"What do you mean?" we all anxiously asked, for his attitude was just cause for alarm.

"Well," he went on, "I have just called Landshut and they are demobilizing the camp today, and the men are all going to their homes."

"What's the matter with that?" I inquired, for this was to my mind the natural thing to do.

"Oh, my," he said, surprised at our lack of understanding, "That car of Red Cross food arrived for you prisoners, and the rest of the camp officials will hook it all before I get back to get my share."

All the way on the journey, Kapp had talked about the very nice girl he knew in Villingen, and that he was surely going to visit her for a few days before he returned to Landshut. So, as we were pulling into Villingen, I told Kapp that I certainly hoped he would have a pleasant visit with his girl friend at Villingen.

"Visit nothing," he came back emphatically, "I'm going to turn you prisoners over to the authorities here and take the first train back to Landshut. There may yet be a little of that Red Cross food left."

Villingen was a real prison camp—believe me it was, compared to those we had been in. They had real spring mattresses, a prisoners' orchestra, a couple of pianos, a library, a tennis court, hand-ball court, basket-ball court, nice place to walk in, and a nice kitchen where prisoners could cook their own recipes, and best of all, they had quite a lot of Red Cross food, even butter. I regretted a plenty that all my prison life had not been spent at that camp, for it was the best I had seen.

When we got to Villingen, we received a fresh supply of rumours as to just when we were going to be released. With all this anticipation, the days were unusually long, for every day was filled with added promises which the Germans never fulfilled. So, after we had been there a few days, I began to think we never were going to get out if we waited for the help of the Germans. So, I decided to have my own "coming out."

I tried to escape for three nights straight, even getting so far as to breaking the lock on an abandoned gate and cutting the barbed wire enclosing the windows, but something always went wrong. Every time we had to run on account of being discovered by the guards. The fourth day, an American artillery colonel, who was the senior officer of the prisoners, called a meeting and stated that the Germans had turned the government or the prisoners over to him, and, as commanding officer, he forbade any more attempts to escape. I thought then and I think now that the colonel was entirely without his rights.

The armistice did not affect our status of prisoners, for there was still a state of war, and, as long as there is a state of war, to my mind there is a corresponding duty on the part of all prisoners to return to their own forces; and no superior officer, regardless of rank, has the right to excuse the failure of any prisoner to perform this duty, and certainly not to forbid even attempting the performance. This colonel stated that, as commanding officer, he had given the parole of all the prisoners. This was again absolutely the assumption of rights not his own. This assumption of our personal privileges as men and soldiers was the only thing that kept several of us from again trying to escape, for a man's word of honour is too serious a thing to permit juggling with, even when given away without his consent.

Finally, the orders came to leave, and one bright morning they assembled us, the Air Service officers being last—probably because that was where we stood in the estimation of the American artillery colonel. The German officer in charge of the camp came out and made a speech about the great friendship of the German and American people, in which he said that the Allies and Germans were both victorious—Germany's victory being in that she had found a new

Republic. But it was not a time for speechmaking—it was a time for action for us, and, like a bunch of race horses, we pawed the earth to get a head start for that train.

To our surprise, they had first-class coaches to carry us out of Germany, although they had taken us in and moved us around in everything from cattle cars to third and fourth class coaches.

We got to Constanz, on the border of Switzerland, and, of course, expected to change trains and go right ahead. To our disappointment, we found that the Americans had not made any preparations to carry us through Switzerland, and we had to wait at Constanz a couple of days until the Americans showed some speed. Believe me, I damned America right, left, laterally, and longitudinally for their lack of preparation. I afterwards was very sorry and found that it was not the fault of the Americans at all. But I was mighty peeved to be forced to eat "Bully Beef" in Germany on Thanksgiving.

I think it was about five o'clock, on the morning of the thirtieth of November, that we crossed the border, and believe me I never want to hear such pandemonium again as those two hundred American prisoners gave as we were pulled out of Germany, and were actually again in the hands of friends. We had shaken hands with our hostess at the "coming out," for I didn't see a single house along our railroad all through Switzerland from five in the morning until midnight that did not have the American flag waving. Everywhere were men, women and children madly waving handkerchiefs and flags as that train went by.

I felt as if I were in heaven. It was wonderful of Switzerland, but, of course, it was the fact that we represented the Great America which caused the demonstration as they had a sincere respect for our friendship.

At Berne, the ladies of the American Red Cross met us and served us hot roast chicken. Take it from me, it was good. Everyone had a ravenous appetite. When we were filled to the brim, the boys got together and appointed me yell leader, and we gave fifteen "raws" for the Red Cross, the Y. M. C A., the Salvation Army, Switzerland, Berne, the Allies, and the U. S. A. The natives thought perhaps that we were lunatics, but those who understood America knew it was the only immediately available way we had of expressing our appreciation. So we repeated our performance at Lucerne, and at Lausanne, and at Geneva.

Hours meant nothing to the austere Swiss on that night, for when we pulled into Geneva at 11 p. m., there was the same tremendous crowd, with American flags, good cheer, and things to eat. All the way along, even from the first, it was the same. At one little town where we stopped for the engine to get water, there was only one little store near the rail-road, but the Swiss man who ran it gave us every bit of wine he had in there, which was about thirty bottles, and then began to feed us cookies. He could speak nothing but German, which was "*Alles for den Amerikaner,*" meaning "Everything for the Americans." And he seemed pleased to have the opportunity to do it. In that part of Switzerland, they speak German, but, of course, around Lausanne and Geneva, French is the common tongue.

But it was a real "coming out." In fact, it was Cesar's Triumphal March, Woodrow Wilson's entrance into Paris, and Pershing on Fifth Avenue, all combined, for we were the King Bees when it came to Swiss chocolate, and they certainly handed it out. I became so ill that I could barely navigate, but it all seemed so much like a dream that I continued to consume chocolate whether I wanted to or not for fear the dream would end.

On the morning of December first, we crossed the border at Bellegarde. There was a big hospital train waiting to meet us, but, for some reason or other, their orders would not permit them to pull out before six or seven that evening. Our destination was some hospital near Dijon. That didn't sound interesting to me. I was tired of being confined, and I felt that it was my duty to join my organization for the war was still on. So, I took some of my most valued friends into my confidence, and relieved them of every cent of money they had, from *pfennigs* to souvenirs, which I finally got exchanged, and got enough French money to get a third-class passage to Paris.

So, when the Geneva-Paris express pulled in, I took my seat. My clothes must have been awful, for I noticed the poor peasant women taking unpleasant sniffs at me. However, my pride had long since ceased to be on my sleeve, so I sniffed right back at 'em. Just before we left, I was sitting back there in that third-class compartment, packed up in a corner like an oiled sardine, when, outside in the companion way I noticed a distinguished looking man, well dressed, with a big diamond flashing. Certainly he belonged in a first-class compartment, and I wondered what he was doing back there among us common peasants. As he stood there a newsboy came along, hollering "*La Liberte,*" and since the sight of a well-dressed man had recalled to my mind the fact that I, too, had once been more or less of a gentleman who could afford a newspaper, I stopped the boy. "*Garcon,*" I said, "*don-*

203

nez moi un journal." That is, "Give me a paper." The lad handed me a paper and also his hand, and so I reached in my pocket and realised that I had spent my last *sous* for that railroad ticket. Quite embarrassed, I handed the paper back and told him I didn't want the paper after all. This man on the outside looked in, and to my great surprise spoke up in English.

"Well," he smiled, "you look like an American."

"Yes, sir," I replied, "I am an American."

"Well," he continued, offering his hand, "I'm an American too. Boggs is my name."

I extended my fist and said, "My name is Lieutenant Haslett"

"Lieutenant?" he said, with surprise, looking for my insignia of rank. "I must say you look more like a buck private." Whereupon I found it was necessary to explain that I had been a prisoner and had just gotten out. He bought the paper for me from the anxious news kid and came across then and offered to give me money or anything else I needed. Modestly I responded that I really didn't need it; that I would be all right, for when I got back to Paris the next morning I would soon be fixed up. Mr. Boggs insisted that I come up to the first-class compartment to meet some very charming American women and some French countesses. I must admit that, even though I did have a lot of self-pride in not wanting to make my appearance under such disadvantageous conditions, yet the opportunity to talk to a real American woman sounded like soft music to my ears.

I was on the point of declining when he pulled out a real Havana cigar, which certainly would have cost him a couple of dollars at the Café de Paris or "Giro's."

"Here," he said, handing it over, "you must want this, since you have probably not had a real cigar for a long time."

I could not resist this invitation, and when I put my teeth on that cigar and took the first puff I condescended right away to permit the charming ladies to be presented to me. The first thing the ladies did was to offer me a piece of chocolate. I would not have touched chocolate for a thousand dollars, for I had had so much of it in Switzerland that it was almost obnoxious. However, I could not tell them that I had been fed up or they would not have had so much sympathy for me, for what I especially craved was sympathy and what I most especially desired was to be petted. So I told them that I was very sorry that I couldn't accept their chocolate for the reason that the doctor had told me not to eat anything at all until I had gone to the specialist at Paris to see if anything was wrong with my stomach.

I soon realised what a bonehead remark I had made, for shortly afterwards Countess B—— pulled out some lovely club sandwiches. There were tears of regret in my eyes as my month watered like a spring—but that doctor gag was my story and I had to stick to it.

We talked quite a while and I smoked another one of this American's good cigars, and then, by means of my olfactory sense, I realised that my clothes were making the air a little uncomfortable in there, so I excused myself and told them that I wished to go back to my compartment, as I felt awfully embarrassed looking so poorly among such lovely and refined people. Of course, they insisted that I stay in their compartment the remainder of the night, as there was plenty of room and I could stretch out and rest my weary bones while they should, like good angels, watch over me. This sounded real, but I knew from a personal standpoint that my welcome had expired as soon as they had seen the curiosity, namely, the prisoner of war, and that it would be more comfortable for all concerned that I hie me back among the peasants.

I had been to Paris quite a number of times. The old saying was that "*all roads lead to Rome*," but the new one of the American Army was "*all Army orders read to Paris*," it being an unwritten law that all army travel orders were via Paris. So in my visits I had naturally learned the customs and rules with respect to reporting to our Military Police of Paris.

The old rule upon entering Paris was that if you intended to stay over twenty-four hours you must go to 10 Rue St. Anne, which was the headquarters of the provost marshal of the American Military Police, and register, stating your hotel, the nature of your business, when you were leaving, and the time. If you did not intend to stay twenty-four hours or over you did not need to register. Of course, I generally managed to stay twenty-three hours and fifty-nine minutes, at which time I was generally broke and had to leave. But this morning, when I arrived at the Gare de Lyons, I was confronted with a tremendous and complete surprise. Preceding me was a line of about fifty officers, ranging in rank from colonel to second lieutenant, and on down to privates, and in front of them was a big desk and two bigger M. P.'s presided over by an officious looking second lieutenant, and above them a sign:

New Regulations, G.H.Q.—No officers or enlisted men under

the rank of brigadier general will be allowed to leave this station or enter Paris without first registering here, giving authority for travel, hotel nature of business, and when officer or man will leave the city,

By order of General Pershing.

Stunned and shocked, I stood on the side lines and watched. Everyone who passed this desk showed written orders and was given a little blue check which the M. P.'s seemed to honour. Things sure looked both black and blue for me. I had no insignia whatever—from appearances I was a private and my uniform was as dirty as a coalscuttle, but at the same time they could tell I was an American. I certainly looked like the last rose of summer after the first winter frost. I figured the small chance I would have of talking my way through that lieutenant provost marshal. Just as sure as could be they would take me up to 10 Rue St. Anne and quarantine me, fumigate me, and hold me for orders. It was the old army game of waiting for orders, and, believe me, that wasn't the object of my visit to Paris. I realised that if I once got to my hotel I could spend a couple of days there without even being seen or known and could eat to the limit of my bank account. I felt that under the circumstances General Pershing would bear me out, provided I could get that high up in presenting my case.

So I decided to make a reconnaissance of the station, hoping for better luck. I sauntered around, by every exit, and there was either a Frenchman there who wouldn't let me by or there was an American who, of course, wouldn't budge. I thought of getting on an outgoing train and being pulled down to the yards and leaving by that way. So I began to walk down the tracks. Finally I found an open gate where the tracks enter for the freight depot.

"Well," I thought, " this will be easy!" I started to walk through when I saw standing in the sentry box a hardboiled buck private—an American. In his hand he had a regular New York billy stick. He saw me, and it was too late to turn back. He walked out and stuck out his jaw, like a bulldog, and said, "Hey, guy, where you goin'?" Of course, he couldn't tell me from a private, so I got just as hard-boiled as he was and stuck out my jaw and said, "Hello, Buddie! What are you doin'?"

"Where yuh going?" he demanded gruffly.

"Damned if I know, Bud," I growled. "I'm getting tired of hanging around Paris. I'm tired of it. I want to get to the front or where the front was. You know, Buddie, they told me when they drafted me into the army I'd get to the front. I've never even heard a gun fire. I've been stationed in the rear all the time, and now the blamed war is over, and I ain't never seen none of it. I'll go back, and my girl will say, 'Reuben, tell me about the war; what were you in?' And, Buddy, won't I feel like the devil when I have to 'fess up and tell them that I was a soldier in Paris?"

I looked at his arm, and I saw that he had a wound stripe. "Looky there!" I snapped out proudly. "You've got a wound stripe, ain't yuh?"

"Yep," he replied, equally proud.

"Gosh, you're lucky,'" I said assuringly. "You've been to the front; tell me about it, for I ain't never had no chance to talk to a real red-blooded guy what's been to the front yet."

This was the prize stroke, for he broke loose and told me his whole story. He said he had been at Château-Thierry, in the Second Division, and was sore because the Marines got all the credit for it, while, as a matter of fact, it was his own regiment that did all the dirty work. He himself, according to his story, had attacked a machine gun nest alone, had got ten prisoners, and, incidentally, got wounded in the hip. I impressed upon him how lucky he was to have gotten through it alive; then I glanced at his chest and I saw upon it the green and yellow ribbon meaning Mexican Border Service.

"What decoration is that?" I asked, curiously, "the Medal of Honour?"

"No," he said, boisterously putting his finger on the ribbon. "You know what that is, don't you?"

"No," I affirmed, "I ain't never seen no decorations."

"Well," he said, realising he had an easy one, "why, that's the *Croix de Guerre.*"

I gripped him by the hand and slapped him on the shoulder and told him he was the most interesting man and the bravest man that I had ever met and that I sure wanted to meet him again, but that I had to browse on today and we would get together some night when we got paid and go to the Folies Bergère and see the theatre. So the old boy offered me a chew of tobacco, took one himself and again proudly shaking his hand I passed on.

I had to walk all the way up to town because I didn't have any money to hire a taxi, nor could I even pay my car fare. Finally I got up to the Place de l'Opera, where I went into my American bank and wrote out a cheque for about two hundred and fifty *francs*, as I still had a little money on deposit there. As is the custom with those

Colonel Brereton, Major Haslett and others being decorated at Coblenz

very shrewd and careful French bankclerks, the Frenchman took the cheque back to consult the books to see if I had that much money on credit. When he came back he looked at me suspiciously over the top rims of his spectacles and said accusingly, "Where did you get that cheque?"

"Well," I replied, surprised at his attitude, "where do you suppose I got it. I just now wrote it."

"Be careful," he answered sarcastically, "don't lie."

"Where do you get that noise?" I demanded, thoroughly insulted.

"Well," he insisted, "we won't cash that cheque. That man is dead."

"Who's dead?" I asked sharply.

"Well, you see," he explained, "our books report that Elmer Haslett was killed in action September 30, 1918."

"Well," I laughed, appreciating the joke, "I'm the guy—been a prisoner of war and have just gotten back and, as is to be expected, I've got to have some money."

"All right," he answered, as if about to accommodate me, "you prove that you are Elmer Haslett."

"I've no papers on me, of course," and I puzzled for a second. "You see, I've been a prisoner of war, but just compare my signature with any previous ones." That wasn't sufficient evidence for him, so I asked him to suggest the means of identity.

"It is very simple," he explained. "Get the Military Police at 10 Rue St. Anne to state that you are Elmer Haslett."

Of course, the prospect of appearing at 10 Rue St. Anne was out of the question, for reasons stated. I must try new means to obtain the wherewithal. With new hopes, I walked over to the Hotel Chatham. They had changed clerks there and so when I asked for a room the clerk told me very politely that they had none. I knew then they simply considered me as an undesirable guest on account of my appearance, but I also knew that if I had a chance to get a room in Paris at all on my present appearance it would have to be at the Chatham, where I had previously been known. I told the clerk that I had been at the Chatham many times and that they certainly knew me, that my name was Elmer Haslett.

"Oh, yes, yes," he said politely, "we know you, Mr. Haslett, but we simply have no rooms."

I asked to see the proprietor, but he wasn't in. Things looked rather bad, when along came the dignified old concierge. Just as big as could be, I walked up and extended my hand to the concierge.

"How are you, Henry?" I said, about to embrace him. He drew back in amazement, looking at me like a powerful judge looks at an overfriendly Bolshevik. But I had his hand, so he couldn't get loose.

"Well, sir," he said sternly, "I don't think I've ever seen you before." I thought of all the woes of poor old Rip Van Winkle—I too had actually changed. But I couldn't give up.

"Come on, Henry, come on," I said. "You know me—I'm Haslett, who used to be here with Len Hammond."

"Oh," he blustered, equally shocked, "I know Lieutenant Haslett, but you're not Lieutenant Haslett."

"I beg your pardon, but I am," I replied, getting a little heated. "I'm getting tired of having people tell me I'm not. Now what I want, Henry, is a room, and the clerk says he has no rooms, and I know damned well he has. I look like the devil, I know. But listen," and I whispered in his ear. "Don't tell it, but I have just gotten back from Germany, where I've been a prisoner of war, and I don't want the newspapers to know it because I want to have a few days refit. You go up and tell him I'm all right and want a room. You know me, Henry. I'll fix it up right with you."

The prisoner sympathy stuff did not have the pull with Henry as the magic little words "I'll fix it right with you." That seems to get by everywhere. So the old boy went over and fixed it up and assigned me to one of the nicest rooms they had. For the rest of the morning I kept two servants busy bringing me food and charging it to my bill. Then I wrote a cheque, dating it before my capture, and proceeded to send it to the concierge. He cashed it and then life was a little more easy.

Just as I was leaving the hotel I ran on to some of my friends— the first boys I had seen since I left Germany, and, of course, they wouldn't let me leave, but took me up and bought me a big dinner. They took me to the Café de Paris and, believe me, I was some sensation, for while I had been eating and had eaten plentifully those few days, I still had a lot to make up for and I had a huge appetite. In fact, it was a continuing appetite. The bill at the *café* for the three of us was something like $45.00, because I ordered everything they had, which, of course, included the necessary emoluments, and fixtures, and all the dainty and choice things both in season and out.

Finally I tore loose and took a taxi down to the Gare de l'Est, where I found practically the same situation as at the Gare de Lyons, only that you had to show orders before you could purchase a ticket

My train left at 3:00 o'clock and it was now about five minutes before time for the train to pull out. I knew it would be impossible to
go through the red tape of getting a ticket O. K.'d, for I had the big
chance of being held. I rushed up to the ticket window and asked for
a ticket to Bar-le-Duc. The lady shook her head and tried to tell me in
English that it was impossible to sell tickets to the Americans without
a purchase authorization check. With apparent surprise I demanded in
French that she speak French or Belgian. Thinking that I was making
remarks about her rotten English, she proceeded to tell me the same
in French.

"Ha! ha! ha! *Madame*," I laughed. "You make me laugh very much.
That is very funny. I am very pleased at your compliment. Do you
think I am American or Belgian?" I had almost forgotten my French,
but it came in very good play, for she fell for it, demanded my pardon
most profusely and immediately forked over a ticket. It was just about
time for the train. I knew I couldn't pull any smooth gag on this hardboiled M. P., so I started to rush through, handing him my railroad
ticket. "Hey," and he grabbed me, "where are you going?"

"I'm going to take this train for Bar-le-Duc," I replied hurriedly.

"Well," he demanded, "whereas your yellow ticket!"

"What yellow ticket?" I said, surprised that such a thing even existed.

"You've got to have a yellow ticket before you can pass through
this gate," he said, emphatically and not permitting argument.

"Here, here's my railroad ticket," I repeated nervously, casting my
eyes on the train.

"I don't care," he said in a voice indicating that his patience was
about gone, "where's your yellow ticket!"

"I haven't got one," I replied. "I didn't know I had to have that."

"You go back there," and he pointed to one of the windows and
explained in detail as to one who was good and dense, "see the M. P.
and get your orders stamped and he will give you a yellow ticket, and
you can't get by this gate until you do."

"Oh, Hell! Come on, Buddy," I said, "I can't do all that I'm just
coming back from leave. If I do all that I'll miss my train. Come on,
Bud, let me by. Why, I'll get K. P. for a week if I don't get there tonight.
It's my last chance. You wouldn't hold up a buddy that way, would
you?" and believe me, I looked appealingly.

He looked at me a moment. The conductor was already blowing his little whistle signal and then he gave up. "Go on! The war is

over," he said. It was the example of the American soldier and the big soft spot they have for their buddies. He couldn't resist the chance to help a pal. So I passed the gates and got on the train and went to Bar-le-Duc. On the train I ran onto a guy I knew and we talked over old times and I got to Chaumont-sur-Aire, which was the old headquarters, and I ran in and saw my old friend, Philip Roosevelt, who was then the Army Pursuit Operations Officer. Then I got on the telephone and called Brereton, who was then up at Longuyon preparing to move to Treves with the Army of Occupation. He was chief of staff for General Mitchell, who was then commanding the Aviation of the Army of Occupation.

"Is this Major Brereton?" I said from force of habit, for he was a major when I knew him last.

"Yes—Colonel Brereton," he corrected.

"This is Lieutenant Haslett," I called.

"WHO?" he fairly yelled.

"Lieutenant Haslett," I replied.

"Who do you mean," he demanded—"Elmer?"

"Yep," I said, "that's right."

"Lieutenant Hell!" he called in old form, "you've been promoted for months and I've been waiting for a month to be decorated with you for Château-Thierry."

"Well, let's not argue over technicalities," I answered. "How am I going to get up there?"

"How are you going to get up here?" he repeated, very surprised.

"Yes," I replied, "how am I going to get up there?"

"Well, Elmer," he said, in his same grand old voice, "you're going up in the king's carriage."

So he immediately sent one of General Mitchell's cars all that distance, and after travelling practically all night over those terrible roads, the next morning at breakfast I had my "coming out." I was back among friends—the dearest friends that man can have—those who with you have upheld the flag and who with an unfaltering trust have faced the common enemy.

LEONAUR

ALSO FROM LEONAUR

AVAILABLE IN SOFTCOVER OR HARDCOVER WITH DUST JACKET

WINGED WARFARE *by William A. Bishop*—The Experiences of a Canadian 'Ace' of the R.F.C. During the First World War.

THE STORY OF THE LAFAYETTE ESCADRILLE *by George Thenault*—A famous fighter squadron in the First World War by its commander..

R.F.C.H.Q. *by Maurice Baring*—The command & organisation of the British Air Force during the First World War in Europe.

SIXTY SQUADRON R.A.F. *by A. J. L. Scott*—On the Western Front During the First World War.

THE STRUGGLE IN THE AIR *by Charles C. Turner*—The Air War Over Europe During the First World War.

WITH THE FLYING SQUADRON *by H. Rosher*—Letters of a Pilot of the Royal Naval Air Service During the First World War.

OVER THE WEST FRONT *by "Spin" & "Contact"* —Two Accounts of British Pilots During the First World War in Europe, Short Flights With the Cloud Cavalry by "Spin" and Cavalry of the Clouds by "Contact".

SKYFIGHTERS OF FRANCE *by Henry Farré*—An account of the French War in the Air during the First World War.

THE HIGH ACES *by Laurence la Tourette Driggs*—French, American, British, Italian & Belgian pilots of the First World War 1914-18.

PLANE TALES OF THE SKIES *by Wilfred Theodore Blake*—The experiences of pilots over the Western Front during the Great War.

IN THE CLOUDS ABOVE BAGHDAD *by J. E. Tennant*—Recollections of the R. F. C. in Mesopotamia during the First World War against the Turks.

THE SPIDER WEB *by P. I. X. (Theodore Douglas Hallam)*—Royal Navy Air Service Flying Boat Operations During the First World War by a Flight Commander

EAGLES OVER THE TRENCHES *by James R. McConnell & William B. Perry*—Two First Hand Accounts of the American Escadrille at War in the Air During World War 1-Flying For France: With the American Escadrille at Verdun and Our Pilots in the Air

KNIGHTS OF THE AIR *by Bennett A. Molter*—An American Pilot's View of the Aerial War of the French Squadrons During the First World War.

AVAILABLE ONLINE AT **www.leonaur.com**
AND FROM ALL GOOD BOOK STORES

07/09

LEONAUR

ALSO FROM LEONAUR
AVAILABLE IN SOFTCOVER OR HARDCOVER WITH DUST JACKET

FARAWAY CAMPAIGN *by F. James*—Experiences of an Indian Army Cavalry Officer in Persia & Russia During the Great War.

REVOLT IN THE DESERT *by T. E. Lawrence*—An account of the experiences of one remarkable British officer's war from his own perspective.

MACHINE-GUN SQUADRON *by A. M. G.*—The 20th Machine Gunners from British Yeomanry Regiments in the Middle East Campaign of the First World War.

A GUNNER'S CRUSADE *by Antony Bluett*—The Campaign in the Desert, Palestine & Syria as Experienced by the Honourable Artillery Company During the Great War .

DESPATCH RIDER *by W. H. L. Watson*—The Experiences of a British Army Motorcycle Despatch Rider During the Opening Battles of the Great War in Europe.

TIGERS ALONG THE TIGRIS *by E. J. Thompson*—The Leicestershire Regiment in Mesopotamia During the First World War.

HEARTS & DRAGONS *by Charles R. M. F. Crutwell*—The 4th Royal Berkshire Regiment in France and Italy During the Great War, 1914-1918.

INFANTRY BRIGADE: 1914 *by John Ward*—The Diary of a Commander of the 15th Infantry Brigade, 5th Division, British Army, During the Retreat from Mons.

DOING OUR 'BIT' *by Ian Hay*—Two Classic Accounts of the Men of Kitchener's 'New Army' During the Great War including *The First 100,000* & *All In It*.

AN EYE IN THE STORM *by Arthur Ruhl*—An American War Correspondent's Experiences of the First World War from the Western Front to Gallipoli-and Beyond.

STAND & FALL *by Joe Cassells*—With the Middlesex Regiment Against the Bolsheviks 1918-19.

RIFLEMAN MACGILL'S WAR *by Patrick MacGill*—A Soldier of the London Irish During the Great War in Europe including *The Amateur Army*, *The Red Horizon* & *The Great Push*.

WITH THE GUNS *by C. A. Rose & Hugh Dalton*—Two First Hand Accounts of British Gunners at War in Europe During World War 1- Three Years in France with the Guns and With the British Guns in Italy.

THE BUSH WAR DOCTOR *by Robert V. Dolbey*—The Experiences of a British Army Doctor During the East African Campaign of the First World War.

AVAILABLE ONLINE AT www.leonaur.com
AND FROM ALL GOOD BOOK STORES

07/09

www.ingramcontent.com/pod-product-compliance
Lightning Source LLC
Chambersburg PA
CBHW032055080426

42733CB00006B/284